H 1

Digitized by the Internet Archive
in 2013

http://archive.org/details/historyoftowntow00jack

Thos Durnan

THE HISTORY OF
THE TOWN AND TOWNSHIP
OF BARNSLEY,

IN YORKSHIRE, FROM AN EARLY PERIOD.

BY ROWLAND JACKSON.

BARNSLEY MARKET PLACE, FROM A PHOTOGRAPH BY G. CAMPBELL.

LONDON:
BELL AND DALDY, No. 186, FLEET STREET.
1858.

DA
690
B24 J14

TO

Godfrey Wentworth, Esquire,

OF WOOLLEY PARK.

SIR,

I FEEL that the favour you confer upon me, in allowing me to dedicate the following small and imperfect work to you, is not the least among many for which I am indebted to your kindness.

The Records containing the early history of the town of Barnsley being almost entirely in your possession, that part of this work which refers to ancient times must have been in a great measure deficient had it not been for the generous manner in which you placed those documents at my disposal, and afforded me facilities for consulting them.

Coupling with the consideration of these favours the close connection of yourself and ancestors with Barnsley, it gives me much satisfaction in being permitted to dedicate these pages to you.

I am, Sir,

Your obliged and obedient servant,

THE AUTHOR.

BARNSLEY, June, 1858.

PREFACE.

An eminent writer* on parochial antiquities, in alluding to these studies, says, " I am sensible there be some who despise this kind of learning, and represent it as dry, barren, and monkish. I leave such to their dear enjoyments of ignorance and ease, but I dare assure any wise and sober man, that historical antiquities, and especially a search into the notices of our own nation, do deserve and will reward the pains of any English student ; will make him understand the state of former ages, the constitution of governments, the fundamental reasons of equity and law, the rise and succession of doctrines and opinions, the original of ancient and the composition of modern tongues, the tenures of property, the maxims of policy, the rites of religion, the characters of virtue and vice, and indeed the nature of mankind."

Some have thought it strange that hitherto no attempt has been made to rescue the past history of Barnsley from oblivion ; but this is easily accounted for, if we take into consideration the great difficulty encountered in obtaining information bearing on the subject, for it must be borne in mind that the place in ancient times

*Kennett.

PREFACE.

was not of the same importance as many of the neighbouring towns; as Doncaster, for instance, a station of eminent note under the Romans, known by the name of *Danum*—Kirkby, now Pontefract, a place of Saxon origin, and the head of this fee, whére Ilbert de Lacy (one of the most noted of those nobles who followed in the train of the Conqueror) erected a stupendous castle, the remains of which still give us an idea of its former greatness—Sheffield, with its stronghold, of which no vestige is now in existence—or Wakefield, memorable as having been the scene of a sanguinary conflict between the rival houses of York and Lancaster.

As Barnsley cannot be said to equal any of the above-mentioned places in connection with great and well known historic events, my duty is to note occurrences of minor importance that have taken place within the township, or which relate to the immediate neighbourhood. In presenting the work to the public, who will be the judges as to whether or not I have done my duty in the matter, I can only say that it would have given me much satisfaction for the task to have been undertaken by some one with greater ability than myself, who could have done more ample justice to the subject; and if this little work is not all that could be wished, I have the consciousness of knowing that much time, and no small amount of labour, have been given to bring to light many interesting particulars which would otherwise most probably never have been recorded. I must not forget to acknowledge the kind assistance afforded by the Rev. Henry Robert Alder, the incumbent of St. Mary's, in allowing me free access to the

PREFACE.

registers. To Mr. George Lawton of York, I am much indebted for ecclesiastical and other information. Mr. Henry Allen Spurr has kindly procured for me extracts from scarce documents, and assisted me with translations of the charters, which without his valuable aid would have occasioned me much trouble and expense. But my thanks are due more particularly to Godfrey Wentworth, Esq., of Woolley Park, who generously placed the Chartularies of Pontefract and Bretton at my service, documents of primary importance—in fact such may be said to be the groundwork of topographical history, being frequently the only source from which we are able to glean information respecting the descent of property in the middle ages. To Mr. George Wentworth I am under great obligation, for the assistance given me in extracting the Charters, which is no easy undertaking; and other gentlemen who have afforded me information bearing on the subject have my best thanks.

Arms and pedigrees are given of the ancient families, which are and have been connected with the township, including the Armitages, Keresforths, Rookes, &c., which I believe will be found correct. These have been compiled from the registers here, and other sources, and I hope the same may prove interesting to many of my readers.

Barnsley, 1857.

GENERAL HISTORY.

CHAPTER I.

"The naked Briton fix'd his wild abode!"

THE spot on which stands the town of Barnsley, and the whole of the surrounding neighbourhood, was in early times one immense forest, traversed by a tribe of Britons, known as the Brigantes, who may be considered as descendants from the original inhabitants of our island. They lived by the chase, and their habitations were of a circular form, and constructed by driving stakes into the ground, which they bound together with pieces of splintered wood; others, who were less provident, found shelter in caves and hollow trees. On the arrival of the Romans, a fierce and protracted struggle ensued between them and these Britons, who are represented as having been a brave and warlike people, and not easily brought to subjection. They were overpowered by Cerealis in the reign of Vespasian, about the year 71. There has been nothing found here to establish the fact of the Romans

Chap. I.

Early inhabitants.

Early History. having been in the immediate neighbourhood. A road is, however, said to have passed near to the site of this town, which touched at Pontefract, and entered the Watling Street, near Castleford. There are traces of a camp at Penistone, and also of earthworks near Darfield, at which place a Roman[1] urn was found towards the latter part of the seventeenth century, which contained gold and other coins. As Doncaster was a station of importance, it is probable that there might be a road from Penistone, leading to Doncaster by way of Darfield, the earthworks there seeming to favour the supposition.

Saxon Period. History is silent respecting Barnsley during the Saxon period; the neighbourhood must then have been almost covered with wood, and cultivation have made little progress, and the only inhabitants probably consisted of a few husbandmen and their families, who would clear and cultivate as much ground from the forest, as was requisite for the support of themselves and their households.

Wild Animals. Of the wild animals which found refuge in this part, perhaps the wolf was the most formidable, and his presence must have caused much uneasiness in the minds of our ancestors; frequent mention is made of wolf-pits in ancient charters which refer to property in this district. By deed executed in the 13th century, John Tyrel of Burghesclive grants to Thomas de Dychtun " *decem et octo acras terre et dimidiam acram et unam perticatam in territorio de Wlvelay* (Woolley), *undecem acre et una perticata jacent in Northbrom ; et una acra jacet juxta Wlfpit.*"

[1] Hunter.

PARISHES AND COUNTIES.

Wolf-pits,[1] or dens, between Dodworth and Silk stone, are also noticed in an early Charter, by which it would appear that the animal was numerous in this locality.

Wolf-pits.

England was divided into parishes about A.D. 636, by Honorius, the fifth archbishop of Canterbury, who entered upon that see in the year 634, and died A.D. 653. Gilbert, the eleventh archbishop, procured a dispensation from the Pope to make cemeteries or churchyards within towns and cities throughout England, about the year 745.

Divisions of the Country.

The parcelling of this country into counties, is said to have been suggested and carried out by order of Alfred. Yorkshire was formed into three districts during the Saxon period, which are now known as the East, North, and West Ridings; these were again sub-divided into wapentakes—the names of those in the last-mentioned division will shortly be given.

The hundreds of the south and wapentakes of the north are identical. Ralph Thoresby, the Leeds historian, citing from Matthew Paris, who himself quotes from Hovenden, gives us the following explanation relative to the origin of the word "Wapentake." He says, that when a person received the government of one of these divisions, at the appointed time and usual place the elder sort met him, and when he had alighted from his horse rose up to him; then he held up his spear, and took security of all present

Wapentakes.

---

[1] Robert de Laci, in describing the boundaries of lands he had given at Dodworth, mentions a certain rivulet called Mervinbrock, and near towards Silkstone, " *luporum fovea*," (Wolves' den, or hole) and a certain tree called in English Lind, and " *morosum fontem*," (the impure well, or spring), and another rivulet called " Helilaiam," which fell into the water which came from Silkstone, and through the valley beyond Huggeside, and as far as Ravensclow.

GENERAL HISTORY.

High Consta-bles. according to custom; whoever came touched his spear with theirs, and by this touch of armour was confirmed in one common interest, and thus from ꝑæꝑnu (weapons) and tac (a touch) or taccaꝑe (to confirm) they were called Wapentakes. The government of these districts was vested in the high constable, whose duty and office were defined by the statute of Winchester, 13 Ed. I., whereby were appointed for the conservation of the peace and view of armour two constables in every hundred and franchise, who were in Latin called " *Constabularii Capitales*," or High Constables. Anciently these officers were appointed by the sheriff, or by the steward of the court leet, or presentment of the jury where there was a custom so to do. Afterwards they were more generally chosen and sworn by the justices of peace in their sessions. The high constable had the direction of the petty constables, head boroughs, and tything men within his hundred; his duty was to keep the peace and apprehend felons and rioters, to make hue and cry after felons, to take care that the watch was duly kept in his hundred, and that the statutes for punishing rogues and vagrants were put in execution. He had to prevent unlawful games, tippling, drunkenness, bloodshed, and affrays; also to execute precepts and warrants, directed to him by justices of the peace, and make returns to the sessions to all the articles contained in his oath or that concerned his office, and cause the petty constables to make their returns. Victuallers and alehouse keepers that were unlicensed were to be returned by him, as also all defects of highways and bridges. At every quarter sessions, his duty was to pay over

WAPENTAKES. 9 Chap. I.

to the treasurer of the county all such money as High Constables. had been received by him for the county rates. At the present day, however, many of the duties that formerly devolved upon the high constable have been abolished or passed into other hands; and now, by 7 and 8 Vic. cap. 33, sec. 1, July 19, 1844, the high constables to be appointed after the passing of that act, are no longer to collect the county rates as heretofore, the precepts for that purpose being thereby directed to be sent from the clerk of the peace to the guardians of unions, by the latter of whom it is to be paid to the treasurer of the county. By section 8, the appointment of high constable is to take place at a special sessions for a division held for hearing appeals against poor rates.

It may amuse some of my readers to peruse the Ancient Rates. particulars of rates made long before poor-law unions or local boards of health were thought of. On the 8th day of April, 44 Eliz., the subjoined assessments were agreed upon at York by her Majesty's council in the north, which consisted of the following persons:—Sir William Mallory and Sir Thomas Fairfax, Knts.; Edward Stanhope and Charles Hales, Esqs.; Drs. Gibson and Bennett, and Mr. Secretary Ferne; some justices of the peace were also present, viz., Sir George Saville, Sir Edward Yorke, and Sir Thomas Lascellés, Knts.; Marmaduke Grimstone, Richard Wortley, Henry Bellassis, Thomas Wentworth, Ralph Beeston, Robert Kaye, John Alured, Thomas Talbot, Richard Aldburgh, Stephen Proctor, William Barnbrough, Thomas Bland, George Twisleton, and Thomas Norcliffe, Esqs.

Rate for the composition of one hundred and ten oxen for the provision of the Royal household,

Chap. I. 10 GENERAL HISTORY.

Ancient Rates. an ox being then valued at seventy-six shillings and eight-pence; and each Riding required to furnish as follows:—

	£	s.	d.
West Riding, xlv oxen, value	clxxii	x	—
North „ xxxvi and a half	cxxxix	xviii	iv
East „ xxviii and a half	cix	v	—

Towards the forty-five oxen the wapentakes in the West Riding were to supply as follows:—

	£	s.	d.
Agbrig and Morley, viii oxen, value	xxx	xiii	iv
Claro, vii and a half . . .	xxviii	xv	—
Staincliffe and Ewcross, vii and a half	xxviii	xv	—
Skyrack, iii and a half . . .	xiii	viii-	iv
Barkstone Ash, iii and a half . .	xiii	viii	iv
Strafford and Tickhill, vi .	xxiii	—	—
Staincross and Osgoldcross, iii and a half	xiii	viii	iv
Ainsty, v and a half . . .	xxi	i	viii
Total for the West Riding	£clxxii	x	—

The last-named assessment was altered in the year 1636, and increased in the West Riding to the sum of £285 19s. 0d., towards which amount the wapentakes contributed as below:—

	£	s.	d.
Agbrig and Morley . . .	xlvii	xiii	iv
Staincliffe and Ewcross . .	xlvii	xiii	iv
Claro	xlvii	xiii	iv
Barkstone Ash	xxiii	xvi	iv
Skyrack	xxiii	xvi	iv
Staincross and Osgoldcross . .	xxiii	xvi	iv
Strafford and Tickhill . .	xxxv	xv	—
Ainsty	xxxv	xv	—
Total . . .	£cclxxxv	xix	—

A rate was levied for the relief of prisoners in the King's Bench and Marshalsea, and to be paid

ANCIENT RATES.

11 Chap. I.

Ancient Rates.

annually. The following amounts were supplied by the different wapentakes in this Riding :—

	£	s.	d.
Agbrig and Morley	—	viii	—
Staincliffe and Ewcross	—	viii	—
Claro	—	viii	—
Strafford and Tickhill	—	vi	—
Skyrack	—	iv	—
Barkstone Ash	—	iv	—
Osgoldcross and Staincross	—	iv	—
Total	£ii	ii	—

An assessment of £43 for the relief of prisoners in York Castle; this amount to be furnished by the whole county: the sum required from each of the Ridings was as follows :—

	£	s.	d.
West Riding	xvii	iv	—
North ,,	xiv	vi	viii
East ,,	xi	ix	iv
Total	xliii	—	—

Towards this amount the wapentakes in this Riding contributed as under :—

	£	s.	d.
Agbrig and Morley	ii	xvii	iv
Claro	ii	xvii	iv
Staincliffe and Ewcross	ii	xvii	iv
Barkstone Ash	i	viii	viii
Skyrack	i	viii	viii
Staincross and Osgoldcross	i	viii	viii
Strafford and Tickhill	ii	iii	—
Ainsty	ii	iii	—
Total	£xvii	iv	—

For the repair of York Castle £200 was required; towards this sum the three Ridings were to furnish as follows :—

GENERAL HISTORY.

Chap. I. 12

Ancient Rates.

					£	s.	d.
West Riding	.	.	.	.	lxxx	—	—
North ,,	.	.	.	.	lxvi	xiii	iv
East ,,	.	.	.	.	liii	vi	viii
Total	.	.	.	:	£cc	—	—

Amounts required from the West Riding wapentakes :—

				£	s.	d.
Agbrig and Morley .	.	.	.	xv	vi	viii
Staincliffe and Ewcross	.	.	.	xv	vi	viii
Claro .	.	.	.	xv	vi	viii
Barkstone Ash	.	.	.	vii	xiii	iv
Skyrack	.	.	.	vii	xiii	iv
Osgoldcross and Staincross	.	.	vii	xiii	iv
Strafford and Tickhill	.	.	xi	—	—
Total .	.	.	.	£lxxx	—	—

The county was charged with a rate of £160; this is stated to be to defray the expenses of carrying saltpetre and providing gunpowder. Towards this amount the Ridings were required to furnish as under :—

				£	s.	d.
West Riding	.	.	.	lxiv	—	—
North ,,	.	.	.	liii	vi	viii
East ,,	.	.	.	xlii	xiii	iv
Total	.	.	.	£clx	—	—

Towards the above amount the different was pentakes contributed, viz. :—

				£	s.	d.
Agbrig and Morley .	.	.	.	x	xiii	iv
Staincliffe and Ewcross	.	.	.	x	xiii	iv
Claro .	.	.	.	x	xiii	iv
Barkstone Ash	.	.	.	v	vi	viii
Skyrack	.	.	.	v	vi	viii
Osgoldcross and Staincross	.	.	v	vi	viii
Strafford and Tickhill	.	.	viii	—	—
Ainsty	.	.	.	viii	—	—
Total	.	.	.	£lxiv	—	—

ANCIENT RATES. 13 Chap. I.

The following extracts are copied from some Ancient Rates. accounts of the seventeenth century, which relate to Barnsley :—·

> " A Bill of disborsement for ye Towne of Barnesley,
>   for the yeare of our Lorde God, 1643."

	s.	d.
For charges to Pontefrett about the salpetre men	vj	iij
Layde downe for beare for the saltpetre men	—	vj
My charges to Pontefrett about the salpetre men	iiij	ix

The county was charged with another rate, amounting to the sum of one hundred marks, to be paid to Sir Edward Yorke, muster-master. Towards this the Ridings contributed as follows :—

	£	s.	d.
West Riding	xxvi	xiii	iv
North ,, ...	xxii	iv	vi
East ,, ...	xvii	xv	vi
Total	£lxvi	xiii	iv

The sum required from each wapentake in the West Riding was as under :—

	£	s.	d.
Agbrig and Morley	iv	viii	xi
Staincliffe and Ewcross . . .	iv	viii	xi
Claro	iv	viii	xi
Barkstone Ash . . .	ii	iv	v
Skyrack	ii	iv	v
Osgoldcross and Staincross . .	ii	iv	v
Strafford and Tickhill . . .	iii	vi	viii
Ainsty	iii	vi	viii
Total . . . :	£xxvi	xiii	iv

There are other assessments, which refer exclusively to the wapentake of Staincross, which will be given hereafter when treating of that division; and should I not be deviating from the subject, I will next proceed to notice a few important historical events.

Chap. II. 14   GENERAL HISTORY.

CHAPTER II.

" Thus, like the rage of fire, the combat burns;
And now it rises, now it sinks, by turns."

The Conquest. ON the death of Edward the Confessor, which took place A.D. 1066, Harold came forward to assume the government of the kingdom, but this high honour it was not his good fortune to enjoy; for another had entered his claim, and pronounced Harold an usurper—this was William the Norman. The son of Godwin, considering himself the rightful successor, disregarded this demand; both he and his army were in high spirits by reason of the victory obtained over the King of Norway at Stamford Bridge, in this county. This triumph was, however, of short duration, and the result of the contest scarcely known to the people, ere his rival had, with a numerous force, set foot on his territory. The brave Saxon, the favourite of the people, no sooner heard of his descent than he advanced to give him battle; a sanguinary struggle ensued, and long it seemed doubtful which way the victory would turn, and whether the Norman or the Saxon should fill the throne. Harold fought nobly, and is said to have slain many of the enemy with his own hand. At length an arrow pierced his brain, and he fell, which threw his army into confusion. The result was that the inhabitants of the south had no other alternative but to acknowledge

THE FEUDAL SYSTEM.

15 Chap. II.

Fiefs.

the Conqueror, and act submissively. The people of the north, and particularly of Yorkshire, William found made of the same stubborn material as the Romans did eleven centuries before; these would not bow to the tyrant. Full of revenge, he swore by the splendour of God's face that a Northumbrian should not be left alive to stir in future insurrections. Yorkshire was made desolate by fire and sword, the estates of the gentry confiscated, and granted lavishly among his followers. This was the foundation in England of the feudal system, which is said to have had its original from the military policy of the northern nations—the Goths, the Huns, the Franks, the Vandals, and the Lombards, who spread themselves all over Europe at the fall of the Roman Empire. Large districts of land were allotted by the conquering generals to the superior officers of the army, and by them dealt out again in smaller portions to the inferior officers and most deserving soldiers. These allotments were called "*Feoda, Feuds, Fiefs, or Fees.*" They were rewards given on condition that the possessor should do service faithfully, both at home and in the wars, to him by whom they were given, for which purpose he, the receiver, took the "*Juramentum fidelitatis,*" or oath of fealty. Every receiver or feudatory was bound, when called upon by the immediate lord of the feud or fee, to do all in his power to defend him; such immediate lord was under the command of his superior, and so upward to the prince or general himself; and the several lords were also bound in their respective gradations to protect the lands they had given. Thus the feudal connection was established; but

Chap. II. 16   GENERAL HISTORY.

Land Tenures. this feudal polity was not received in England universally till the reign of William the Norman. In the latter part of the year in which the ": Domesday Book" was made, a council was held by the Conqueror of all his nobility at Sarum, when all the principal landowners submitted their lands to the yoke of military tenure, became the King's vassals, and did homage and fealty to him. This was probably the era of introducing feudal tenure by law. This new polity does not seem to have been imposed by William, but to have been freely adopted by the general assembly of the whole realm. Besides the oath of fealty, the vassal, upon the lands being given to him, did homage to the lord thus :—" Openly and humbly kneeling, ungirt, uncovered, and holding up his hands between those of his lord who sat before him, and there professing that he did become his man from that day forth, of life, and limb, and earthly honour, and then received a kiss from his lord."

Different kinds of Tenures. There were amongst our ancestors four principal species of tenure. Bracton, who wrote in the reign of Henry III., says :—" Tenements are of two kinds, frank tenements and villenage; and of frank tenements some are held in consideration of homage and knights' service; others in free socage, with service of fealty only; and again of villenage, some are pure and others privileged. He that holds in pure villenage shall do whatever is commanded of him; the other kind of villenage is called villein socage, and these villein socmen do villein service but such as is sure and determined."

The most honourable species of tenure was knights' service. To make a tenure by knights' service, a certain quantity of land was necessary,

THE FEUDAL SYSTEM. 17 Chap. II.

which was called a knight's fee (" *Feodum mili-* Gen. History.
tare "), the measure of which was, in the third year
of Edward I., estimated at twelve ploughlands, and
its value twenty pounds per annum. He who held
this quantity of land was bound to attend his lord
to the wars for forty days in every year, if called
upon.

By statute passed in the twelfth year of
Charles II., cap. 24, the military tenures were
abolished; and all sorts of tenures held of the
King or others were turned into free socage,
copyholds excepted.

B

Chap. III. 18   GENERAL HISTORY.

Family of Laci.

CHAPTER III.

> " No trace is left of the invading Dane,
>   Or the arm'd follower of the Norman Knight,
>   Gone is the dwelling of the Saxon Thane,
>   And Lord and Baron with their feudal might."

OF those who followed in the train of the Conqueror, few stood higher in the favour of their royal master than the noble family of Laci, whose share of the plundered property must have been considerable, as it appears from Domesday[1] that Ilbert had one hundred and sixty-four manors in the counties of York, Lincoln, and Notts. He was a tenant *in capite*, that is, he held his lands immediately of the King, which were confirmed to him by William in the tenth year of his reign. He was founder of the

---

[1] The Domesday survey was made by order of the Conqueror, and the part relating to Yorkshire compiled about the year 1080. It was completed by the King's justiciaries, who, upon the oaths of the sheriffs, the lords of each manor, the priests of every church, the reeves of every hundred, the bailiffs and six villeins, were to inquire into the name of the person who held each manor in the time of the Confessor, who was the present possessor, how many hides of land were in the manor, how many carucates in demesne, how many homagers, or villeins, or *cottarii*, or *servi*, what free men, how many tenants in socage, the quantities of wood, meadow, and pasture, what mills and fish ponds, how much added or taken away, what the value in the Confessor's time, what the present value, and how much each freeman or socman had or has. This valuable record is in the Exchequer.

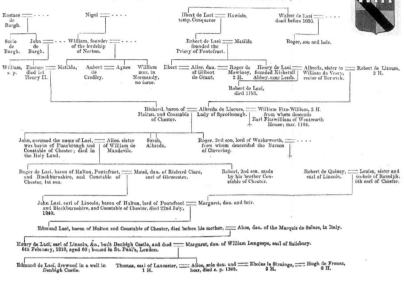

PEDIGREE OF THE FAMILY OF LACI, LORDS OF PONTEFRACT AND BLACKBURNSHIRE.

Arms—Quarterly *Or* and *Gules* a Bend *Sable*, over all a Label of Five Points *Argent*.

THE FAMILY OF LACI. 19 Chap. III.

honour of Pontefract, and held much land in this Gen. History.
locality, which, previous to the Norman conquest,
was enjoyed by Ailric the Saxon, and gave the head
of his fee its name from the resemblance it bore to
Pontfrete, his birthplace.

Ilbert had also a brother who accompanied the
expedition, to whom lands were given in Hereford-
shire and other counties. He died before the survey was completed, and his possessions descended
to his eldest son, Roger, who held one hundred and
twenty lordships.

Annexed is a pedigree, showing the course the
Honour of Pontefract took in this family.

Ilbert died in the early part of the twelfth century. Robert, his son, the founder of the Priory of
Pontefract, succeeded to his vast possessions, which
were confirmed to him by the king.

Rufus had agreed with his brother Robert that, The contest be-
if he were the survivor, he should succeed to the tween Henry
I. and Ro-
throne; but Robert, at the time of the death of bert of Nor-
Rufus, being engaged in the Crusades, Henry, the mandy.
youngest son of the Conqueror, finding the people
much attached to him, assumed the sovereignty
himself, and was solemnly crowned. Robert, on
his return to Normandy, hearing what had trans-
pired in England during his absence, embarked
with a considerable army to enforce his claim; and
Henry, it appears, was not unprepared to resist
him. The parties met, but wisely resolved not to
involve the nation in civil war. The rival claims
were compromised, and a reconciliation at once
effected—Robert agreeing to waive his right to the
throne on being paid annually a stipulated sum,
and Henry promising to pardon all who had
espoused the cause of his brother; but as soon as

Chap. III. 20   GENERAL HISTORY.

Family of Laci. the nation had assumed its former tranquillity, Henry thought it safest to be rid of those who had taken part with Robert. Amongst those unfortunate individuals was Robert de Pontefract, and his son Ilbert, who were banished the kingdom. Dodsworth says:—"*Anno* 1102, *Henricus Rex, Robertum Malletum et Yvonem de Grentsmill, Robertum de Pontefracto, filium Ilberti de Laceio, et potentiorem omnibus Robertum de Belismo, &c., ad judicium summonivit.*"

Robert de Laci summoned to judgment. And again he informs us, that "*Rex Robertum de Pontefracto, et Robertum Malletum, placitus impetivit et honoribus expoliatos extorres expulit.*"

The King having expelled Robert de Laci and his son, gave the castle and honour of Pontefract to Henry Traverse, who enjoyed these honours and estates but a few days, he being murdered by one of his servants.

Hugh de la Val next held these possessions, as appears from a charter by which he grants to the monks of Pontefract the " church of Ledesham, and Ledestone, and Whitewode, and Dodeworde, and in Foxeholes six bovates of land, and in Silkestone six bovates of land, of the gift of Ailric; and the church of Silkestone, with the things thereto belonging, of the gift of Swein the son of Ailric; and moreover of his gift the church of Caltorne, with two parts of the tithes of the whole of his lordship." This charter was confirmed by Henry, the king, who signed the sign of the holy cross as a witness to it.

After a few years' banishment, Robert de Laci was restored to his estates and honours. He died towards the close of the reign of Henry I., and was succeeded by his son Ilbert, who adhered faithfully to King Stephen; and after the battle of Northal-

THE FAMILY OF LACI.   21   Chap. III.

lerton, in which his nephew Robert, the last of the old line of Laci, took a distinguished part, he obtained a pardon on behalf of all his servants, and reversal of all forfeitures whatsoever.

The time of Ilbert's death is not known. Leaving no issue, his estates went to his brother Henry, who was engaged in the battle of Teverbrai in the sixth year of Henry II. ; in the latter part of whose reign he died, and was buried in the abbey of Kirkstall, near Leeds.

On the death of Robert de Laci, which took place A.D. 1193, Albreda de Lizours, his half-sister, succeeded to the estates, and, marrying Richard Fitz-Eustace, carried them into that family.

Dodsworth[1] gives us the following account of the descent of the Lacis, lords of Pontefract and Blackburnshire, which he professes to have taken, in the year 1620, from an old manuscript formerly belonging to the abbot of Kirkstall.

" Now after the Conquest, and all things were brought together, William the Conqueror gave to a certain Ilbert de Laci, knight, who came out of Normandy at his conquest, the lordship of Blackburnshire, and to his heirs, as an hereditary possession, with the lordship and honour of Pontefract, with many other lands. Now the same Ilbert built in his castle which he had made at Pontefract a certain chapel, which he caused to be dedicated in honour of St. Clement, by Thomas, who was then archbishop of York. He also founded in the same chapel a certain chantry, and appointed canons, with a dean, to serve for ever in the same place; and endowed the chapel itself with lands, revenues,

---

[1] The original is in Latin.

Chap. III. 22   GENERAL HISTORY.

Dodsworth's account of the Laci Family.

tithes of sheaves, and fowls from the brood belonging to him, with many other things; and caused the said chapel to be decreed and made free by our lord Pope Alexander the Third, then head of the Church universal, as in a bull of the said lord the Pope is more fully contained.

"Now the son and heir of this Ilbert was Ilbert the younger, who was succeeded in his inheritance by Henry de Laci, brother and heir of the same Ilbert the younger; which Henry founded the monastery of Kirkstall, of the Cistercian order, first at Barnoldwyke, and then transferred the same house to the aforesaid Kirkstall, where they dwelt in the twelfth year of the reign of King Stephen.

"This Henry was succeeded by Robert, his son and heir, who died in the fourth year of Richard I., and in the year of our Lord 1193, 12 Kal. Septembris;[1] which Robert de Laci, the son and heir of Henry de Laci, in the reign of Henry II., who was called the son of the Empress, began to erect the castle of Clyderhon, in Blackburnshire, in which castle he caused to be built a certain chapel in honour of the blessed Michael the Archangel; in which chapel, by the assent and license of Galfridus, then dean of Whalley, the elder, he ordained Divine service to be celebrated and the sacraments to be administered among his respective tenants, shepherds, and foresters; whereby the same his tenants, shepherds, foresters, and other servants living distant from the said church, in the said church, by the chaplain there serving, should receive the holy sacrament, and pay the parochial dues, as the other parishioners in divers chapels in the same parish did render."

[1] 21st August.

THE FAMILY OF LACI. 23 Chap. III.

Gen. History.

In another part of the said book :—

"Genealogy of the lord Henry de Laci, Earl of Lincoln.

Genealogy of De Laci, Earl of Lincoln.

"A certain knight, Nigel by name, came with Hugh, Earl of Lincoln, who brought with him five brothers, viz.—Hordardus, Everdus, Wolmerus, Horswinus, and Wolfanus.

"This Nigel by name had one son, called William, who was founder of the lordship of Norton, at Runcona. This William begat a certain son, known as William the younger, who was married beyond the sea in Normandy. He left no heir, but had two sisters, named Agnes and Matilda, between whom the hereditary possession of Halton was divided; and there came a certain soldier, called Eustace, and espoused Matilda, which Eustace was slain in Wales; and one Aubert de Credley was betrothed to the other sister, viz., Agnes de Gantes. The aforesaid Matilda had by Eustace one son, called Richard, who took to wife the sister of Robert de Laci, who was called Albreda de Lizours; of whom he begat John, constable of Chester, the founder of Stainlow, and brother of Robert the Hospitaller, and also two daughters, Sarah and Albreda. The aforesaid John, the founder, betrothed Alice, sister of William de Maundevile, of whom he begat Roger, surnamed 'Hell;' and this Roger begat John, constable of Chester, who took to wife Margaret, daughter of Robert de Quincy, grand-daughter of Ralph, Earl of Chester; and on her, when made Earl of Chester, this John also begat Edmund. · Edmund begat Henry, the noble Earl of Lincoln, and founder of Whalley, who begat one son, Edmund, who died quickly, and one daughter, Alice the countess, whom

Chap. III. 24   GENERAL HISTORY.

Family of Laci. a noble man, Thomas, viz., Thomas Earl of Lancaster, espoused.

2nd Rufus.   "In the year of our Lord 1089, Ralph Pagnel founded the priory of the Holy Trinity, at York.

12th Stephen. 1147.   "The Savignian Order was joined together, and the abbey of Kirkstall was founded on the feast of the Holy Virgin.

15th Henry II. 1169.   "The Order of Hospitallers began.

18th Henry II. 1172.   "The Abbey of Stainlow was founded.

19th Henry II. 1173.   "John de Laci died in the Holy Land. He was the founder of Stainlow.

13th John. 1211.   "Died Roger de Laci, second founder, on the feast of St. Remigius, to whom succeeded John, his son, afterwards Earl of Lincoln through his wife.

24th Hen. III. 1240.   "John de Laci, Earl of Lincoln, Constable of Chester, and Lord of Halton, died on the feast of Magdalene.

42nd Hen. III. 1258.   "Died Edmund de Laci, son of John, fourth founder; to whom succeeded Henry, his son. The bones of these are at Whalley.

42th Edw. I. 1296.   "On the feast of St. Ambrose the Bishop, by the license of our lord the King, the abbot and convent of Stainlow were translated to the monastery called Whalley, by Henry, Earl of Lincoln."

From the foregoing account it will be seen that the family of Laci was one of importance, and took an active part in the affairs of the country. Henry[1] was the last male of his house. He bequeathed to Alice, his only surviving daughter and heiress, the whole of his possessions, and, if no issue, he entailed the same on the King and his heirs; so that the honour of Pontefract ultimately came to the Crown.

[1] Henry de Laci, Earl of Lincoln, towards the close of the thirteenth century, resided at London, and had a mansion in Lincoln's Inn Fields.

CHAPTER IV.

THE WAPENTAKE OF STAINCROSS.[1]

THE Wapentake of Staincross is one of the smaller divisions of the West Riding, the whole of which was given to Ilbert de Laci. One volume of the Harleian Manuscripts is entirely taken up with matters relating thereto; amongst which are notices of charters, charges of land, and courts held at Barnsley, from the reign of Henry III. to the time of Henry VI., particulars of which will be given hereafter.

Manorial Courts.

In the book from which I have extracted the rates, it is said that there are usually two high constables in this wapentake, which is part of the duchy and honour of Pontefract; and the bailiff is here appointed by the farmer of the liberties belonging to the said honour, which is granted by lease upon a rent reserved under the duchy-seal; and that Barnsley is the only particular liberty within the wapentake, and is likewise part of the duchy, and hath a particular bailiff for the liberties there.

High Constables.

Ailric held a great portion of the land in this division in the time of the Confessor. He was lord of the following places in the middle of the eleventh century:—Birchworth, Cawthorn, Clayton, Cum-

---

[1] It is supposed that there was formerly a stone-cross placed where the wapentake courts were held, and from which the name is derived.

Chap. IV. 26 GENERAL HISTORY.

Staincross. berworth, Hoyland, Hunshelf, Penistone, Pilley, Silkstone, Skelmanthorpe, Thurgoland, Thurlestone, Wortley.

The whole of his possessions were seized by the Conqueror, and given to Ilbert de Laci, the founder of the honour of Pontefract.

Ailric the Saxon. When this Norman lord parcelled out his lands, Ailric appeared as an applicant, and was accepted as one of his tenants, but had not as much land granted to him in this wapentake[1] as he had enjoyed prior to the Conquest. It is rather singular that he should have succeeded to the property he had previously held, if we take into consideration the estimation in which the Saxons were held by the new-comers, and the treatment they received from them. Ailric cannot have been actuated by the same spirit as the majority of the Saxon chiefs, and the conferring of this favour upon him must have been in a great measure owing to his peaceful disposition. We know little of him, and what we are able to obtain is from charters of his descendants. He held of the honour of Pontefract the following places in the wapentake of Staincross:— Cawthorne, Silkstone, Hoyland, Clayton, Penistone, Hunshelf, Denby, Brierley, Hiendley, with part of Shafton and Carlton, and is supposed to have resided at Cawthorne. He had issue Swein, who made a donation of the church of Silkstone to the monks of Pontefract, of which an account will be given hereafter. Swein had one son, Adam, who about the middle of the twelfth century founded the priory of Monk Bretton.

[1] The jurors say that the Earl of Lincoln and his seneschals let the wapentakes of Staincross and Osgoldcross at a high rent, and for a very grievous sum of money.—*Rotuli Hundredorum.*

THE WAPENTAKE OF STAINCROSS. 27 Chap. IV.

In connection with this wapentake, is an old Gen. History. document which furnishes us with a list of the names of armed men serving in this division in the reign of Elizabeth, which I give verbatim.

Musters taken of the Privat Men and Towne Soldiors within The Militia. the wapentacke of Staincrose at Barnsleyc, the iiij[th] of December, 1587, by Richard Wortleye and George Woodroff, Esquiers.

Thurlstone.—*Privat Men.*—P. Edwarde Riche, F. ; P. Willm. Marshden, F. ; P. John Skott, F. ; A. Willm. Skott, F. ; Nicholas Lee, his man. *Town Soldiors.*—A. Edward Fyrthe, F. ; P. Willm. Thomson, F. ; A. John Michell, F. ; P. John Nicholls. F.

Thurgoland.—*Privat Men.*—P. Thomas Cudworth, F. savinge a better man ; P. Nicholas Ellison, F. ; B. Willm. Dughtyman, F. *Town Soldiors.*—B. John Hurste ; C. Thomas Crawshaye ; P. Nicholas Tetlowe ; to shewe themselves furnyshed upon Thursdaye next at Wortleye.

Stainbroughe.—*Privat Men.*—P. John Cutler, F. ; C. Richarde Wadsworthe, F. *Town Soldior.*—C. Roger Warde, F.

Langsett.—*Privat Men.*—P. John Preste, F. ; P. John Haighe, F. ; to come to Wortleye upon Thursday. *Town Soldior.*—P. Raufe Townrowe, F., has the daye till Thursdaye.

Worsbroughe.—*Privat Men.*—P. Rob. Castelfurthe, F. ; William Tingle, his man ; P. Roger Elmhurste, F. ; Averay Norton, his man ; P. William Walker, F. ; William Warame, his man ; P. Roger Ellison, F. *Town Soldiors.*—P. William Huchingson, F. ; C. Roger Howaye, F. ; C. Robert Sycks, F. ; C. John Jenkyngson, F.

Notton.—*Privat Men.*—P. Robert Scawberte, F. ; B. Richard Gill, F. *Town Soldiors.*—P. Thomas Brodhead, F. ; B. Brian Sunyer, F.

Hymsworthe.—*Privat Men.*—P. Thomas Wood, F. ; Richard Ranskall, his man ; A. Samuel Ashton, F. ; John Bedfurthe, his man. *Town Soldiors.*—P. John Hirst ; C. Robert Oplif ; to be at Wooleye upon Thursday.

Wortleye.—*Privat Men.*—A. John Heye, F. ; Thomas Woode, his man ; C. Thomas Ayton, F. *Town Soldiors.*—P. William Wyntterbotham, F. ; C. John Woodheade, F.

Highe Hoyland.—*Privat Men.*—P. John Weste, F. ; B. Roberte Bilcliffe, F. *Town Soldior.*—C. Robert Smythe, F.

Chap. IV. 28 GENERAL HISTORY.

The Militia. South Hyndleye.—*Privat Men.*—P. Roberte Norfolcke, F.; John Anderson, his man. *Town Soldior.*—P. Christopher Wolfenden, F., to be at Woolleye to-morrow.

Kesper.—*Privat Men.*—John Allot to shewe Thomas Taylor, his man, at Woolleye upon Thursday. *Town Soldiors.*—C. John Hogson, F., to bring another soldior to-morrow for Jagger to Wooleye; A. John Turner.

Ingburchworthe.—*Privat Men.*—P. John Mickeltwhate, F.; Raufe Charlesworthe, his man. *Town Soldiors.*—P. John Mickeltwhate, younger, F.; Godfraye Swyndinge, his man.

Denbye.—*Privat Men.*—P. Thomas Jenkynson, F.; Richard Willmson, his man; P. John Michell, F. *Town Soldiors.*—A. Raufe Clayton, F.; C. Lawrance Hawcksworth, F.; C. Richard Owdom, F.

Cawthorne.—*Privat Men.*—P. Willm. Champneye, F.; C. Thomas Grenne, F.; P. Thomas Catlowe, F.; C. Willm. Grene, F. *Town Soldiors.*—P. Edmond Haighe, F.; C. Willm. Hawcrofte, F.; C. Richard Gawthrope, F.; P. Richard Rawling, F. Armor.

Tankersleye.—*Privat Men.*—C. Michaell Clerke, F. *Town Soldiors.*—C. Richard Lynleye, F.; C. Edward Skott, F.

Penystone.—*Privat Men.*—P. Willm. Wadsworthe, F. *Town Soldior.*—C. John Bilclyffe, F.

Silkstone.—*Privat Men.*—C. Willm. Swyfte, F.; B. Thomas Oxlye, F.' *Town Soldior.*—P. John Edson, F.

Oxspringe.—*Privat Men.*—B. Richard Marsden, F.; C. Raufe Jessope, F.; Adam Botham, his man. *Town Soldior.* —C. Thomas Hall, F.

Hunshelf.—*Privat Men.*—P. John Greaves, F.; A. Raufe, Wadsworth, F. *Town Soldiors.*—P. John 'Silvester, F.; A. Lawrance Lynleye, F.

Cumberworth-half.—*Privat Man.*—A. Raufe Burdit, F. *Town Soldior.*—A. Amore Lockwoode, F.

Bretton-half.—*Town Soldior.*—D. John Rove, not F.

Hoylland Swayne.—*Privat Men.*—B. John Moxson, F.; C. John Holme, F. *Town Soldior.*—P. Willm. Catling, F.—The man appears not.

Barnsleye.—*Privat Men.*—P. Thomas Kesfurthe, F.; P. Willm. Rushworthe, F.; P. John Jenkynson, F.; P. Richard Norfolke, F.; John Dyche, his man; C. Roberte Thwaite, F.; John Bradleye, his man. *Town Soldiors.*—P. Raufe Birkenshaye, F.; C. John Rouke, F.; C. Godfraye Roodes, F.; C. Richard Chapell, F.

THE WAPENTAKE OF STAINCROSS. 29 Chap. IV.

Brearleye.—*Privat Men.*—C. Mr. Jarvas Rayneye, F. ; The Militia. Henrye Porter, his man; A. Willm. Pyt, F.; Willm. Wilkynson, his man. *Town Soldiors.*—C. Francis Sanderson, F.; Matthew in his place; B. George Woode, F. ; to be shewed at Woolleye upon Thursday.

Ardsleye.—*Privat Men.*—A. Willm. Ellyott, F. ; B. Willm. Parkyne, F. *Town Soldiors.*—P. Thomas Morton, F.; A. Nicholas Goodaile, F.

Munckburton.—*Privat Men.*—P. George Woode, F.; Thomas Allot, his man. *Town Soldiors.*—C. Francis Swyfte, F.; A. Francis Foxe, F.

Carlton.—*Privat Men.*—B. Richard Hyncliffe, F. ; A. Roberte Pytte, his man. *Town Soldiors.*—A. Thomas Silverwoode, F. ; C. Thomas Lyster, F.

Havercrofte.—*Privat Man.*—A. George Gille, F. *Town Soldior.*—C. Willm. Stocks, F.

Cudworthe.—*Privat Men.*—P. Edward Lynleye, F.; John Turton, his man; A. Edward Brownleye, F. ; Thomas Jessope, his man ; B. Thomas Slacke, F. ; James Sycks, his man. *Town Soldiors.*—C. Richard Willay, F. ; B. Edwarde Howden, F. ; A. Thomas Porter, F.

Clayton.—*Privat Men.*—P. Peter Hawcksworthe, F.; Thomas Hawcksworthe, his man ; B. Richard Clayton, F.; Arthurr, his sone, his man. *Town Soldiors.*—P. Henrye Ellis, F.; A. Mathewe Oxleye, F.

Barghe.—*Privat Men.*—P. Raufe Jenkynson, F. ; Charles Haslowe, his man; P. Robert Marsh, F.; P. Richard Marsh, F. *Town Soldiors*—C. Thomas Wolfenden, F. ; B. Willm. Barrowe, F.

Darton.—*Privat Men.*—P. Nicholas Burditt, F. ; B. Thomas Adye, F. *Town Soldiors.*—P. Robte. Denton, F. ; John Lepton in his place; C. Thomas Haighe, F.; Willm. Copley in his place.

Wynttersett.—*Privat Man.*—A. James Barber, F. *Town Soldior.*—C. Nicholas Johnson, F.

Dodworthe.—*Privat Men.*—C. John Hobson, F. ; C. Richard Hobson, F. *Town Soldiors.*—C. Richard Skorrer, F.; C. Thomas Moxson, F.

Ryell.—*Privat Man.*—B. Robert Sympson, F.

Woolleye.—*Privat Men.*—P. Raufe Hellywell, F.; P. Mr. John Popleye, F.; Nicholas Savill, his man. *Town Soldiors.*—B. Lawrance Langton, F. ; P. Willm. Waynwrighte, F.

Royston.—*Privat Men.* .... *Town Soldior.*—C. George Clerke, F.

Chap. IV. 30   GENERAL HISTORY.

The Militia. Shafton.—*Privat Men.* .... *Town Soldiors.*—A. Richard Clerkson, F.; Wyllm. Renolds in his place.

Privat Souldiors . .	71	Towne Soldiors . . .	70
Armyd Picks . . .	37	Armyd Picks . . .	20
Calivers[1]	12	Calivers.	32
Bills.	11	Bills.	6
Archers	11	Archers.	12

Totall Some, CXLI.

Rates.   In the forty-second year of the reign of Elizabeth, it was agreed that the justices of every wapentake, or the greater part of them, should meet at Wakefield, at Whitsuntide, to consult respecting soldiers' pensions, assessments, and other matters; and there to deliver to the clerk of the peace a particular estreat and perfect assessment of every township within their several wapentakes, to remain for a precedent to direct other justices to make equal assessments for the West Riding when occasion should require. Amongst the rates then agreed upon was one to be levied on the wapentake of Staincross, amounting to the sum of forty-four shillings and two pence. It is not stated for what purpose this was required. The townships contributed as under:[2]—

	s.	d.		s.	d.
Barnsley . .	ij	ij	Hemsworth . .	j	vij
Cawthorne . .	ij	ij	Cudworth . .	j	vij
Worsbrough . .	ij	ij	Thurgoland . .	j	vij
Thurlestone . .	ij	ij	High Hoyland .		ix
Wortley . . .	j	vij	Havercroft . .		ix

[1] A particular kind of musket formerly used.

[2] There is evidently an error in these rates, as the total will not agree with the amount given above.

THE WAPENTAKE OF STAINCROSS.

	d.			d.
Stainbrough	ix	Clayton	. . .	xiij
Cumberworth	viij	Dodworth	. . .	xiij
Ryhill	viij	Darton	. . .	xiij
Winterset	viij	Denby .	. . .	xiij
Shafton .	viij	Hoyland Swein	. .	xiij
Gunthwait	v	Hunshelf	. . .	xiij
Ingbirchworth	v	Kexbrough	. . .	xiij
Oxspring	v	Langset	. .	xiij
Bretton .	iiij	Silkstone	. . .	xiij
Chevet .	iiij	Notton	. . .	xiij
Ardsley	. xiij	Penistone	. . .	xiij
Monk Bretton	. xiij	Roystone	. . .	xiij
Carlton	. xiij	Hiendley	. . .	xiij
Bargh .	. xiij	Tankersley	. . .	xiij
Brierley	. xiij	Woolley	. . .	xiij

Lame soldiers were provided for by a special rate, and several acts of Parliament were passed which relate to their pensions.

The statute of 33 Eliz., cap. 4, enacts, " that no parish shall be assessed for the relief of maimed soldiers above six pence, or under one penny, and so that they shall not exceed two pence, one parish with another."

By the statute of 39 Eliz., cap. 21, it is ordered, " that no parish shall be rated at above eight pence, or under two pence; in order that the amount may not be above four pence, taking one with another."

The statute of 43 Eliz., cap. 3, says, " that no parish shall be charged more than ten pence, or under two pence; so that the total shall not amount to more than six pence, one parish with another."

The weekly contributions of different places in Staincross wapentake towards this assessment, in the year 1601, stood as follows :—

Chap. IV. 32 GENERAL HISTORY.

Rates.

	d.			d.
Barnsley . . .	vj	Hemsworth . . .	vj
Penistone . . .	x	Darton . . .	iiij
Silkstone . . .	viij	Tankersley . . .	iiij
Roystone . . .	viij	Hoyland . . .	iiij
Fieldkirk . . .	viij	Woolley . . .	ij
Cawthorne . . .	vj		

I append a few extracts from documents which relate to lame soldiers' money, in connection with Barnsley, with copies of some receipts relating thereto, together with other matters.

s. d.

January 12, 1623. More payd to George Wood, chiefe constable, for laime soldiers' money. . . . . . . iiij —

1634. Leayde downe by Edward Oxley and mysealf, for laime souldiers, at Rotheram seshons . . . iiij iiij

And payde the High Constable, at Barnsley seshons . ij iij

vij die Octobris Anno 1634. Rec. the day and yeare above said, of the church-wardens of Barnsley, for laime souldiers due at Michaelmas seshons . . . . . . iiij iiij

I say, rec. the above,

By me,

WILL. PLATTS.

xiij die Octo-bris, 1635. Rec. of the churchwardens of Barnsley, for laime souldier money, for the sesshons holden at Don-kester the daye and yeare aforesaid, the sum of . iiij iiij

ARTR. PLATTS.

1636. Payde Robert Wood, lame shouldger money, at Rotheram seshons . . . . . . viij v

1648. Payde to Mr. Price, ye High Constable, for three querters, iiijs. vjd. ye querter, being for ye maimed souldiers . . . . . . xiij vj

1649. Payde to Robert Wood, for his bill for laime soul-diers, at Michaelmas . . . . . x ix

It would appear by a document from which the subjoined is taken, that the amount previously collected for the relief of lame soldiers was not sufficient to meet the demand :—

THE WAPENTAKE OF STAINCROSS. 33 Chap. IV.

Rates.

WHEREAS. I have rec. an order from severall of his Matie Justices of ye Peace of this Riding, in pursuance of an Act of Parliament, intituled "An Act for the reliefe of poore maymed souldiers," and upon due consideration thereupon, and of ye excessive number of petitioners for pentions raymaining upon y^r severall fiyles of these and of ye last generall sessions houlden att Pontefract ye eight day of Aperill last, of theire poore necessitous condition, it is ordered by ye said Justices y^t ye utmost power be given by ye said Act to charge ye Ridinge for ye use abovesaid bee putt in execution, namely y^t every P^{'ish} or chapellrie y^t hath a distinct p'och'all officer bee charged three times as much to y^t w^h they were before by virtue of a statute made ye 43 yeare of Queene Elizabeth raine, and it is ordered to be continued soe till the next Genrall sessions houlden att Pontefract. These are therefore in his Maties name to require and charge you ye severall churchwardens of ye Parishes hereunder written, to apeare att Barnsley upon Wednesday the 24th of this instant Sep. att the house of Will. Simpson, then and there to pay unto me before 12 of ye clocke of ye s^d day the severall somes here expressed. herein you are not to faile, as you tender his Maties servis and will answer ye contrary.

A.D. 1662.

Wollye, Sept. ye 16.

From

Tho. Ellis.

	For lame Soldiers.			For Prisoners in the King's Bench.			For ye Castle of York.		
Darton . .	£1	6	0	£0	1	7	£0	1	7
Barnsley . .	0	17	4	0	1	1	0	1	1
Tankersley .	0	13	0	0	0	9	0	0	9

Then received of the churchwardens of Barnsley the sume of xvijs. iiijd. beinge theire due proportion for laime soldiers.

Sep. ye 27, 1662.

I say, received by me,

Tho. Ellis.

For a quittance iiijd.

The last notice I have seen of this rate is in the accounts of James Allen, who held the office of churchwarden in 1679. The amount is there set down at eight shillings and eight pence, and for acquittances four pence.

c

GENERAL HISTORY.

Chap. IV. 34

Rates. I subjoin copies of other receipts, of an earlier date and different description :—

Barnsley, 14th Nov., 1627. Receyved the daie and yeere above said of the Constable of Barnsley vij*s*. according to my warrant to him directed, and for the acquitance ij*d*.

J. Baitman.

The first day of Aprill, 1628. Receyved the daye and yeare above said of the Constabb. of Barnesly, for the M^r and Govnor of the House of Correction, for his wages due unto him the next seshons, the some of ij*s*.

By me,

John Swinden.

Decimo Octavo die Junii, Anno D'ni., 1628. Received the day and yeare above written of William Wright, constable of Barnesley, the some of x*s*. iiij*d*. assessed upon your sayde towne by his Ma$^{tie's}$ Justices towards the repayre of six Bridges ordered at the last general seshons houlden at Wakefield the 22 day of Aprill last paste.

I say received the same abovesaid, and ij*d*. for the acquitance.

By me,

Godfr. Ellissonne.

viii daye of October, 1628. Received the daye and yeare above said of Petter Robinsonn the some of seaven shilling and sixe pence, for outhoune (outowing) monaye deu to his Matie att Mychallmass last.

I saye, received by me,

John Hinchlife.

xxv of November, 1629. Received of the Constables of Barnesley towards the repaire of Horburie and Hampesthwaite Bridges, towards his Ma$^{tie's}$ provision of . . . towards the reluife of prisoners in Yorke Castle, for Captaine Phillips' pension, for the Govner of the House of Correction for carrying prisoners to sevrall seshons and for his fee, the sume of x*s*. x*d*. Quittance ij*d*.

By me,

Willm. Wordsworth.

The Militia. I have not been able to ascertain the period when the organisation of the militia furnished by the wapentakes of Staincross, Strafford, Tickhill,

THE MILITIA. 35 Chap. IV.

Agbrig, and Osgoldcross took place. Macaulay *The Militia.*
states that, " shortly after the Restoration, two acts of
Parliament were passed, by which the militia was
put on a different footing. Every person who had
an income of five hundred pounds per annum
derived from landed property, or possessed personal estate to the value of six thousand pounds,
was required to provide, equip, and support one
horseman; while others, who had fifty pounds a
year issuing from property, or had personal estate
amounting to the sum of six hundred pounds, were
bound, in like manner, to furnish one pikeman or
musketeer. The services of the standing army were
dispensed with, and the militia is said to have been
the only force which this country possessed for
many years after the termination of the civil wars.
Its strength was estimated at near one hundred
and thirty thousand men, under the direction of
the Sovereign, and officered by the lords-lieutenant
and their deputies, who fixed the time for drilling,
which was not to exceed fourteen days in the year.
For disobedience or breach of discipline, the magistrates had power to inflict penalties. "

Sir Michael Wentworth's regiment was raised in
the wapentakes before mentioned. I have been
favoured with a copy of his muster-roll, executed
about the year 1680, which shows who were
chargeable at that period. It is headed—

" Militia "—Sr. Michaell Wentworth's Regimt., within the *Muster Roll of*
wappentakes of Agbrigg, Staincross, Osgoldcross, Strafford, *Sir Michael*
and Tickhill. *Wentworth's
Regiment.—
1680.*

(The Letters P. and M. denote Pikeman and Musketeer.)

STAINCROSS.

Ardsley.—Richard Micklethwait, P.; John Prince, P.;
Richard Mawhood, M. non. app.

Chap. IV. 36   GENERAL HISTORY.

The Militia.

Muster Roll of Sir Michael Wentworth's Regiment.— 1680.

Barnsley.—Richard Ellinson, P.; Thomas Waid, M.; Mrs. Usher, P.; George Leggett, M.; Thomas Rhoades, M.; William Baggaley, M.

Bargh.—John Barber, P.; Richard Marsh, P. non. app.; John Rooke, non. app.

Brierly.—George Hellenley, M.; Robert Holgate, M.

Cumberworth,—Thomas Anley, M.; Joseph Mosley, M.

Clayton.—Alex. Bothomley, M.; Matthew Swallow, P. non. app.; Thomas Baitson, M. non. app.

Cudworth.—Thomas Ramsden, M.

Cawthorne.—Josias Micklethwait, M.; Robert Smith, M.; William Littlewood, P.; Daniel Hinthman, M.

Denby.—Robert Blackburn, M.; Thomas Burdet, M.; Samuel Clayton, M.; John Hawkesworth, M.; Thomas Hague, junior, M.

Darton.—Mr. William Beaumont, charge to H. P.; Matthew Brown, M.

Dodworth.—Thomas Senior, M.; Thomas Brooke, P.; John Hobson, M.; John Rawson, M. non. app.; William Brooke, M.

Hoyland Swaine.—John Sanderson, M.; John Green, P.; John Sotwell, P.

Hemsworth.—Thomas Ramsden, P.; Michael Leake, M.

High Hoyland.—Mr. William Herne, M.

South Hiendley.—Matthew Goodwin, P.

Havercroft.—Mr. John Gill, M.

Hunshelf.—John Greaves, P.; George Walker, M.; John Wordsworth, M.

Ingbirchworth.—John Micklethwait, P.

Kexbrough.—Mr. William Cotton, M.

Langsett.—Samuel Cockin, P.; John Newton, M.; Isaac Wordsworth, M.

Oxspring.—Richard Marsden, M.

Penistone.—Josias Wordsworth, M: non. app.

Ryhill.—Richard Slack, M.

Monk Bretton.—Mr. William Crookes, M.; Jonathan Broadhead; George Wood, M.

Roystone.—Widdow Bramhall, M.

Stainborough.—Richard Wordsworth, P.; Nicholas Creswick, M. non. app.

Silkstone.—Mrs. Wood, M.; Henry Lee, M.; Mr. Francis Burdet, M.; John Coldwell, P.

Shafton.—John Oxley, M.

Thurlestone.—Silvanus Rich, P.; Mr. Wilson, P.; Daniel Rich, P.; William Hague, M.; Francis Hague, M.

·THE MILITIA. 37 Chap. IV.

Thurgoland.—Mr. Mirfield, P. ; Francis Morton, M. ; Thomas Hobson, P.

Woolley.—Mrs. Prince, P. ; Mary Wheatley, P.

Worsborough.—John Allot, P. ; William Skyers, M. ; Daniel Ellis, M. ; William Adams, P.; Mr. Milner, M. ; John Bingley, M.

The Militia.

Muster Roll of Sir Michael Wentworth's Regiment.—1680.

The names of the sev'all principalls of the foot Armes to the Militia of this division of Agbrigg:—

Aketon.—Mr. John Holdsworth, M.

. Almondbury.—Callas Phillipson, M.; Richard Armitage, M. ; Abraham Beaumont, M. ; Mr. Thomas Darby, M.

Battley.—Sam. Foxcroft, P. ; Timothy Haton, M. ; James Shepley, M. ; Natha. Booth, M.

West Ardesley.—Robt. Casson, M. ; Lawrence Robinson, M.

East Ardesley.—Charles Cooper, P. ; Benjamin Deiton, M.

Crigglestone.—Thomas Johnson, P. ; Jonas Burnett, M. ; Chr. Rhodes, M. ; Mr. Clayton, M.

Cumberworth.—John Cowdill, M. ; William Oxley, M.

Crosland.—Geo. Dawson, M. ; Jos. Hague, M.

Crofton.—Mrs. Mary Oley, M. ; James Clayton, jun., P. ; Thomas Mason, M.

Dewsbury.—Robt. Bedford, M. ; John Nettleton, P. ; Jos. Oldroyd, M. ; James Dawson, P. ; Chr. Dixon, M.

Dalton.—Luke Shaw, M. ; Ath. Langley, P. ; Richard Thewless, M. ; George Beaumont, M.

Emley.—Mrs. Ashton, P. ; John Richinson, M. ; Thomas Wheatley, M.

Flocton Nether.—Will. Rhodes, M.

Ov. Flocton.—George Beaumont, M. ; John Oates, M.

Farnley.—John Wood, P.

Horbury.—Mrs. Leake, P. ; Mr. Longley, P. ; John Walker, M. ; Will. Langfield, M.

Hothersfield.—Daniel Cooper, M. ; Thomas Clarke, M. ; Mr. Will. Brooke, P.

Honley.—Josias Newton, M. ; Richard Littlewood, M. ; Richard Morton, P.

Homforth.—Jonas Kay, M. ; George Linley, M.; Matthew Morehouse, M. ; John Newton, M. ; Luke Wilson, M. ; Humphrey Crosland, M.; Richard Matthewman, P. ; Jonathan Ellis, M.; John Earnshaw, M. ; James Hinchliffe, M. ; John Armitage, P. ; Edmund Broddel, P.

Kirkburton.—John Fitten, M. ; Mr. Joseph Briggs, M.

Chap. IV. 38 GENERAL HISTORY.

The Militia.

Muster Roll of Sir Michael Wentworth's Regiment.— 1680.

Lepton.—Geo. Shaw, M.

Methley.—Richard Laverack, M.; John Farrer, P.; Will. Roberts, M.; Mr. Thorril, P.; Tho. Smith, M.; Mr. John Shann, P.; Mr. Prickett, M.

Meltham.—Edward Tayler, P.; John Armitage, P.

Morley.—Matthew Scatcher, M.; Tho. Craster, M.

Middleton - cum - Thorpe.—William Cassan, P.; Francis Proctor, P.

Marsden.—John Woodhead, P.; John Hague, sen., M.; John Marsden, M.; John Hague, jun., M.

Murfield.—Mr. Geo. Thurgoland, M.; Mr. Tho. Darby, M.; Tho. Shepley, P.; Robt. Holdworth, P.; Joshua Hurst, M.; Joseph Jepson, M.; Mrs. Anne Beaumont, M.; John Hall, M.; John Ledgerd, M.

Norminton.—Mr. Rich. Edmund, M.; Mrs. Nichols, M.; Mrs. Levitt, M.

Ossitt.—Will. Hopwood, P.; Rich. Foster, M.; Edward Bradford, M.; Antho. Whitley, M.; Will. Wilson, M.; Rob. Bradford, M.

Quarmby.—John Tayler, M.; John Dyson, M.; Geo. Dyson, M.; Edw. Aneley, M.; Tho. Denton, P.; John Hague, M.; James Walker, M.

Quick.—John Buckley, P.; Robt. Whitehead, M.; John Garthside, P.; Hen. Buckley, M.; Ralph Andrews, M.; Enuck Andrew, M.; Geo. Garthside, M.

Rothwell.—Mr. Idle Clerk, M.; John Foreman, M.; James More, M.; Tho. Wrigglesworth, M.; Anth. Laburne, M.; Rob. More, M.; John Clareburn, P.; Ann Cogghill, M.; Will. Bosvill, M.; Abraham Fenton, M.; Roger Swift, M.; Henry Clareburn, M.; Mr. Kitchin, M.

Sandall.—Jos. Hall, P.; John Webster, M.; Widd. Shan, M.

Soutill.—Mr. Oates, P.; Will. Hall, M.

Sharleston.—Will. Heater, M.

Shelly.—Mr. John Sykes, P.; Will. Tinker, M.; Will. Mosley, M.

Shepley.—Rich. Matthewman, M.; John Wortley, M.; Tho. Ferth, M.

Stanley.—Mr. Gervase Hatfield, P.; Gideon Mand, M.; John Kent, M.; Joseph Wordsworth, P.; Daniel Mande, P.; Mr. Rich. Grice, P.

Thornhill.—William Empson, P.

Thurstoland.—John Cowdill.

Wakefield.—Mr. William Lawson, M.; Daniell Hoyle, M.;

THE MILITIA. 39 Chap. IV.

The Militia.

Muster Roll of Sir Michael Wentworth's Regiment.— 1680.

Mr. Char. Nayler, M.; Mr. Jeremy Spinke, M.; Mr. Richard Norfolke, sen., P.; Rich. Shaw, M.; Mr. Withers, M.; Rich. Ellis, P.; Rich. Norfolke, jun. M.; Rich. Harrison, P.; Matt. Meager, M.; Mr. Jos. Watkinson, P.

Warnfield.—Will. Mason, M.; John Gelder, P.; Thos. Shepherd, P.

Wolten.—John Kinoston, M.; Mr. Clayton, M.

Whitley.—Geo. Thurgoland, M.; Tho. Shes.

The names, &c., within the Wappentake of Osgoldcross:—

Addingfleet.—Mr. Charles Hall, M.; Mr. Thos. Robinson, M.

Ackworth.—William Lambe, P.; Philip Austwick, M.; Rob. Huitt, P.; Jeremy Bolton, P.

Balne.—John Hudson, M.; John Crooks, P. non ap.

Bramwith.—Thos. Stones, P.; Will. Watson, M.

Begghall.—Theop. Brooke, P.; Tho. Rainer, M.

Burghwallis.—Mr. Sutton, M.; John Pinder, M.; Tho. Shirtcliffe, M.

Cowick.—Cuthbert Rickard, M.; Will. Stables, P.

Cradlingstubbs.—Mrs. Bedford, M.

Carleton.—John Hitchin, M.

Castleford.—John Lake, M.

Campsall.—Thos. Fletcher, M.; Tho. Middleton, P.; John Robinson, M.; Rob. Rusby, M.

Darrington.—Rich. Cookson, M.; Rich. Heaton, M.

Egbrough.—Will. Bateman, M.

Ferry Fristone. — Nich. Bywater, M. non. app.; Rich. Thompson, M.

Fetherstone.—Rob. Shillitoe, M. non. app.

Goule.—John Empson, P.; Will. Empson, M.; Will. Mitchell, M.; Will. Thompson, M.

Goudale.—Rich. Grime, M. non. app.

Houke.—Will. Godfrey, M.; Rob. Mitchell, M. non. app.

Heck.—Geo. Schackleton, P. non. app.

Haldenby.—Geo. Danber, M.

East Hardwick.—John Lambe, M.

Hensall.—Char. Hudderfall, M.; Will. Ferth, charg. to Ho.

Houghton.—Henry Bingley, M. non. app.; James Ward, M.

Kellington.—Rich. Stokeham, P.; John Skelton, M.

Knottingley.—Sam. Pooll, charg. to Ho.; Will. Browne, M.; John Browne, M.; Mr. Sykes, M.

Kirksmeaton.—Mrs. Rasby, P.; Mr. Oates, M.

Norton-cum-Fenwick.—Will. Mittin, M.

Chap. IV. 40   GENERAL HISTORY.

The Militia.

Muster Roll of Sir Michael Wentworth's Regiment.— 1680.

Ousleet.—Rich. Warksope, M.

Owston.—John Harrison, M.; Tho. Shirtcliffe, P. non. app.

Preston Jagling.—Mr. Crofts, M. non. app.; Daniel Wigfall, P.; Timothy Rhodes, M.; Matt. Roebuck, M.

Pollington.—John Gathorne, M.

Pontefract.—Mr. Knowles, M.; Mr. Sam. Tayler, M.; Mr. Rich. Austwick, M.; Geo. Holdcote, M.; Mr. Coates, M.; Mr. Rob. Ward, M.; Mr. Burgess, M.; John Johnson, M.; Mr. Taton, M.; Mr. Leo. Stables, P.

Rawcliffe.—Tho. Bafton, M.; Mr. John Adams, P. non. app.; Mrs. Gathorne, M. non. app.

Redness.—John Wressle, M.; Tho. Thompson, M.; Tho. Harrison, M.

Smeaton Parva.—Mich. Woodhouse, M.

Swinfleet.—Tho. Stephenson, char. to Ho.; Rob. Mitchell, char. to Ho.; Robert Empson, M.

South Kirkby.—Rob. Shillitoe, M.; John Houldgate, P.

South Empsall.—Will. Horncastle, M.; John England, M.

Snaith.—Rob. Balland, M.; Geo. Gleady, M.

Skellow.—Will. Harrison, M.

Thorpe Audline.—Mr. Sam. Saltonstall, M. non. app.; Mr. John Wood, M. non. app.; Will. Roberts, M.

Whitgift.—Heires of Mr. Bullard, P.; John Stephenson, M.; Tho. Wressell, M.

Womersley.—Will. Ellin, M.; John Ellin, M.

Whitley.—John Turner, P.

The names, &c., within the Wappentakes of Strafford and Tickhill :—

Austerfield.—Tho. Hoyland, P.; John Swailes, P.

Armethorp.—

Aston-cum-Aughton.—Mr. Barnham West, M.

Attercliffe-cum-Darnall.—John Stainforth, P.; Joseph Nicholson, M.

Auston-cum-Memb.—Charles Hutton, M.; John Kirke, P.; Rob. Wright, M.; Joshua Pitts, M.

Adwick-sup-Street.—John Rawson, P.

Bilham.—Mr. Rob. Turner, M.

Barnby-sup-Dunn.—Will. Wintringham, M.; Rob. Seaton.

Brodsworth-cum-Pigburne.—Mr. Wentworth, M.; Mr. John Holme, P.

Bentley-cum-Arksey.—Mr. Jennings, M.; Mr. Wildbore, P.;

THE MILITIA. 41 Chap. IV.

Mr. Bradford, P.; Mr. Triffit, M.; Rich. Adwick, M.; Mr. Hall, M.; Will. Handley, M.

Bramley.—Tho. Webster, M.

Brampton-Bierley.—Mr. Ellis, M.; Tho. Waide, M.; Rob. Wharum, P.

Braithwell.—Tho. Waterhouse, M.; Tho. Boswell, M.

Barmbrough.—John Roberts, M.

Bradfield.—John Greaves, P.; John Woodhead, M.; Will. Milner, M.; John Ibbotson, M.; Mr. Rob. Hall, char. to Ho. M.; Daniel Rich, M.; Matthew Hemce, M.; Mr. John Foster, M.; Charles Wilson, M.; Fran. Morton, M.; Tho. Stead, M.; Tho. Berley, M.; John Stead, M.; John Marritt, M.; Mr. Morewood, P.; Jonathan Shaw; Edw. Revell, M.; Will. Shaw, M.

Brampton.—Mr. Nath. Revell, M.

Bawtry.—Tho. Lund, M.; Mr. Michaell Wharton, M.

Bolton.—Reynold Watson, P.; Will. Shepherd, M.; Ambrose Bingley, P.; John Tyas, M.

Brightside-Bierley—Hugh Nutt, P.; Rob. Hold, M.

Cadeby.—Henry Tong, P.

Cantley.—Tho. Mouldson, M.

Clayton.—Reuben Thompson, P.

Conisbrough.—Mr. Saxton, M.; Mr. Wasse, M.; Will. Blackburne, M.; Will. Boswell, P.; Joshua Snawden, M.

Dalton.—Tho. Hurst, M.

Dynnington.—Tho. Tagg, M.; John Bayles, M.

Darfield.—Rob. Wainwright, char. to Ho., M.; William Marsden, M.; Mr. Fran. Raney, M.; Tho. Marsden, P.; Mrs. Dixon, P.

Doncaster.[1]—Mr. Rich. Shepherd, M.; Mr. Geo. Raisine, P.; Mr. Daniell Hull, P.; Mr. Will. Bassett, M.; Mr. Will. Bell; Mr. John Burton, M.; Mr. Rich. Clay, P.

Blaxton-cum-Awkley.—Tho. Tuke, M.

Hextrop-cum-Balby.—Mr. Wass, P.; John Walker, M.

Ecclesfield.—Timo. Twybell, M.; Geo. Phillips, M.; Nicho. Shirtcliffe, M.; Will. Stainforth, M.; Rob. Carr, M.; John Yealand, M.; Mr. Watts, M.; Will. Smith, M.; Tho. Creswick, M.

Ecclesall.—Mr. Henry Bright, M.; Mr. Tho. Bright, P.; Mr. Alex. Ashton, P.

Fishlake.—Mr. Will. Pinkney, M.; Edw. Wormley, M.; Mr. Tho. Parkins, M.; John Johnson, M.

The Militia.

Muster Roll of Sir Michael Wentworth's Regiment.— 1680.

[1] The corporation, three musketeers and one pikeman.

Chap. IV. 42 GENERAL HISTORY.

The Militia.

Muster Roll of Sir Michael Wentworth's Regiment.—1680.

Firbeck.—Nonus Parker.

Greasbrooke.—Edw. Satherthwaite, P.; Rob. Heyward, M.

Hamphall Stubbs.—Mrs. Margarett Rollston, P.; Mrs. Dorothy Wharton, M.

Houghton Magna.—Henry Bingley, M.; Tho. Box, P.

Houghton Parva.—John Deane, P.

Hutton Pannel.—Mr. Tho. Stanhope, P.; Mr. Fran. Heaton, M.; Will. Conway, M.

Hutton Roberts.—Mr. Robt. Banks, P.

Hansworth.—Cuthbert Browne, M.; Phillip Challenor, M.; Burrowes Tippett, M.; Tho. Stacy, M.; Rich. Woodrove, P.; Joseph Newbold, M.; Alex. Fenton, M.

Harthill.—Mr. Edw. Carver, P.; John Symonet, P.

Hoyland.—Rich. Townsend, M.; Nich. Tilney, P.

Hoyland Swaine.—John Green, P.; Will. Sanderson, M.; Jo. Solwell, P.

Hatfield.—John Bradbury, Esq., M.; John Harvey, Esq., M.; Mr. Hatfield, P.; Tho. Outbridge, M.; John Cooke, M.

Hallam-cum-Ecclesall. — Geo. Fox, M.; Rob. Hall, M.; Marma. Stacy, P.; Henry Bright, M.; Mr. Ashton, M.

Houghton-Levitt.—Mr. Roger Lee, M.

Kimberworth.—John Murgateroyd, M.; Rob. Kent, M.

Kirk Sandall.—Mr. Shepherd, P.

Laughton-le-Morthen.—Edw. Laughton, P.; Sam. Misterton, M.; Rob. Seaton, M.; Rich. Leadbeater, M.

Langfield.—James Gibson, M.; John Ingham, M.; Jeremy Ingham, P.

Letwell.—Mr. Tho. Chadwick, M.

Marrh.—Mrs. Lewis, M.; Lord Dencoate, M.

Maltby.—Roger Fretwell, M.; James Pashley, M.; Roger Lee.

Rawmarsh.—Mr. Adams, P.; Mr. Youle, P.; Mr. Goodwin, M.; Mrs. Ellis, P.

Rotherham.—Mr. Charles Tucker, P.; Mr. John Mandeville, M.; Cornelius Clarke, P.; Will. Stephenson, M.; Mr. John Malin, M. non app.

Rossington.—Mr. Jackson, M.; Tho. Best, M.

Stainforth.—Francis Elwick, M.; Tho. Simpson, M.

Stenby-cum-Helleby.—Mr. Hunt; Geo. Pashley, M.

Swinton.—Tho. Barhouse, P.; Henry Waller, P.; Darcy Stones, M.

Sikehouse.—Will. Huscroft, M.; Joseph Pooll, M.; John Thirsby, M.

THE MILITIA. 43 Chap. IV.

Stansall Wellenley-cum-Wilsike.—Lawrence Wharton, gent., M.

Sandall.—Mr Will. Scorah, M.

Sheffield.—Rob. Henshey, P.; Malin Soresby, M.; Will. Cooke, M.; Joseph Shemeild, M.; Rob. Boughton, M.; Joshua Baynes, M.

Thorne.—Edw. Forster, M.; Will. Forster, M.; Will. Darling, M.; Seth Southwell, M.; John Darling, M.

Thurnsco.—Dr. Spencer, M.; Mr. Rob. Pierpoint, M.

Thryburrh.—Mr. Yarbrough Rearsy, M.; Charles Loughton, gent., M.

Tinsley.—Will. Harrison, sen., M.; Will. Harrison, jun., M.

Todewicke.—Mr. Rich. Lambert, M.

Tickell.—Mr. Nich. Wilson, M.; Mr. John Slyman, M.; Rob. Damins, P.; Will. Lambert, M.; Mr. Will. Loughton, M.; Fran. Smith, P.; Will. Repey, M.

Ulley.—Nich. Stones, land sold, M.; Will. Allerton, M.

Wickersley.—Benjamin Adams, M.; Rich. Kent, M.

Woodsetts-cum-Gillingwells.—John Nelson, P.; Hen. Rushforth, M.

Whiston.—Tho. Roarston, M.; Mr. John Cart., M.; Rob. Wild, M.

Wales.—Will. Rogers, M.

Wath.—Tho. Carr, M.

Warmsworth.—Tho. Adame, P.; Tho. Rookesby, M.

Wentworth.—Tho. Hodgkinson, M.; Will. Holl, M.

Wombwell.—Will. Armitage, M.; Mr. Townsend, M.; Mr. Taylor, M.

Sir Michael Wentworth was afterwards Captain of a troop of horse, and served under the Earl of Peterborough.

HISTORY OF BARNSLEY.

CHAPTER V.

*"Where once the forest tree upreared its head,
The chimney casts its smoke-wreath to the skies."*

Chap. V.

Situation of Barnsley.

BARNSLEY, the subject of this history, is a flourishing market town, in the parish of Silkstone, wapentake of Staincross, honour of Pontefract, in the West Riding of the county of York. Its situation is partly on the summit and partly on the slope of a hill which rises boldly from the bank of the river Dearne, and from the top again declines in almost every direction. Upon the whole, it may be considered a healthy place, which is attributable in a great measure to the lofty situation on which it is built, affording a good natural, drainage; added to which, the sanitary regulations of the Board of Health, though far from being perfect, have done much towards preventing the spread of those epidemic diseases which cause such devastation in large towns.

Instances of Longevity.

In 1769 we have a rare instance of longevity in this place, mentioned in the "Mirror," in the person of Martha Preston, who died at the age of 125. I have searched the registers here, but find no account of her burial. It unfortunately happens, too, that the baptismal records of the year in which she would be born are illegible. There is also a stone in St. Mary's grave-yard, recording the death of Mary Wilkinson, the midwife, in 1761, aged 102.

POPULATION. 45 Chap. V.

Population.

Subjoined is an account of the population of Barnsley, at different periods:—

	1750.	1801.	1811.	1821.	1831.
Population	1,740.	3,606.	5,014.	8,284.	10,330.

In 1801, were grown in the township the following numbers of acres of corn, &c.:—Wheat, 369; barley, 123; oats, 183; beans, 33; potatoes, 6.; turnips and rape, 82:—Total, 796.

The town had been divided into two ecclesiastical districts previous to the taking of the census in 1841, and in that year the population, &c., was stated to be as follows:—

	Inhabited Houses.	Unin- habited.	Houses Building.	Males.	Females.	Total.	Grand Total.
St. Mary's	851	22	12	2,141	2,196	4,337	12,307.
St. George's	1,529	24	16	4,046	3,924	7,970	

The quantity of land occupied as arable, pasture land, and gardens, in this year, was $2116a.\ 3r.\ 31p.$

Another district was afterwards formed, and in 1851 the population was enumerated as below:—

St. Mary's	6,126
St. George's	4,729
St. John's	4,060
Total	14,915

showing an increase of 2,608 inhabitants between the years 1841 and 1851, during which period 504 houses had been erected, making the number of occupants to each dwelling somewhat under five persons. The population of the township now, A.D. 1857, exceeds 17,000 souls. The total number of acres of land in the township is 2,385, including the hamlets of Keresforth, Old Town, and Pogmore, which places will be separately treated of hereafter.

Few places can equal this in beautiful scenery, such a variety of hill and dale, and in so pleasing

Scenery.

HISTORY OF BARNSLEY.

Chap. V. 46

Scenery. a combination of fertile pasture lands and corn fields, interspersed with remains of the ancient forest, through which the river Dearne winds its serpentine course. The pedestrian is soon out of the smoke of the town; and if health be the object of his pursuit, he at once enjoys a bracing air and cheering prospect, or should he be a naturalist, objects are not wanting to attract his attention, and add to his stock of knowledge.

Manufactures. Barnsley formerly ranked high as a place for the manufacture of wire. This branch of business began to decline towards the close of the last century; before that time, however, the linen trade had been introduced, which is now the staple trade of the town, and gives employment to several thousand of its inhabitants. The locality is rich in **Minerals.** minerals, particularly coal, but the trade has been only recently developed by railway communication, in every direction immense quantities being now transmitted by that means; and in consequence of this facility for transit, many new collieries have been opened, which promise to repay the spirited proprietors the capital they have invested. The wire trade, manufacture of linen, and coal mines, will afterwards receive attention.

Origin of the Name. As to the origin of the name of Barnsley, I would propose to account for it in the common sense way as being derived from the Saxon "*Berne*" (a barn or storehouse), and "*Ley*" (a field), possibly so denominated from the situation of the granaries of some of our early ancestors. In the last century it was called Black Barnsley, or Bleak Barnsley, either from the smoke of its forges, its lofty situation, or from its proximity to the neighbouring moors, which, like Blackheath, have a sooty appearance.

THE DOMESDAY SURVEY.

47 Chap. V.

The time is uncertain when mankind first set- When first Inhabited.
tled here,—it must, however, have been of ancient
date, as, from the early mention of a mill, it would
seem that the population was of a fixed character
in the time of the Confessor, when Barnsley was
royal property, and comprised part of the soke
of Tatshalla. I have met with several names which
are of Saxon origin, but whether the progenitors
of these families partially cleared the forest and
laid the foundation of the town, cannot be determined. The earliest mention we have of the place
is in the Norman survey, called Domesday.

EXTRACT.

In CREVESFORDE 7 BERNESLAI The Domesday Survey.
e similit soca ptin ad Tateshalla.

V. car. træ ad gld. 7. III. car. poss ibi.
ee. Nc e ibi | uill. cu. II. car. 7. I ac
pti. Silua past. dim leu lg. 7 tntd lat.

That is—" In Keresforth and Barnsley is a like
soke[1] belonging to Tateshalla; five carucates of
land to be taxed, and three ploughs may be there.
There is now there one villein,[2] with two ploughs

---

[1] *Soca*, or soke, was a territory or precinct within which
the *saca*, or *sac*, which was the power or privilege of hearing
and determining causes and disputes, levying forfeitures and
fines, executing laws, and administering justice, was exercised.
Soca, soke, commonly means franchise, liberty, or jurisdiction;
and sometimes a rent paid for using the land, with some privilege or liberty, or for protection of the land.

[2] So called from the word *villa*, because the villein generally
lived in a village, and was employed in works of the most
sordid kind, such as carrying out dung, ditching the lord's

Chap. V.   48   HISTORY OF BARNSLEY.

The Domesday Survey and one acre of meadow. The wood pasture is half a mile long, and as much broad."

In consequence of both places being included in the passage, it is not easy to say what was the exact state of each at that period; but we may presume, from Keresforth standing first, that it must have been of the greater importance of the two; the *Geld*[1] was charged on five hundred acres of land, which required five ploughs for the cultivation thereof; there was one acre of meadow, and a wood three-quarters of a mile[2] in length and the same in breadth, in which cattle might graze; the remainder comprising thick forest, of which Hevening or Mottram Wood, which has never been cleared, formed a part.

Barnsley and Keresforth comprised a portion of the honour of Pontefract, and of the grant to Ilbert de Laci, who reserved the former for a family whose founder probably came into England at the Norman invasion, and, like Ailric and his descendants, were considerable benefactors to the religious houses.

demesnes, and cultivating his lands. The services of the villein were not only base, but uncertain as to the time and quantity. He could acquire no property in land or goods; but if he purchased either, the lord might enter upon, oust the villein, and apply them to his own use, unless they were disposed of before the lord had seized them. In fact, the villeins were slaves; and when property was sold, those appendant thereto were included in the bargain, and passed to another master.

[1] The *Geld*, which so often appears in Domesday, was a yearly tax of two shillings upon every hide of arable land in the kingdom, which "Webb" informs us was first imposed in the reign of Ethelred, about A.D. 991. The Domesday shilling was equal in weight to three shillings of the present day.

[2] The Domesday mile was a mile and a half of our present measure.

Carta Caduth de Capreciria

Nouerint presentes et futuri qd Ego
Cad de Capnrara et soror mea Breatry
concessim et dedim deo et sco Ich et monachi de
Pontose villam de Buellaya in botho
mplano in molendino in aquo ipsius
et in omnib; q' ad eam pertinet in purim
et perpetuam elemosinam p' animab; nrís et
antecessor nrp q hedum· animab; siben
meis sordano et uxor· Concesserde ciom nob
phil monachi de sorte qs pro hanc elemo
sinam qd facim unm monachum p' mane
nra et abum p' sorore mea scim p' me amp
obiere quicuidam ocew pro big q' etiam
concesserur monacatu Un dog nobilo ad re
coguinonem huj ro dederuno mo· eidem secca
mee decm marcas angenti à mres et dimid
tin pellicea monachor et banig dederunt
euam sodano silio meo p' prellione hur rei
palesridum Unum silio meo Ricardo
Hanc donotionem Ego Cad de caprecinia meo
sterra sigillo g'mno Qd' si qis hedum meoy
infringe p'sumendo quodam Anime mee
et seeory mog inhoc minuere rempraihy de le
ar eum deus debrource Then p· de lasg·
mat p'lenye Bonnano scaeth à manlde
wairelusl Arnoldo psbuo Robio psluo
Henry Maloil Lr bagor Thom dapisf·
et Unllotce a Lie sil leising et Rt hijneeif

GIFT OF THE TOWN TO THE MONKS.   49   Chap. V.

In their possession the manor of Barnsley did *Ancient Charters.* not long continue, for we find that it was bestowed on the monks of Saint John of Pontefract. This took place in the reign of Stephen. Ralph, son of Toroldus, was the benefactor. I give a translation and fac-simile of the charter referring to the transaction, which is in the possession of Mr. Wentworth.

TRANSLATION OF THE CHARTER OF RALPH DE CAPRECURIA. *Ralph de Caprecuria.*

Know all men, now and hereafter, that I, Ralph de Caprecuria, and my sister Beatrix, have granted and given to God and to the monks of Saint John of Pontefract the town of Barnsley, with the woodland, the open land, the mill, the waters, the meadows, and all things which belong to it, in pure and perpetual alms, for the salvation of our souls and those of my ancestors and heirs, my sons Jordan and Richard consenting. I have granted also to you, the aforesaid monks of Pontefract, this perpetual alms for the making of one monk for my mother, another for my sister, and a third for me when I shall have died, who shall pray with you for us. The monastery shall allow me to become a monk when I shall desire; and as an acknowledgment for this grant, the monks have given my said sister ten marks of silver, and shall annually give to me the robe of a monk and the boots of the order; they have given also to my son Jordan, for this grant, a palfrey; and to my son Richard, five marks of silver. This gift, I, Ralph de Caprecuria, have confirmed with my seal; but if any one of my heirs shall infringe, by taking away in any manner soever from the soul of me and of my sister, may God blot him out of the book of life.* WITNESSES : Henry de Laci, in whose presence this donation was made; Matilda his mother; Arnald the priest; Robert the priest : Henry Waleis; Richard Bagot; Thomas the steward, and William his brother; Richard son of Leising; and Richard Franceis.

This grant was confirmed to the monks by the chief lord, Henry de Laci, as appears by the charter next given.

* This charter is literally translated; therefore the reader must excuse the inelegance of the diction. This indulgence must also be granted in other instances.

D

Chap. V.　50　　　　　HISTORY OF BARNSLEY.

Pedigree of the
Caprecuria
Family.

PEDIGREE OF THE DE CAPRECURIA FAMILY.

Toroldus, temp. Conqueror === - - - -

Ralph === - - - -　　Beatrix.　　Richard.

Jordan, living 1174. === Avicia, sister of Ranulph the Sheriff.

Simon.　　Ralph, founder of Wallingwells Priory.

Ranulph de Newmarch === Lettice.

Mabel.　　Robert === Albreda === Adam de Sancta Maria, 2 H.
St. Quintin, 1 H.

Robert === Isabel.
Furnes.

DONATIONS TO THE MONKS.

51 Chap. V.

Ancient Charters.

Henry de Laci.

, **Omnibus** Sanctæ Matris ecclesiæ filiis Henricus de Laceio salutem. Noverit Universitas vero quod ego Henricus de Laceio pro amore Dei et pro salute animæ meæ et omnium antecessorum et heredum meorum concessi et presenti carta mea confirmavi Deo et Sanctæ Mariæ et sancto Johanni et Monachis meis de Pontefracto Deo ibidem famulantibus Villam de Berneslaya cum omnibus pertinentibus suis quam simul dedimus Deo et prefatis Monachis ego Henricus de Laceio et Radulphus de Caprecuria in puram et perpetuam eleemosinam, liberam solutam et quietam ab omni seculari servicio et ex actione et ego et heredes mei ad quietabimus eam in omnibus locis et in omnibus rebus sicut liberam eleemosinam per totam. **Hiis Testibus**—Jordano Folioth et Henrico fratre suo, Willielmo de Ramevill, Occone de Tilli, Adamo de Wenvilla, Willielmo de P'stun, Henrico Hacest, Willielmo elemosinario, Lamberto medico, Roberto dispensatore, Aschetillo de Hewic et Warnero.

TRANSLATION.

Translation.

To all sons of Holy Mother Church, Henry de Laci sends greeting. Know truly all the world, that I, Henry de Laci, for the love of God and for the salvation of my soul and of all my ancestors and heirs, have granted, and by this my present charter confirmed, to God, and Saint Mary, and Saint John, and to my Monks of Pontefract serving God there, the Town of Barnsley with all its appurtenances, which I, Henry de Laci, and Ralph de Caprecuria, have given at the same time to God and to the aforesaid Monks in pure and perpetual alms, free discharged and quit from all secular service, and from disturbance both I and my heirs will keep quit the same, as free alms. THESE BEING WITNESSES: Jordan Folioth, and Henry his brother, William de Rameville, Occo de Tilli, Adam de Wenville, William de P'stun, Henry Hacest, William the almoner, Lambert the physician, Robert the steward, Aschetill de Hewic and Warner.

Jordan confirms the grant of Ralph (his father), and gives up all claim and right which he has in the town of Barnsley. A copy and translation of his charter are subjoined :—

CARTA JORDANI DE CAPRECURIA.

Jordan de Caprecuria.

Et autem quod ego Jordanus de Caprecuria confirmavi quam habui in Berneslaya quitam clamo de me et heredibus

HISTORY OF BARNSLEY.

Chap. V. 52

Ancient Charters.

Jordan de Caprecuria.

meis in perpetuum Deo et monachis de Pontefracto pro salute mei et antecessorum meorum et uxoris meæ et heredum meorum. Insuper donationem ejusdem Villæ de Berneslaya cum omnibus appendicibus quam donaverunt eis Beatrix amita mea et Rad. de Caprecuria pater meus concedo et dono et hac mea carta confirmo in omnibus. Ipsi autem monachi Sancti Johannis de Pontefracto pro gratia hujus concessionis et donationis decem marcas argenti mihi dederunt et annuatim dabunt pelliceam mihi et botas monachi et unum monachum pro me fecerunt et me monachum facient quando voluero. Quicunque heredum meorum aliquid impedimentum facerit de me et hac mea donatione et elemosina maledictionem Dei incurret et meam. Hæc pax et compositio inter me et eosdem monachos facta in Capella Sanctæ Mariæ Magdalene in Doncastera coram Justiciario Regis Ric. de Lucio, Rogero Archiepo Ebor, Henrico de Lascy, Williemo de Vesci, Roberto Clico. Vicecomite, Turstano de Sutton, Magistro Roberto Morel, Willielmo Vavasore, Jord. Foliot, Ric. Bagot, Rob. Dispensatore, Joh. fil. Will. Elemosinar.

Translation.

TRANSLATION OF THE CHARTER OF JORDAN DE CAPRECURIA.

And moreover that I, Jordan de Caprecuria, have confirmed, and that which I had in Barnsley, I quit claim from me and my heirs for ever to God and the monks of Pontefract, for the salvation of me and of my ancestors, and of my wife, and of my heirs. Moreover, the gift of the same town of Barnsley, with all its appendages, which Beatrix my aunt and Ralph de Caprecuria my father gave to them, I grant and give and by this my charter confirm in all things myself. Nevertheless, the monks of Saint John of Pontefract, for the favour of this grant and donation, have given to me ten marks of silver, and shall annually give to me the robe and boots of a monk, and they have made one monk for me, and shall make me a monk whenever I will. Whosoever of my heirs shall in anywise impede this my gift and alms shall incur God's curse and mine. This agreement and composition made between me and the same monks in the chapel of Saint Mary Magdalene in Doncaster, in the presence of Richard de Luci the Justiciary of the King, Roger Archbishop of York, Henry de Laci, William de Vesci, Robert Clerk, sheriff, Thurstan de Sutton, Master Robert Morel, William Vavasour, Jordan Foliot, Richard Bagot, Robert the steward, and John son of William the almoner.

DONATIONS TO THE MONKS. 53 Chap. V.

Barnsley is next mentioned in three Royal charters, executed in the reign of Henry II., which I give somewhat curtailed.

Ancient Charters.

CARTA HENRICI REGIS ANGLIÆ.

King Henry II.

Archiepiscopis Episcopis Comitibus Baronibus Justiciis Vicecomitibus et omnibus fidelibus suis salutem. Sciatis quod ego pro amore Dei et pro salute animæ meæ et Matildæ Reginæ et Willielmi filii mei et omnium antecessorum et heredum meorum concessi et hac présenti carta mea confirmavi Deo et Sancte Marie et Sancto Johanni Evangelisto et monachis de Pontefracto Deo ibidem famulantibus villam quandam, scilicet Doddeworde cum omnibus pertinentibus et libertatibus suis quæ sita est in Silkestona et Berneslay &c., &c. 𝕳𝕚𝕚𝕤 𝕿𝕖𝕤𝕥𝕚𝕓𝕦𝕤—Ebor. archiepiscopo, Rogero Salesbiensi. episcopo, Roberto Cestrensi epo., Ric. Herefordensi epo., Ricardo de Brus, Ganfrido cancellario, Ganfrido de Clintona, Roberto de Oilli, Thoma de Sancto Johanni, Hugh Bigod, Willielmo de Munfichet, Hugh de Bretoil, Roberto de Sigillo.

Inter 7 & 16 Hen. II.

TRANSLATION.—CHARTER OF HENRY, KING OF ENGLAND.

Translation.

To the archbishops, bishops, earls, barons, justices, sheriffs, and all his lieges, greeting. Know ye, that I, for the love of God and for the salvation of my soul, and of Matilda the Queen, and of William my son, and of all my ancestors and heirs, have granted, and by this my present charter confirmed, to God and Saint Mary, and Saint John the evangelist, and the monks of Pontefract there serving God, a certain town, namely Doddeworde, with all its appurtenances and liberties, which is situate in Silkstone and Barnsley, &c., &c. THESE BEING WITNESSES : The Archbishop of York; Roger, Bishop of Salisbury; Robert, Bishop of Chester; Richard, Bishop of Hereford; Richard de Brus; Ganfred the Chancellor; Ganfred de Clintona; Robert Oilli; Thomas de Saint John; Hugh Bigod; William de Munfichet; Hugh de Bretoil; Robert de Sigillo.

CARTA HENRICI REGIS ANGLIÆ.

King Henry II.

Henricus Rex Angliæ et Dux Normandie et Aquitain et Comes Andegau Archiepiscopis Episcopis Justiciis Comitibus Vicecomitibus et omnibus Ministris suis salutem. Noverit Universitas vero quod ego Henricus Rex justis postulationibus religiosorum monachorum de caritate qui in monasterio

Chap V.   54   HISTORY OF BARNSLEY.

Ancient Charters.

King Henry II.

Beati Johannis Apostoli et Evangelisti de Pontefracto Deo assidue et devote deserviunt attentius annuens omnes possessiones et bona quœ in presentia juste et canonice possident et alia quœ justis modis in futurum adipisci possint eis in eleemosinam perpetuam concedo et presenti scripto munienti confirmo. Ad majorem ergo evidentiam illis ducentur exponenda vocabulis scilicet situm ecclesiæ ipsorum monachorum in Pontefract, et ibidem vii acras cum mansuris suis et in Brackenhil xiii acras et Ecclesiam omnium Sanctorum in eadem villa et quicquid ad eam pertinet et Ecclesiam de Ledesham et quicquid ad eam pertinet et dimidium ejusdem villæ de Ledesham et Ledestona et Witewode et Dodworde et Kelingleia cum omnibus pertinentibus suis et villam de Berneslaya cum omnibus pertinentibus suis &c., &c. 𝕳𝕚𝕚𝕤 𝕿𝕖𝕤𝕥𝕚𝕓𝕦𝕤—Thoma Cancellario, Hugone Episcopo Dunel, Rainal. filio regis Henrici, et Comite Cornwallia, Hugone Bigod, Henrico de Hesexia, Ricardo de Luci, Ricardo de Huinar. Apud Northamt.

Translation.

TRANSLATION.—CHARTER OF HENRY, KING OF ENGLAND.

Henry,* King of England, Duke of Normandy and Aquitaine, and Earl of Anjou, to the archbishops, bishops, justices, earls, sheriffs, and all other his servants, greeting. Know truly all the world, that I, Henry, King, assenting to the just demands of the religious monks of charity, who in the monastery of the blessed John the Apostle and Evangelist, of Pontefract, diligently and devoutly serve God, do grant, and by this present writing confirm to them, in perpetual alms, all the possessions and goods which now justly and canonically they possess, and all others which by just means they may in future acquire; therefore, for the sake of more effectual evidence, they shall be taken to be expressed in these words, namely, the site of the church of the monks themselves in Pontefract, and in the same place seven acres with the dwellings thereon, and in Brackenhil thirteen acres and the church of All Saints in the same town, and whatsoever to the same belongs, and the church of Ledesham and whatsoever to the same belongs, and half of the same town of Ledesham, and Ledestone, and Witewode, and Dodworde, and Kelingleia, with all their appurtenances, and the town of Barnsley with all its appurtenances, &c., &c. THESE BEING WITNESSES : Thomas,

* Of the sons of Henry II., only five are mentioned in History, viz., William, Henry, Richard, Geoffrey, and John; it is evident, however, from this charter, that he had another named Rainulphus.

DONATIONS TO THE MONKS. 55 Chap V.

the Chancellor ; Hugh, Bishop of Durham ; Rainal., son of King Henry, and Earl of Cornwall ; Hugh Bigod ; Henry de Hesex: Richard de Luci ; Richard de Huinar.   At Northampton.

Ancient Charters.

ITEM CARTA EJUSDEM HENRICI.

King Henry II.

Henricus Dei Gratia Rex Angliæ Dominus Hiberniæ Dux Normandiæ et Aquatain Comes Andegau.   Archiepiscopis Episcopis Abbatibus Prioribus Comitibus Baronibus Justiciis Vicecomitibus præpositis Ministris et omnibus Ballivis et fidelibus suis salutem.   Inspeximus cartam Henrici regis domini nostri in his verbis.   "Henricus Dei Gratia Rex Angliæ Dux Normandiæ et Aquitaine et Comes Andegau archiepis-copis episcopis abbatibus comitibus baronibus justiciis vice-comitibus et omnibus fidelibus suis salutem.   Sciatis me con-cessisse et presenti carta mea confirmasse Deo et Ecclesiæ Sancti Johannis de Pontefracto et monachis ibidem Deo servientibus omnes donationes terrarum et hominum et eleemosinarum quæ donatæ eis fuerunt in ecclesiis et in omnibus aliis rebus et posses-sionibus scilicet situm ecclesiæ eorum in Pontefracto et ibidem septem acras cum mansuris earum et in Brackenhil tresdecem acras et in eadem villa Ecclesiam omnium sanctorum cum capellis et terris et ceteris pertinentibus et Ecclesiam de Ledes-ham cum capella de Fareburn et cum terris et ceteris pertinen-tibus et medietatem prefatæ villæ de Ledesham et Ledestonam et Wottewood et Doddeworde et Berneslayam, &c., &c.   Hiis Testibus—Thoma Cancellario, Henrico Episcopo Wintoniensi, Roberto Comite Leycestriæ, Hugone Epo. Dunelm., Ric. de Hume, Ric. de Luci, Henrico de Essex, Henrico de Laceyo. Apud Northamtonia."   Nos igitur has concessiones et donationes ratas et gratas habendas eis prædictis monachis concedimus et confirmamus pro nobis et heredibus nostris.

8th Jan. 14th Hen. II.

𝕳iis 𝕮estibus—Henr. de Burgo, Comite Kanc., Justicio Angliæ ; Philipo de Albimaco, Waltero de Everin, Godfrido de Crauncumb, Henrico de Capella, Galfrido de Caur, et aliis. Datum per manum venerabilis patris Ricardi, Cicestriæ Epis-copi, Cancellarii nostri, apud Lincoln, octavo die Januarii, anno regni nostri quarto decimo.

TRANSLATION.—ALSO CHARTER OF THE SAME HENRY.

Translation.

Henry, by the Grace of God King of England, Lord of Ireland, Duke of Normandy and Aquitaine, and Earl of Anjou. To the archbishops, bishops, abbots, priors, earls, barons, jus-

Chap. V. 56   HISTORY OF BARNSLEY.

Ancient Char-
ters.

King Henry II.

tices, sheriffs, officers, and all his bailiffs and lieges, greeting. We have looked upon the charter of our Lord, King Henry, in these words: "Henry, by the Grace of God King of England, Lord of Ireland, Duke of Normandy and Aquitaine, and Earl of Anjou, to the archbishops, bishops, abbots, earls, barons, justices, sheriffs, and all his lieges, greeting. Know that I have granted, and by my present charter confirmed, to God and the church of Saint John of Pontefract, and the monks there serving God, all the donations of lands and men (homagers), and of alms, which have been given to them in churches and in all other chatels and possessions, namely, the site of their church in Pontefract, and seven acres there with the dwellings thereon, and in Brackenhil thirteen acres, and in the same town the church of All Saints, with the chapels and lands, and other appurtenances, and the church of Ledesham, with the chapel of Fareburn, and with the lands and other appurtenances, and a moiety of the aforesaid town of Ledesham, and Ledeston, and Wottewode, and Dodworth, and Barnsley, &c., &c. These being Witnesses: Thomas, the Chancellor; Henry, Bishop of Winchester; Robert, Earl of Leicester; Hugh, Bishop of Durham; Richard de Hume, Richard de Luci, Henry de Essex, Henry de Lacy. At Northampton." These grants and donations rightfully and freely to be held by the aforesaid monks, we therefore do grant and confirm for ourselves and our heirs.

These being Witnesses: Henry de Burgo, Earl of Kent, Justiciar of England; Philip de Albimaco, Walter de Everin, Godfrey de Crauncumb, Henry the chaplain, Galfrid. de Caur, and others. Given by the hand of the venerable father Richard, Bishop of Chichester, our Chancellor, at Lincoln, the eighth day of January, in the year of our reign the fourteenth.

Other Dona-
tions to the
Monks.

My next step will be to record other donations to the monks, of property situate within the township of Barnsley, which appear to have been considerable; copies of the charters I give *in extenso*, with full translations of such as refer to property still known by the same name; with respect to the others, I presume that giving the substance thereof, together with the names of the witnesses, will suffice.

Whether these benefactions answered the pur-

DONATIONS TO THE MONKS.

57 Chap. V.

pose for which they were intended by the donors, is a subject into which it is not my place to enter in this work; every one must form his own opinion on the matter. There can be no doubt but that the persons who bestowed property on these houses did so with a good motive, and under the impression that spiritual good would accrue from gifts of this nature; be this, however, as it may, we cannot in justice but admit that the monks had as much right to these benefactions as any religious body (episcopal or otherwise) have at the present day to their endowments; and though no doubt some abuses were corrected by the suppression of the religious houses, yet we must regard Henry VIII.'s conduct more as that of a devastating spoliator than of a zealous believer in, or sincere agent in carrying out, any system of Christianity.

Ancient Charters.

Monastic Property.

Though many of these charters are without date, we may arrive at something near the time they were executed by comparing them with others which are dated and attested by the same parties. The two following were executed in Henry II.'s reign:—in the first of these, the name of Jordan Folioth appears as a witness, in which capacity we meet with him in Jordan de Caprecuria's charter, and amongst the persons who attest the other is the name of Robert de Laci, who it will be remembered died in the year 1193, and was the last of the old line of that family.

CARTA RICARDI DE CRAVENA.

Richard de Craven.

Sciant presentes et futuri quod ego Ricardus de Cravena et Matilda uxor mea in perpetuum quietum clamavimus de nobis et heredibus nostris dominis nostris priori et conventui de Pontefract omne jus et clamium quod habuimus vel aliquo modo

Chap. V. 58 HISTORY OF BARNSLEY.

Ancient Charters.

Richard de Craven.

habere potuimus in boscis de Berneslaya cum omnibus quercubus ubique per totum territorium de Berneslay stantibus et crescentibus tam juxta nos. quam ten. de nobis libere et quiete integre et honorifice cum omnibus libertatibus et aisamentis ville de Berneslay pertinentibus salua nobis et heredibus nostris libra communia de via fori usque divisas de Keresford versus west et communia pastura per totam divisam de Berneslay extra claustra predicti prioris et conventus de Pontefract ita quod nec nos nec heredes nostri de cetero aliquod jus vel clameum vel demandam in predictis boscis et quercubus habere vel exigere possimus. Pro hac autem quieta clamatione dederunt nobis prior et conventus de Pontefract unam marcam argenti propriis manibus et sua gratia concesserunt quod quando persona advenit dominici porci nostri in propria curia nostra mitti sine contradictione aliquid quieti erunt de panagio. Et ego ante dictus Ricardus de Cravena et Matilda uxor mea et heredes nostri hanc quietam clamationem predicto priori et conventui contra omnes homines in perpetuum warantizabimus et si forte contingat quod nos aut heredes nostri hanc quietam clamationem confringere velimus obligamus omnia bona nostra infra villam de Berneslay et extra dominis nostris priori et monachis de Pontefracto donatio eisdem monachis satisfaciemus de predicta marca argenti et insuper dabimus nomine pœnæ ad opus Ecclesiæ Beati Johannis de Pontefracto xl solidos argenti. 𝕳𝖎𝖎𝖘 𝕿𝖊𝖘𝖙𝖎𝖇𝖚𝖘—Henrico Walensis tunc senescallo, Jordano Folioth, Roberto de Stapilton, Willielmo de Bretton, Henrico de Seyvile, Galfrido de Ledesham, Ricardo de Marton, et aliis.

Translation.

TRANSLATION.

Charter of Richard de Craven, whereby he, and Matilda his wife, quit claimed to the Prior and Convent of Pontefract all right and claim which they had in the woods of Barnsley, with all the oaks standing and growing throughout the whole territory of Barnsley, both on their own (Richard and Matilda's) land and that of their tenants, with all the liberties and easements belonging to the town of Barnsley, saving to them (Richard and Matilda) and their heirs, free common of the highway leading to Keresforth towards the west, and common of pasture throughout all the district of Barnsley, without the inclosures of the aforesaid Prior and Convent, so that they (Richard and Matilda) and their heirs should have no more claim or demand on the aforesaid woods and oaks. For that

DONATIONS TO THE MONKS. 59 Chap. V.

release (quit claim) the Prior and Convent gave them one mark of silver. Some part of this charter is monkish Latin, and seems to be something respecting a parson and tithe pig. The said Richard and Matilda warranted the above to the said Prior and Monks, and bound all their goods within and without the town of Barnsley to the said Prior and Monks, that if this charter shouldbe infringed by them or their heirs, they would repay the said mark of silver, and would give to the Church of Saint John of Pontefract forty shillings in silver. WITNESSES: Henry Walensis, then seneschal, Jordan Folioth, Robert de Stapilton, William de Bretton, Henry de Savile, Galfrid de Ledesham, Richard de Marton, and others.

Ancient Charters.

Richard de Craven.

I have seen a deed by which Agnes, daughter of Thomas de Rydale, grants to Peter de Craven one bovate of land in Northorp. To this deed is affixed an impression of her seal in green wax, which is in an excellent state of preservation, and bears the words—

Agnes de Rydale.

S : Agnes de Ridale.

The device is a fleur-de-lis, and amongst the witnesses to this charter appears the name of Ricardus de Craven.

CARTA RAINERI MARESCALLI.

Sciant. presentes et futuri quod ego Rainerus Marescallus reddidi Deo et Sancto Johanni et Monachis de Pontefracto et quietas clamavi de me et de hæredibus meis in perpetuum illas duas bovatas terræ in Berneslay cum omnibus pertinentibus suis quas bovatas de eis libere tenebam et confirmavi hanc meam cartam hoc meo sigillo. Similiter mater mea Godith et frater meus Adam eandem terram quietam clamaverunt prædictis monachis in perpetuum. Monachi vero in perpetuum mihi dederunt tres marcas argenti et receperunt me et uxorem meam et filium meum et matrem meam Godith et fratrem meum Adam et animam patris mei in orationes suas. Hoc autem sicut præscriptum est warentizabimus ego et heredes mei prædictis monachis contra omnes homines. Adamo vero fratri meo dederunt ipsi monachi in testimonium hujus rei duodecim denarios. His Testibus—Radulpho Figa, Willielmo filio Hervei, Roberto de Lascy, Jordano de Ledestun, Waltero de

Rainerus Marescallus.

Chap. V. 60 HISTORY OF BARNSLEY.

Ancient Char-
ters.

Tuliis, Ervino Gundwino, Gilberto de Bagghil, Wid. de Aula Rogero dispensatore, et aliis.

R. Marescallus.

Translation.

TRANSLATION.

Charter of Rainerus Marescallus, by which he releases and quits claim to the monks of Saint John of Pontefract those two bovates of land in Barnsley which he held of them, likewise his mother Godith and his brother Adam quit claim the same land to the said monks.' Nevertheless, the monks gave to him (Rainerus) three marks of silver, and received him and his wife and son, and his mother Godith and brother Adam, into their prayers. The said monks gave to Adam the sum of twelve pence. WITNESSES : Ralph Figa, William son of Herveius, Robert de Laci, Jordan de Ledeston, Walter de Tuliis, Ervin Gundwin, Gilbert de Bagghil, Wid. de Aula, Roger the Steward, and others.

Andrew, son of
William of
the Old Town.

CARTA ANDREÆ FILII WILLI. DE HOLDTONA.

Sciant presentes et futuri quod ego Andreas filius Willi. de Holdtona dedi et concessi et hac presenti carta mea confirmavi in puram et perpetuam eleemosinam pro salute animæ meæ et antecessorum meorum Deo et Beato Johanni Apostolo et Evangelisto de Pontefracto et monachis ibidem Deo servientibus unam bovatam terræ in territorio de Berneslay scilicet illam bovatam quam Willielmus pater meus quondam tenuit. Tenend.

2 John.

et habend. libere quiete et pacifice cum tofto et crofto et omnibus libertatibus et aisamentis ad unam bovatam terræ pertinentibus intra villam de Berneslay et extra. Et ut hæc donatio et confirmatio rata sit et stabilis ego prædictus Andreas sigillum meum huic scripto apposui. Et ego prænominatus Andreas et hæredes.mei prædictam bovatam terræ cum.pertinentibus contra omnes homines warantizabimus et defendemus. His Testibus— Domino Johanne de Saivile, Domino Roberto de Holand, Roberto de Bergh, Johanne de Rupe, Roberto de Turs, Andrea Tinctore, Ricardo de Bergh, et aliis.

Translation.

TRANSLATION.

Charter of Andrew, son of William of the Old Town, granting to the monks of St. John of Pontefract, for the salvation of his soul, and of his ancestors, one bovate of land in the territory of Barnsley, which William, his father, formerly held. WITNESSES : Domino John de Savile, Domino Robert de Hoyland, Robert de Bergh, John de Rupe, Robert de Turs, Andrew the Dyer, Richard de Bergh, and others.

DONATIONS TO THE MONKS. 61 Chap. V.

CARTA HENRICI RASUR DE BRETTON.

Ancient Charters.

Sciant presentes et futuri quod ego Henricus Rasur de Bretton concessione Aliciæ uxoris meæ dedi et concessi et hac presenti carta mea confirmavi Deo et Beato Johanni Apostolo et Evangelista de Pontefract et monachis ibidem Deo servientibus, terram jacentem juxta pontem de Berneslay versus aquilonem quæ vocatur Stephene Crimbil cum omnibus libertatibus et aisiamentis de quibus aliquo tempore saisati fuimus tam ad terram nostram quæ vocata Lagelay quam ad istam prenominatam terram pertinentibus. Tenendas et habendas in puram et perpetuam eleemosinam pro salute animarum nostrarum et antecessorum nostrorum. Et ne ego predictus Henricus vel Alicia uxor mea aliquid jus vel clamium contra tenorem istius cartæ revocare possimus sigilla nostra huic scripto apposuimus. Hiis Testibus—Roberto de Berch, Roberto de Terribus, Hugone filio Johannis de Bretton, Henrico Portbref, et Adamo clerico de Berneslay, et aliis.

Henry Rasur de Bretton.

TRANSLATION.

Translation.

Charter of Henry Rasur de Bretton, granting to the monks of St. John of Pontefract (with the consent of Alice, his wife), the land situate nigh to the Bridge of Barnsley, towards the north, which is called Stephene Crimbil, with all the liberties and easements belonging thereto, and to the land called Lagelay, to hold in pure and perpetual alms, for the salvation of the souls of the said Henry and Alice, and of their ancestors. WITNESSES: Robert de Berch, Robert de Terribus, Hugh son of John de Bretton, Henry Portbref, Adam clerk of Barnsley, and others.

We have next an agreement between Edusa de Barnsley and the monks of Pontefract.

Edusa de Barnsley.

Anno ab incarnatione D'ni mccxxii. ad festum Sancti Michæl. Hec est conventio facta inter priorem et monachos de Pontefract ex una parte et Edusam de Berneslay qui fuit uxor Hugonis de Baggehyl ex alia. Sciant quod prefata Edusa in plena viduitate sua dimisit et concessit predictis priori et monachis usque ad terminum sex annorum capitale suum messuagium cum omnibus edificiis et totam terram cum omnibus pertinentibus suis quam habuit vel habere potuerit tam de dotario quam de custodia filii sui in territorio de Berneslaya, pro hac autem concessione dederunt prefati prior et monachi predictæ

Chap. V. 62   HISTORY OF BARNSLEY.

Ancient Char-
ters.

Edusa de
Barnsley.

Eduse xx solidos et caritatis intentioni unum quartum frumenti et unum windel pisor vero sex annis predicta terra cum pertinentibus suis remanebit soluta et quieta prefatæ Eduse et filio suo sine impedimento vel contradictione prioris et monachorum. Saluis predictis priori et monachis servitio et firma quæ debent habere de eadem terra. Insuper prenominata Edusa vel filius suus reddet in fine sex annorum usque expensas quas prior et monachi posuerint in sustentationem et reparationem domorum. Et ut conventio firma sit et stabilis hoc scriptum sigillorum suorum appositione roboraverunt. 𝕳iis 𝕿estibus—Gilberto de Notton, Willielmo filio suo, Alano fitz Ranulf tunc ballivo de Staincros et de Osgotecros, Radulpho de Savile, Henr. de Savile, Ricardo de Marton, et aliis.

Translation.

TRANSLATION.

In the year of the incarnation of our Lord, 1222, at the feast of St. Michael. This is the agreement made between the prior and monks of Pontefract, on the one part, and Edusa de Berneslay, who was wife of Hugh de Baggehil, on the other part. Be it known, that the aforesaid Edusa, in her full widowhood, hath demised and granted to the aforesaid prior and monks for the term of six years, her capital messuage, with all the buildings and all the land, with all their appurtenances, which she hath or which may fall to her, as well of her dowry as of the guardianship of her son, in the territory of Berneslay; and for this grant the aforesaid prior and monks have given to the aforesaid Edusa twenty shillings, and for the purpose of charity one quarter of corn and one windel of peas, but in six years the aforesaid lands, with the appurtenances, shall remain discharged and undisturbed to the aforesaid Edusa and her son, without impediment or objection on the part of the prior and monks, saving to the aforesaid prior and monks the service and (firma) which they ought to have from the same land. Moreover, the before-named Edusa, or her son, shall restore, at the end of six years, the amount of the expenses which the prior and monks have laid out in the upholding and reparation of the the buildings. And that this agreement may be firm and stable, they have confirmed this writing by the application of their seals. THESE BEING WITNESSES: Gilbert de Notton, and William his son, Alan Fitz Ranulf, then bailiff of Staincross and of Osgoldcross, Ralph de Savile, Henry de Savile, Richard de Marton, and others.

DONATIONS TO THE MONKS.

63   Chap. V.

CARTA JOHANNIS FILII ADAMI DE SEPELAY.

Ancient Charters.

Sciant presentes et futuri quod ego Johannes filius Adami de Sepelay pro salute animæ meæ et omnium antecessorum et hæredum meorum dedi concessi et hac presenti carta mea confirmavi Deo et Sancto Johanni Apostolo et Evangelisto de Pontefracto, et monachis ibidem Deo servientibus in perpetuam eleemosinam decem acras terræ in territorio veteris Berneslay illas scilicet decem acras quæ vocantur Oldfeld tenendas et habendas præfatis monachis in perpetuum sine impedimento vel reclamatione mei vel hæredum meorum libere et quiete integre et pacifice cum omnibus ædificiis et omnibus aliis pertinentibus ad præfatas decem acras intra villam et extra. Reddend. inde annuatim capitalibus dominis viginti denarios ad festum Sancti Martini pro omni servitio. Insuper dedi concessi et hac carta mea confirmavi prædictis monachis in perpetuam eleemosinam unum angulum adjacentem præfatis acris quem ego tenui de heredibus Adami filii Rogeri de Berneslay uno denario annuatim ad festum Sancti Martini pro omni servitio reddendo quem denarium prædicti monachi persolvent hæredibus præfati Adami nomine meo. Et ut hæc mea donatio firma sit et stabilis huic cartæ sigillum meum pro me et hæredibus meis apposui. Hiis Testibus—Alano de Smytheton tunc ballivo de Staincross et Osgotecros, Gilberto de Notton, Henrico de Tancreslay, Willielmo de Bretton, et aliis.

John de Sepelay.

7 Hen. III.

TRANSLATION.

Translation.

Charter of John, son of Adam de Sepelay, granting to the monks of St. John of Pontefract, for the salvation of his soul, and of all his ancestors and heirs, ten acres of land in the territory of Old Barnsley, known by the name of Oldfeld, to hold to the aforesaid monks for ever, without hindrance from him or his heirs, with all the buildings and other appurtenances belonging to the said ten acres, within and without the town, rendering thereout yearly to the chief lords twenty pence at the feast of St. Martin, in lieu of all services. Moreover, granting to the same monks in perpetual alms one enclosure adjoining to the aforesaid acres, which he held of the heirs of Adam, son of Roger of Barnsley, rendering one penny annually at the feast of St. Martin, in lieu of all service, which penny the aforesaid monks were to pay to the heirs of the aforesaid Adam, son of Roger, in his (Adam de Sepelay's) name. WITNESSES: Alan de Smytheton, then bailiff of Staincross and Osgoldcross, Gilbert

Chap. V. 64 HISTORY OF BARNSLEY.

*Ancient Char-
ters.*

de Notton, Henry de Tankersley William de Bretton, and others.

*Henry Port-
bref.*

CARTA HENRICI FILII WILLIELMI PORTBREF.

Sciant presentes et futuri quod ego Henricus filius Willielmi Portbref dedi concessi et in perpetuum quietum clamavi de me et de hæredibus meis priori et monachis de Pontefracto Willielmum filium Hugonis hominem meum nativum meum cum omnibus catallis suis et cum tota familia sua. Et hanc donationem

7 Hen. III.

meam ego Henricus et heredes mei prædictis priori et monachis warantizabimus contra omnes homines. Hiis Testibus—Alano filio Rand., tunc ballivo, Willielmo filio Adami, Roberto de Deneby, Adamo de Holand, Adamo de Oldfeld, et aliis.

Translation.

TRANSLATION.

Charter of Henry, son of William Portbref, giving to the prior and monks of Pontefract, William, the son of Hugh, his man, with all his chattels and his family. Witnesses—Alan, son of Rand., then bailiff; William, son of Adam; Robert de Deneby; Adam de Holand; Adam de Oldfeld, and others.

*Henry Port-
bref.*

CARTI HENRICI FILII WILLIELMI PORTBREF.

Sciant presentes et futuri quod ego Henricus filius Willielmi Portbref pro salute animæ meæ et omnium antecessorum et heredum meorum dedi concessi et presenti carta mea confirmavi et in perpetuam quietam clamavi sine retenemento de me et de heredibus meis Deo et Sancto Johanni et Priori et monachis de Pontefract in puram et perpetuam eleemosinam unam bovatam terræ in territorio de Berneslay cum omnibus pertinentibus suis intra villam et extra illam scilicet quam Rogerus filius Arnoldi tenuit et ego Henricus et heredus mei warantizabimus predictam bovatam terræ prenominatis monachis contra omnes homines. Hiis Testibus— Alano filio Rand. tunc ballivo, Willielmo filio Adami, Roberto de Deneby, Adamo de Oldfeld, et aliis.

Translation.

TRANSLATION.

Charter of Henry, son of William Portbref, quit claiming from him and his heirs to the Prior and monks of St. John of Pontefract, for the salvation of his soul, and of all his ancestors and heirs, one bovate of land in the territory of Barnsley, with all the appurtenances, viz., that which Roger, son of Arnold, held. WITNESSES: Alan, son of Rand., then bailiff; William, son of Adam; Robert de Denby; Adam de Oldfeld, and others.

PEDIGREE OF THE FAMILIES OF CLARKE AND CHAPPEL[1] OF BARNSLEY.

ARMS OF CLARKE—*Argent on a Bend Gules between three Pellets, as many Swans Proper.*

Martin Clarke of Barnsley, living 1570. === .... === Roger Chappel === Alice, buried March of Barnsley. 31, 1571.

Christopher Clarke of Barnsley, bur. Mar. 5, 1627. === Margaret, mar. April 11, 1588, bur. Jan. 23, 1636. === John Chappel of Barnsley. === Elizabeth Green, mar. June 15, 1579, bur. May 20, 1603. === Oliver had issue. === Margaret Bower, mar. Feb. 11, 1583. === Richard, bur. Nov. 11, 1615, had issue. === Margaret Jesson, mar. Jan. 31, 1592. === Agnes, bap. 3rd July, 1569.

Francis, d. y. Robert. Christopher. — Grace. Ann. — Martin Clarke of Barnsley, bap. Nov. 12, 1603, buried Mar. 27, 1651, from whom the Clarkes of Moorside are supposed to descend. === Isabel. — John, bap. Sept. 30, 1592, bur. May 13, 1636. === Frances, bur. May 18, 1634. — William, mar. Eliz. Spibin, and had issue. Thomas. — Ann. Margaret. Elizabeth. — Elizabeth Flather, 1 W. mar. Feb. 3, 1606. — Robert Chappel of Barnsley, bap. May 1, 1584, bur. July 7, 1645. === Agnes General, 2 W., mar. Sept. 11, 1628.

Martin, mar. and had issue. — Thomas, d. y. Josias. — Sarah, Ellen, d. y. Isabel. — John Clarke of Barnsley, bap. Nov. 23, 1628, buried January 20, 1705. === Elizabeth Thompson, mar. March 5, 1656, bur. Sept. 9, 1684. — John Chappel bap. Sept. 28, 1610. === .... === Sarah Rooke, 1 W. bur. 1643. — Thomas. — Elizabeth Chappel, 2 W. bur. 1646. === Ann Usher, 3 W. mar. Feb. 19, 1679. — Ann. Elizabeth. Ellen. — John. Francis, d. y. William. Robert. — Richard, bur. Nov. 15, 1666.

Jonathan, John Clarke bap. April of Barnsley, 24, 1684. bap. July 18, 1661, buried January 11, 1745. === Isabel Slack, mar. Nov. 1, 1685, buried September 12, 1706. — John, bap. Nov. 16, 1681, bur. 1713. === Frances Allen, mar. Jan. 29, 1698. — Jonas, bap. May 31, 1648, bur. Nov. 28, 1681. === .... — Mary.

Martin, bap. Oct. 23, 1693, mar. and had issue. — Ann, Isabel, d. y. — John, d. y. Henry. — William, bap. Nov. 26, 1695, bur. Dec. 27, 1776. — Ann Lawton, mar. Aug. 24, 1720. — Joshua, mar. and had issue. — John Clarke, of Barnsley, yeoman, bp. July 22, 1703, bur. Nov. 30, 1783. === Sarah Marsh, died Dec. 30, 1794, aged 75. — Richard Chappel, of Barnsley, only son, bap. May 25, 1681, bur. July 3, 1743. === Mary, bur. Jan. 22, 1741.

Martha, mar. John Alderson. Sarah mar. Ben. Cauwood. — John Clarke of Barnsley, bap. June 15, 1741, died June 4, 1808. === Frances Hill of Smithley, died April 13, 1810, aged 70. — George Clarke of Barnsley, banker, died 1814, aged 70. — Richard Chappel of Barnsley, mercer, bap. Sept. 3, 1724, bur. Sept. 3, 1766, and was the last male of this family. === .... — Elizabeth, Ann, d. y. — John, bap. May 27, 1731.

Sarah, mar. William Winter. — Dorothy, mar. William Beatson. — Fanny, mar. Wm. Wilkinson. — John Clarke of Barnsley, died Nov. 13, 1851, aged 79. — Hannah Brameld, died Jan. 26, 1842, aged 59. — Joseph. — John Ellis of Barnsley, apothecary. === Ann Chappel, only child, bap. Feb. 20, 1761, mar. Dec. 20, 1786.

Robert Cauwood of Barnsley. === Martha, died 1834. — Thomas Richardson. === Sarah. — James Parker. === Elizabeth. — John Clarke, only son, died Sept. 9, 1834, aged 17. — Edward Parker. === Ann.

John Stocks Raywood === Annie, only daughter.

Annie. Lucy.

William Parker. John. Charles. Edward. One daughter.

[1] Johnston says that this was the chief family at Barnsley in 1570.

DONATIONS TO THE MONKS. 65 Chap. V.

Ancient Charters.

CARTA HENRICI PORTBREF DE BERNESLAY.

Henry Portbref de Berneslay.

Sciant presentes et futuri quod ego Henricus Portbref de Berneslay dedi et concessi et hac presenti carta mea confirmavi in puram et perpetuam eleemosinam pro salute animæ meæ et antecessorum meorum Deo et Beato Johanni Apostolo et Evangelisto de Pontefracto et monachis ibidem Deo servientibus unam bovatam terræ in territorio de Berneslay scilicet illam bovatam quam Rogerus de Monte quondam tenuit. Tenend. et habend. libere quiete et pacifice cum tofto et crofto et omnibus aliis libertatibus ad unam bovatam terræ pertinentibus intra villam de Berneslay et extra. Et ut hæc donatio et confirmatio rata sit et stabilis sigillum meum huic scripto apposui. Et ego prædictus Henricus et heredes mei prædictam bovatam terræ prædictis monachis contra omnes homines warantizabimus et defendemus. **Hiis Testibus**—Domino Johanne de Sevile, Rainero de Wambwelle, Roberto de Berch, Roberto de Turs, Roberto de Haltona, Andrea tinctore, et aliis.

TRANSLATION.

Translation.

.Charter of Henry Portbref, granting in pure and perpetual alms, for the salvation of his soul, and of all his ancestors, to the monks of St. John of Pontefract, one bovate of land in the territory of Barnsley, which Roger de Monte formerly held. WITNESSES: Dominus John de Sevile, Rainer de Wambwelle, Robert de Berch, Robert de Turs, Robert de Halton, Andrew the dyer, and others.

CARTA ROBERTI DE BERGH.

Robert de Bergh.

Sciant præsentes et futuri quod ego Robertus de Bergh dedi et concessi et in perpetuum quietum clamavi de me et hæredibus meis et confirmavi Deo et Sancto Johanni de Pontefract et monachis ibidem Deo servientibus pro salute animæ meæ et antecessorum meorum redditum duodecim denariorum quem Rogerus de Berneslay solebat reddere mihi annuatim ad festum Sancti Oswaldi. Et præterea totum servitium plenarie sine retenemento mei vel hæredum meorum de terra illa quam predictus Rog. de Berneslay tenuit de me in Wilmerstordh. Tenend. et habend. prædictus monachis in puram et perpetuam eleemosinam liberam et quietam ab omni servitio et consuetudine. Ego vero Rob. de Bergh et hæredes mei prædictis monachis de Pontefract. prædicta redditum et servitium contra omnes warantiz-

E

Chap. V.   66   HISTORY OF BARNSLEY.

Ancient Charters.

Robert de Bergh.

abimus. Et ne ego Rob. vel hæredes mei contra concessionem hujus cartæ venire possimus huic scripto pro me et hæredibus meis sigillum meum apposui. **Hiis Testibus**—Nichol. de Wyrthlay, Henr. de Tancreslay, Rad. de Turkerland, Adamo de Oldfield, Regnero de Wambwelle.

Translation.

TRANSLATION.

Charter of Robert de Bergh, granting to the monks of St. John of Pontefract, for the salvation of his soul, and of all his ancestors, a rent of twelve pence, which Roger de Bernesley used to pay him annually, at the feast of St. Oswald. And besides, the whole service, entirely, without reservation to himself or his heirs, from that land, which Roger de Barnesley formerly held of him in Wilmerstordh. To be held and possessed by the same monks in free and perpetual alms, free and quit from all service and custom. WITNESSES : Nicholas de Wrythlay, Henry de Tancreslay, Ralph de Turkerland,[1] Adam de Oldfield, Regner de Wambwelle.

The subjoined charters are undated ; they probably belong to the reign of Hen. III.

William, son of Ulf.

CARTA WILLIELMI FILII ULFI.

Sciant presentes et futuri quod ego Willielmus filius Ulfi dedi concessi et presenti carta mea confirmavi Gerardo de Berneslay vel ubicunque vel cuicunque assignare velit iv denarios à monachis de Pontefracto in die Sancti Andreæ annuatim percipiendos quos ipsi monachi solebant mihi reddere pro una bovata terræ in Doddeword. Pro hac autem concessione et confirmatione dedit mihi prædictus Gerardus xxxs. iid. propriis manibus. Et ego præfatus Willielmus filius Ulfi et hæredes mei warentizabimus prædicto Gerardo vel ubicunque vel cuicunque assignare velit prænominatos iv denarios contra omnes homines. **Hiis Testibus**—Willielmo filio Everardi, Rogero Diacono de Silkeston, Ricardo de Stagno, Thoma de Stagno, Adamo de Berneslay, Johanne fil. Michaelis, et aliis.

Translation.

TRANSLATION.

Charter of William, son of Ulf, granting to Gerard of Barnsley, and his assigns, fourpence, to be annually received from

[1] Thurgoland.

DONATIONS TO THE MONKS. 67 Chap. V.

the monks of Pontefract on Saint Andrew's day, which the said Ancient Charters.
monks used to pay him (William) for one bovate of land in
Doddeworde. For that grant the said Gerard gave him thirty[1]
shillings and twopence. Witnesses: William son of Everard,
Roger the Deacon of Silkstone, Richard de Stagno, Thomas de
Stagno, Adam de Berneslay, John son of Michael, and others.

CARTA ADAMI FILII ROGERI DE BERNESLAY.

Adam, son of Roger de Berneslay.

Sciant presentes et futuri quod ego Adamus filius Rogeri de
Berneslay dedi concessi et presenti carta meœ confirmavi Deo et
Sancto Johanni de Pontefracto et monachis ibidem Deo servientibus in puram et perpetuam eleemosinam pro salute animœ meœ
et omnium antecessorum et hœredum meorum octo acras terræ
cum pertinentibus in Milneholm et in Milneker in territorio de
Berneslay et carucas quas pater meus inde habuit prefatis monachis sursum reddidi et quietas de me et heredibus meis in perpetuum clamavi. Hiis Testibus—Rogero decano de Ledesham,
Willielmo filio Everardi, Rogero de Silkiston, Roberto de Stainburgh, Willielmo de Kamesal, Waltero de Byrum, et aliis.

TRANSLATION.

Translation.

Know all men now and hereafter, that I, Adam, son of Roger
de Berneslay, have given, and by this my present charter have
confirmed, to God and St. John of Pontefract, and the monks
serving God there, for the salvation of my soul, and of all my
ancestors and heirs, eight acres of land, with their appurtenances,
in Milneholm and Milneker, in the territory of Barnesley, and
the ploughs which my father had thence I have moreover restored to the aforesaid monks, and quit claimed from me for ever
and my heirs. Witnesses: Roger deacon of Ledesham, William
son of Everard, Roger de Silkiston, Robert de Stainburgh,
William de Kamesal, Walter de Byrum, and others.

CARTA GREGORII DE ALTONA.

Gregory de Altona.

Sciant presentes et futuri quod ego Gregorius de Altona
dedi concessi et presenti carta mea confirmavi et quietam

---

[1] Thirty shillings and twopence seems a large sum for fourpence a year; this would be about one per cent. per annum at
the present day, and might perhaps be the common rate of
interest at that period.

Chap. V. 68 HISTORY OF BARNSLEY.

Ancient Charters.

Gregory de Altona.

clamavi de me et heredibus meis sine retenemento Deo et Sancto Johanni de Pontefracto et monachis ibidem, Deo servientibus totam terram meam in Berneslay quam tenui de eisdem monachis in territorio de Berneslay habendam et tenendam præfatis monachis in perpetuam eleemosinam cum omnibus aisamentis et libertatibus ad eandem terram pertinentibus. Et ego prenominatus Gregorius et hæredes mei warrantizabimus præfatis monachis predictam terram cum omnibus pertinentibus suis contra omnes homines. *His Testibus*—Rogero clerico de Silkeston, Adam de Oldfield, Ricardo de Marton, Gerardo de Berneslay, Henrico filio Rogeri, Andrea tinctore, et aliis.

Translation.

TRANSLATION.

Charter of Gregory de Alton, granting to the monks of St. John, of Pontefract, all his land in the territory of Barnsley, which he held of the same monks, to hold to them in perpetual alms. WITNESSES : Roger clerk of Silkstone, Adam de Oldfield, Richard de Marton, Gerard de Berneslay, Henry son of Roger, Andrew the dyer, and others.

Adam de Falthwait.

CARTA ADAMI DE FALTHWAIT.

Sciant presentes et futuri quod ego Adamus de Falthwait pro salute animæ meæ et omnium antecessorum et heredum meorum. dedi concessi et hac presenti carta mea confirmavi in puram et perpetuam eleemosinam Deo et Sancto Johanni de Pontefracto et monachis ibidem Deo servientibus unum toftum in Berneslay de dimidia acra terræ juxta terram Gerardi filii Bernardi et terram Pagani in orientali parte tofti Hugonis de Baggehyl et dimidiam acram in Collegrimewellerodes et dimidiam acram super Kirke-toftes et dimidiam acram super Langlandes et unam perticam super Clailandes, tenend. et habend. præfatis monachis in perpetuum libere et quiete et absolute ab omni servicio seculari et consuetudine. Et ego prænominatus Adamus et hæredes mei warentizabimus præfatis monachis prædictas acras terræ contra omnes homines. *His Testibus*— Johanne de Birkin, Rogero clerico de Silkestona, Roberto de Turs, Rainero de Wambwelle, Adamo de Oldfeld, et aliis.

Translation.

TRANSLATION.

Charter of Adam de Falthwait, granting to the monks of St. John of Pontefract, for the salvation of his soul, and of all his

DONATIONS TO THE MONKS. 69 Chap. V.

ancestors and heirs, one toft in Berneslay, consisting of half an acre of land next the land of Gerard, son of Bernard, and the land of Pagan, in the eastern part of the Toft of Hugh de Bagghyl, and half an acre in Collegrimewellerodes, and half an acre on Kirke Toftes, and half an acre on Langlands, and one perch on Clailands, free from all secular service. WITNESSES : John de Birkin, Roger clerk of Silkstone, Robert de Turs, Rainer de Wambwelle, Adam de Oldfeld, and others.

Ancient Charters.

Adam de Falthwait. Translation.

As the succeeding Charter refers to places well known at.the present day, I think a full translation of the same will not be out of place.

CARTA GERARDI DE BNESL.

Gerard de Berneslay.

Sciant presentes et futuri quod ego Gerardus de Bnesl. assensu et voluntate Adami primogeniti filii mei pro salute animæ meæ et omnium antecessorum et heredum meorum dedi concessi et hac presenti carta mea confirmavi Deo et Scto. Johi. de Pontefracto et monachis ibidem Deo servientibus in pptuam. elemosinam unam bovatam terre cum pertinentibus suis in territorio de Bneslaya. illam scilicet quam Ric. de Milnthorp tenuit et quatuor acras terræ in Milneker cum pertinentibus suis et totam terram cum pertinentibus suis quam ego tenui in Hevening de qua terra unum caput percutit super boscum versus aquam de Dirne et aliud caput percutit super Suini Hyl et terram Ricardi filii Adami et unum toftum in Bneslaya, quod Henricus de Mora et Matilda vidua tenuerunt de me termino in vita sua et non hereditarie et terram quæ vocatur Crimblis quam ego tenui de Johe. de Cellario et heredibus suis pro tribus denariis annuatim divisione solvendis pro omni servicio quos tres denarios prefati monachi reddent predicto Johanni et heredibus suis et duas acras et dimidiam cum omnibus edificiis quas tenui de Ada. fil. Rogi. et heredibus suis pro xii denariis annuatim reddendis mediet. ad Penticost et mediet. ad festum Scti. Martini quos xii denarios dicti monachi reddent annuatim heredibus prænominati Adami illas scilicet duas acras et dimidiam quæ jacent inter terram Ricardi de Marton versus north et terram Gerardi filii Thomæ versus South et terram ubi grangia mea fundata fuit quam tenui de Gerardo filio Thom. pro uno denario annuatim reddendo quem denarium prefati monachi persolvent heredibus predicti Gerardi hæc omnia supra dicta

Chap. V. 70 HISTORY OF BARNSLEY.

Ancient Charters.

Gerard de Berneslay.

habebunt prænominati monachi et tenebunt libere et quiete in perpetuum cum omnibus ad præfatas terras infra villam et extra pertinentibus. Et ego prenominatus Gerardus et heredes mei omnia predicta prefatis monachis warentizabimus contra omnes homines. 𝕳iis 𝕿estibus—Alan de Smytheton, Nichol. de Wyrthlay, Henrico de Tancreslay, Willelmo de Bretton, Radulph de Rupe, Ricardo de Marton, et aliis.

Translation.

TRANSLATION.

Know all men, present and to come, that I, Gerard de Berneslay, with the consent of Adam my first-born son, for the salvation of my soul, and of all my ancestors and heirs, have given, granted, and by this my present charter confirmed, to God and to Saint John of Pontefract, and the monks there serving God, in perpetual alms, one bovate of land, with its appurtenances, in the territory of Berneslay, namely, that which Richard de Milnthorp held, and four acres of land in Milneker, with their appurtenances, and all land, with the appurtenances, which I held in Hevening, of which land one end joins on the wood over and against the water of Dirne, and the other end joins on Swine Hill and the land of Richard the son of Adam; and one toft in Berneslay, which Henry de Mora and Matilda his mother held of me for the term of their lives, and not hereditarily; and the land which is called Crimblis, which I held of John de Cellarius and his heirs, for three pence yearly, to be paid for all service, which three pence the aforesaid monks shall pay to the aforesaid John and his heirs; and two acres and a half, with all the buildings, that I held of Adam son of Roger, and his heirs, for twelve pence yearly, to be paid half at Pentecost and half at the feast of Saint Martin, which twelve pence the aforesaid monks shall pay yearly to the heirs of the before-named Adam, namely, the two acres and a half which lie between land of Richard de Marton towards the north, and land of Gerard son of Thomas towards the south, and the land where my farm grange was, which I held of Gerard the son of Thomas, for one penny, payable yearly, which penny the aforesaid monks shall pay to the heirs of the aforesaid Gerard; and all things above mentioned the aforesaid monks shall have and hold freely and quietly for ever, with all things to the aforesaid lands within the town and without appertaining. And I, the aforesaid Gerard, and my heirs, all things aforesaid to the same monks will warrant against all men. THESE BEING WITNESSES: Alan de Smytheton, Nicholas de Wyrthlay, Henry de

DONATIONS TO THE MONKS. ·71 Chap. V.

Tancreslay, William de Bretton, Ralph de Rupe, Richard de Marton, and others.

Ancient Charters.

CARTA ROBERTI FILII GERARDI DE BERNESLAY.

Sciant presentes et futuri quod ego Robertus filius Gerardi de Berneslay sursum reddidi et de me et heredibus meis in perpetuum quietum clamavi dominis meis priori et conventui de Pontefract. omne jus et clamium quod habui vel unquam habere potui in duabus acris terræ cum pertinentibus suis quas de eisdem prius tenui in territorio de Berneslay, quæ jacent in Heyinges et quas recipi de eisdem in exambium pro medietate de Gresroda. Pro hac vero quieta clamatione et sursum redditione dederunt mihi dicti monachi decem solidos argenti propriis manibus. Et ne ego Robertus vel heredes mei in perpetuum aliquid jus vel clamium in dictis duabus acris terræ et earum pertinentibus vindicare possimus huic scripto sigillum meum pro me et heredibus meis in perpetuum apposui in testimonium. Hiis Testibus—Ricardo de Craven, Andrea tinctore, Henrico Portbref, Roberto de Veteri Villa, Ricardo de eadem, et aliis.

Robert, son of Gerard de Berneslay.

TRANSLATION.

Charter of Robert, son of Gerard de Berneslay, releasing and quit claiming to the Prior and Convent of Pontefract, all his right and claim in two acres of land he had theretofore held of them in the territory of Berneslay, which lay in Heyinges (Hevenings), and which he received from them in exchange for half of Gresrode. For that surrender the said monks gave him ten shillings of silver. WITNESSES: Richard de Craven, Andrew the dyer, Henry Portbref, Robert of Old Town, Richard of the same place, and others.

Translation.

CARTA DIANÆ FILIÆ ROGERI DE BERNESLAY.

Sciant presentes et futuri quod ego Diana filia Rogeri de Berneslay reddidi quietam clamavi et confirmavi de me et hæredibus meis priori et monachis de Pontefracto totam terram quam tenui in Doddeworde infra villam et extra tam in bosco quam in plano. Pro hac autem quieta clamatione dederunt mihi prædicti prior et monachi duas marcas argenti. Et ne ego vel hæredes mei contra hanc quietam clamationem prædictam venire possimus hanc cartam sigilli mei appositione roboravi.

Diana, daughter of Roger de Berneslay.

Chap. V. 72   HISTORY OF BARNSLEY.

Ancient Char-
ters.

Diana, daugh-
ter of Roger
de Berneslay.

Hiis Testibus—Johanne de Birkin, Roberto Walensi, Adamo de Rameville, Thoma filio suo, Willielmo de Stapilton, Gilberto de Notton, Hugone filio Walteri, Magistro Raimundo, Ricardo de Medelay, Willielmo de Kamesal, et aliis.

Translation.

TRANSLATION.

Charter of Diana, daughter of Roger de Berneslay, releasing and quit claiming to the Prior and Monks of St. John of Pontefract all the land she held in Doddeworde, within and without the town, both wood and open land, in consideration of which the monks gave her two marks of silver. WITNESSES: John de Birkin, Robert Walensis, Adam de Rameville, Thomas his son, William de Stapilton, Gilbert de Notton, Hugh son of Walter, Master Raimund, Richard de Medelay, William de Kamesal, and others.

Matilda
daughter of
Adam the
steward.

CARTA MATILDÆ FILIÆ ADAMI DISPENSATORIS.

Omnibus Christi fidelibus ad quos presens scriptum pervenerit Matilda filia Adami Dispensatoris de Berneslay salutem in Domino.

Noverit Universitas vero me remississe et quieta clamâsse priori et conventui de Pontefracto duo quartaria frumenti et duas sceppas siliginis et dimidiam marcam argenti in quibus idem prior et conventus annuatim mihi in vitæ meæ terminum per cartam suam tenebantur et insuper duas acras terræ de dominio suo cum una domo in Berneslay quas in vitam meam similiter concesserant eisdem quietas clamavi. Et ne ego Matilda in dictis quartariis frumenti cum duabus sceppis siliginis dicta marca argenti domo et duabus acris terræ jus aliquid vel clamium in perpetuum vindicare possim presens scriptum sigillo meo signavi et illud cum carta quam de dicto priore et conventu habui propriis manibus sursum reddidi eisdem. Pro hac autem remissione et quieta clamatione dederunt mihi dicti prior et conventus in magna necessitate mei quatuor marcas argenti propriis manibus. **Hiis Testibus**—Roberto de Berch, Rogero Capellano de Berneslay, Adamo de Berneslay clerico, Henrico Portbref, Andrea tinctore, et aliis.

Translation.

TRANSLATION.

Charter of Matilda, daughter of Adam the steward of Berneslay, releasing and quit claiming to the Prior and Convent of St.

DONATIONS TO THE MONKS. 73 Chap. IV.

John of Pontefract, two quarters of bread corn, and two measures of fine flour, and half a mark of silver, which were payable to her yearly for her life by the aforesaid Prior and Convent; and moreover, two acres of land of their lordship in Barnsley, which they had likewise before granted to her for her life, she quit claimed to them; and the said Matilda gave up to the said Prior and Convent a charter she had from them. They paid to her for the above release in her great necessity four marks of silver. WITNESSES: Robert de Berch, Roger the chaplain of Berneslay, Adam de Berneslay clerk, Henry Portbref, Andrew the dyer, and others.

Ancient Charters.

Matilda, daughter of Adam the steward.

CARTA MATILDÆ FILIÆ ADAMI DISPENSATORIS.

The same.

Sciant presentes et futuri quod ego Matilda filia quondam Adami dispensatoris de Berneslay quondam uxor Ricardi de Cravena in mea legitima potestate et libra viduitate dedi concessi sursum reddidi et quietum clamavi in perpetuum de me et hæredibus meis Deo et Sancto Johanni Apostolo et Evangelisto de Pontefracto et monachis ibidem Deo servientibus pro salute animæ meæ et antecessorum meorum tenementum meum de Berneslay et de Veteri Villa quod quoddam tenementum Adam pater meus de eisdem monachis quondam tenuit. Tenend. et habend. dictis monachis in puram et perpetuam eleemosinam libere quiete honorifice pacifice et integre sine ullo retenemento mei vel heredum meorum cum omnibus redditibus aschætis et cum omnibus aliis libertatibus et aisamentis ad dictum tenementum pertinentibus in bosco et plano in pratis et pasturis et cæteris communibus suis infra villam et extra sicut dictus Adam pater meus et ego ipsum tenementum libere et integre unquam tenuimus vel de jure tenere debuimus vel potuimus. Ut igitur hæc mea donatio concessio sursum redditio et quieta clamatio ad perpetuam firmitatem obtineat præsens scriptum meum sigilli mei appositione roboravi. Hiis Testibus—Domino Adamo de Everingham, Domino Roberto de Stapilton, Domino Johanne de Hoderode, Domino Johanne de Sevile, Adamo de Holand, Johanne de Rupe, Roberto de Turs, et aliis.

TRANSLATION.

Translation.

Charter of Matilda, daughter of Adam the steward of Berneslay, and formerly wife of Richard de Craven, of her lawful power and free widowhood, granting and quit claiming for ever, to the monks of St. John the Apostle and Evangelist of Pontefract, for

Chap. V. 74   HISTORY OF BARNSLEY.

Ancient Charters.

the salvation of her soul, and of her ancestors, her tenement of Berneslay and of Old Town, which tenement Adam her father formerly held of the same monks. To hold to them in pure and perpetual alms, freely and quietly, without any reservation, with all rents, escheats, and other liberties and easements thereto belonging, in wood and plain, in meadows and pastures, and other commons within the town and without, as her father Adam and she herself held, or might or ought to have held, the same tenement. WITNESSES: Dominus Adam de Everingham, Dominus Robert de Stapleton, Dominus John de Hoderode, Dominus John de Sevile, Adam de Holand, John de Rupe, Robert de Turs, and others.

Matilda, daughter of Adam the steward.

Gerard, son of Thomas de Berneslay.

CARTA GERARDI FILII THOMÆ DE BERNESLAY.

Sciant presentes et futuri quod ego Gerardus filius Thomæ de Berneslay concessi et hac mea presenti carta confirmavi Gerardo filio Rogeri de Berneslay et hæredibus suis totam illam terram cum ædificiis quam tenuit de patre meo in villa de Berneslay scilicet quæ jacet inter terram quam idem Gerardus tenuit de ecclesia in qua mansit et Hencroft unde unum caput buttat super viam quæ vadit per mediam villam versus north et aliud caput super terram meam quam tenui de domino priore. Tenend. et habend. de me et de heredibus meis sibi et heredibus suis in feudo et hereditate libere et quiete et honorifice solventi inde annuatim mihi et hæredibus meis unum denarium pro omni servicio et demando silicet unum obolum ad Pentecost et unum obolum ad festum Sancti Martini. Ego autem et hæredes mei warantizabimus illi et hæredibus suis prædictam terram cum ædificio contra omnes homines. Pro hac autem concessione et confirmatione dedit mihi idem Gerardus ii solidos de recognitione. Hiis Testibus—Rogero de Keresford, Adamo de Oldfeld, Johanne filio ejusdem, Symone filio Arnoldi, Henrico filio Rogeri de Bretton, et aliis.

Translation.

TRANSLATION.

Charter of Gerard, son of Thomas de Berneslay, granting to Gerard, son of Roger de Berneslay, all that land, with the buildings, which he (Gerard, son of Roger) held of his (Gerard, son of Thomas) father in the town of Berneslay, viz., that which lay amongst the land which the same Gerard, son of Roger, held of the church, in which he dwelt, and Hencroft, whereof one end butted on the way leading through the middle of the town towards the

DONATIONS TO THE MONKS. 75 Chap. V.

north, and the other end on his land which he held of the lord Ancient Char-
prior. To hold to him and his heirs in fee and inheritance freely ters.
and quietly, paying thereout annually one penny in lieu of
all service, viz., one halfpenny at Pentecost and one halfpenny Gerard, son of
at Martinmas. For that grant the same Gerard, son of Roger, Thomas de Berneslay.
gave him two shillings as an acknowledgment. WITNESSES:
Roger de Keresford, Adam de Oldfeld, John son of the same,
Symon son of Arnold, Henry son of Roger de Bretton, and
others.

CARTA GERARDI FILII THOMAE DE BERNESLAY. The same.

Sciant presentes et futuri quod ego Gerardus filius Thomæ
de Berneslay dedi concessi et hac presenti carta mea confirmavi
pro salute animæ meæ et omnium antecessorum meorum Deo et
Ecclesiæ Sancti Johannis de Pontefracto et monachis ibidem
Deo servientibus, quandam placiam terræ in villa de Berneslay
quæ jacet juxta curiam eorundem monachorum versus west haben-
tem decem et septem percatas et quinque pedes in longitudine et
duas percatas in latitudine cujus caput buttat super cimite-
rium et aliud super ortum meum. Tenend. et habend. præfatis
monachis in puram et perpetuam eleemosinam in perpetuum. In
hujus rei testimonium pro me et heredibus meis sigillum meum
huic scripto apposui. Hiis Testibus—Henrico de Sevile, Hugone
de Berch, Ricardo de Cravena, Ricardo de Marton, Henrico Portbref, et aliis.

TRANSLATION. Translation.

Charter of Gerard, son of Thomas de Berneslay, granting,
for the salvation of his soul, and of all his ancestors, to the
monks of St. John of Pontefract, a certain plot of land in the
town of Berneslay, which lay nigh to the court of the same monks
towards the west, measuring seventeen perches and five feet
in length, and two perches in breadth, whereof one end butted on
the burial ground and the other on his (Gerard's) garden. To
hold to the aforesaid monks in pure and perpetual alms for ever.
WITNESSES: Henry de Sevile, Hugh de Berch, Richard de
Craven, Richard de Marton, Henry Portbref, and others.

CARTA GERARDI DE BERNESLAY. Gerard de Berneslay.

Sciant presentes et futuri quod ego Gerardus de Berneslay
tenco de priore et monachis de Pontefracto unam bovatam

Chap. V. 76 HISTORY OF BARNSLEY.

Ancient Charters.

Gerard de Berneslay.

terræ in territorio de Berneslay termino quamdin illis placeat et non hæreditarie illam scilicet quam Willielmus filius Rad. ante me tenuit. Reddendo inde annuatim præfatis priori et monachis iv solidos medietatem ad festum Sancti Martini et medietatem ad Pentecost. Iterum teneo de eisdem priore et monachis in eadem villa de Berneslay unam dimidiam bovatam terræ termino quamdin illis placeat et non hæreditarie illam scilicet quam Thomas de Milnthorp et Hugo filius Leuke ante me tenuerunt. Redden. inde annuatim præfatis priori et monachis xv denarios medietatem ad festum Sancti Martini et medietatem ad Pentecost. Præfati vero monachi capient quando voluerint predictam bovatam terræ et dimidiam sine impedimento mei vel hæredum meorum salvo mihi et heredibus meis croppo bladi mei. Et ne ego Gerardus vel heredes mei post mortem meam aliquid jus aut clamium in prædictis bovata terre et dimidia de accommodatione vendicare possimus hanc cartam sigilli mei oppositione roboravi. 𝕳𝖎𝖎𝖘 𝕿𝖊𝖘𝖙𝖎𝖇𝖚𝖘— Johanne Tyrel, Rogero clerico, Waltero de Byrum, Ricardo de Marton, Gerardo de Berneslay, Adamo de Oldtona, Roberto dispensatore, et aliis.

Translation.

TRANSLATION.

Charter of Gerard de Berneslay, declaring that he held of the prior and monks of Pontefract one bovate of land in the territory of Berneslay, during their pleasure, and not hereditarily, that, namely, which William the son of Radulf held before him, rendering thence annually to the aforesaid prior and monks four shillings, half at the feast of St. Martin and half at Pentecost. Moreover, that he held of the same prior and monks, in the said town of Berneslay, one-half of a bovate of land, at their pleasure, and not hereditarily, viz., that which Thomas de Milnethorp and Hugh the son of Leuke held before him, rendering thereout yearly to the aforesaid prior and monks fifteen pence, half at the feast of St. Martin and half at Pentecost. And that the aforesaid monks should retake whenever they willed the aforesaid bovate and a-half of land, without impediment from him or his heirs, saving to him and his heirs his crop of corn. WITNESSES: John Tyrel, Roger the clerk, Walter de Byrum, Richard de Marton, Gerard de Berneslay, Adam de Oldton, Robert the steward, and others.

DONATIONS TO THE MONKS.

77 Chap. V.

CARTA HENRICI FILII ROGERI DE BERNESLAY.

Ancient Charters.

Sciant presentes et futuri quod ego Henricus filius Rogeri de Berneslay et heres mei nunquam exigemus aliquod annuatim in quercubus bosci de Berneslay occasione tenementi quod de Priore et Conventu de Pontefract teneo in eadem villa. Qiis Testibus—Thoma de Torneton, Rainer de Wambwell, Adamo filio Rogeri, Thoma de Stagno, Ricardo de Baghil, et aliis.

Henry, son of Roger de Berneslay.

TRANSLATION.

Translation.

Charter of Henry, son of Roger de Berneslay, declaring that he and his heirs would never demand anything yearly in the oaks of the wood of Berneslay by reason of the tenement which he held of the prior and convent of Pontefract in the same town. WITNESSES: Thomas de Torneton, Rainer de Wambwell, Adam son of Roger, Thomas de Stagno, Richard de Baghil, and others.

CARTA WALTERI PRIORIS DE PONTEFRACTO.

Walter, the Prior of Pontefract.

Sciant presentes et futuri quod ego Walterus prior de Pontefracto et ejusdem loci conventus dedimus concessimus et presenti carta confirmavimus Adamo de Falewait et hæredibus suis vel cui assignare voluerit unum toftum in Berneslay de dimidia acra terræ inter terram Gerardi filii Bernardi et terram Pagani in orientali parti tofti Hugonis de Baggehil et dimidiam acram in Collegrimewellrodes et dimidiam acram super Kirketoftes et dimidiam acram super Langlandes et unam percatam super Claylandes. Tenendas et habendas prefato Adamo et heredibus suis vel cui assignare voluerit libere et quiete cum communia prefate ville de Berneslay quantum ad tantum tenementum pertinet saluis nobis boscis nostris. Reddendo inde annuatim unam libram cymini ad festum Sancti Egidii pro omni servicio. Et ne prefatus Adamus vel heredes sui sive assignati sui in perpetuum contra tenorem hujus cartæ venire possint huic scripto quod penes nos retinemus sigillum suum apposuit. Qiis Testibus—Johanne de Birkin, Rogero clerico de Silkeston, Roberto de Turs, Rainero de Wambwelle, Adamo de Oldfeld, Ricardo de Marton, et aliis.

TRANSLATION.

Translation.

Charter of Walter the prior of Pontefract, and the convent of the same place, granting to Adam de Falewait and his

Chap. V. 78 HISTORY OF BARNSLEY.

Ancient Charters.

heirs and assigns, one toft in Berneslay, of half an acre of land between the land of Gerard the son of Bernard and the land of Pagan, in the earstern part of the toft of Hugh de Bagghil, and half an acre in Collegrimewellrodes, and half half an acre on Kirke Toftes, and half an acre in Langlandes, and one perch on Claylandes, to hold to the said Adam, his heirs and assigns, freely and quietly, with common of the aforesaid town of Berneslay, so much as appertains to such a tenement, rendering annually one pound of Cummin at the feast of St. Egidius in lieu of all services. WITNESSES : John de Birkin, Roger clerk of Silkstone, Robert de Turs, Rainer de Wambwell, Adam de Oldfeld, Richard de Marton, and others.

Walter the Prior.

The same.

CARTA WALTERI PRIORIS DE PONTEFRACTO.

Sciant presentes et futuri quod ego Walterus prior de Pontefracto et ejusdem loci conventus dedimus concessimus et hac carta nostra confirmavimus Henrico filio Rogeri de Berneslay et heredibus suis unum toftum in Berneslay de duabus acris terræ juxta Bernesclif et quindecem acras terræ in campis scilicet in W'dalecroft decem acras et quinque acras in essarto quod fuit Willielmi filii Radulfi tenendas et habendas de nobis libere et quiete cum communi pasturæ ejusdem villæ exceptis quercubus in bosco de Berneslay.- Redden. inde nobis annuatim dimidiam marcam argenti pro omni servicio medietatem ad Pentecost et medietatem ad festum Sancti Martini. Pro hac autem donatione et concessione dedit nobis predictus Henricus xx solidos. Hiis Testibus—Thoma de Thorneton, Rainer de Wambwelle, Johanne de Rokelaya, Ricardo de Stagno, Thoma fratre suo, et aliis.

Translation.

TRANSLATION.

Charter of Walter the prior of Pontefract, and the convent of the same place, granting to Henry the son of Roger de Berneslay and his heirs, one toft in Berneslay of two acres of land, near Bernesclif, and fifteen acres of land in the fields, to wit, in W'dalecroft ten acres, and five acres in the essart which was of William the son of Radulph, to hold freely and quietly, with common of pasture of the same town, the oaks in the wood of Berneslay excepted, rendering thereout yearly half a mark of silver in lieu of all service, half at Pentecost and half at the feast of Saint Martin. For this grant the aforesaid Henry gave twenty shillings. WITNESSES : Thomas de Thorneton, Rainer de Wambwelle, John de Rokelay, Richard de Stagno, Thomas his brother, and others.

DONATIONS TO THE MONKS. 79 Chap. V.

CARTA HUGONIS FILII HERBERTI DE SILKISTON.

Ancient Charters.

Omnibus Sanctæ Matris ecclesiæ filiis Hugo filius Herberti de Silkiston salutem. Noverit universitas vero quod ego teneo de priore et monachis de Pontefracto xxxii acras terræ de essartis in territorio de Berneslay terminum in vita mea et non hæreditarie ita quod post mortem meam prædictæ acræ prædictis priori et monachis solute et quiete remanebunt sine omni impedimento vel retenemento de me vel de heredibus meis cum tota melioratione quam ibi posuero. Et quia de supradictis xxxii. acris in territorio de Berneslay partem dimisi Rogero de Berneslay partem Thomæ de Bertun ad tenend. de me terminum in vita mea ne idem Rogerus et Thomas aut heredes sui in eodem tenemento post obitum meum jus aut clamium habere possint præsentem cartam hujus rei veritatem continentem sigilli mei munimine roboravi. Hiis Testibus—Johanne de Birkin, Willielmo de Stapilton, Ricardo de Fareburn, Willielmo de Brodecroft, Willielmo filio Eur, Ricardo de Stagno, et aliis.

Hugh, the son of Herbert de Silkiston.

TRANSLATION.

Translation.

Charter of Hugh, the son of Herbert, to all the sons of Holy Mother Church, sending greeting, and declaring that he held of the prior and monks of Pontefract thirty-two acres of land of assarts,[1] in the territory of Berneslay, for the term of his life, and not hereditarily, so that after his death the aforesaid acres might freely and quietly remain to the aforesaid monks without hindrance from him or his heirs, with all the improvement made by him there. And because of the said thirty-two acres, he had demised part to Roger de Berneslay, and part to Thomas de Bertun, to hold of him during his life, lest the said Roger or Thomas should after his death have any right or claim in the same tenement, he fortified that charter with his seal. WITNESSES: John de Birkin, William de Stapilton, Richard de Fareburn, William de Brodecroft, William son of Eur, Richard de Stagno, and others.

[1] In the mention of assarts, or essarts, we have probably the earliest notice of increasing cultivation. Essart was a forest phrase for a cultivated spot, from the French "*assartir*," to make plain.

Chap. V.   80   HISTORY OF BARNSLEY.

Ancient Charters.

CARTA JOHANNIS DE CELLARIO DE BRETTON.

John de Cellario de Bretton.

Sciant presentes et futuri quod ego Johannes de Cellario de Bretton dedi et concessi et hac mea presenti carta confirmavi Gerardo de Berneslay filio Averdi et heredibus suis vel cui assignare voluerit duos Crimbles in campis de Bretton illos scilicet qui spectant ad duas assartas meas scilicet Lamerod et Langelay quas teneo de domino priore de Bretton. quæ jacent juxta molendinum de Berneslay unum crimble buttat super molendinum et aliud caput super aquam et unum caput unius crimble buttat super Dirne et aliud caput super pontem. Tenend. et habend. de me et de heredibus meis illi et heredibus suis in feudo et hereditate libere et quiete et honorifice. Solven. inde annuatim mihi et heredibus meis tres denarios ad Annunciationem Beatæ Mariæ pro omni servicio et exactione. Ego autem et heredes mei warentizabimus prædicto Gerardo et heredibus suis vel cui assignaverit predictos Crimbles contra omnes homines. Pro hac autem donatione et concessione dedit mihi idem Gerardus duos solidos de gersumma. Hiis Testibus—Johanne filio Hugonis de Bretton, Roberto de Pul, Henrico filio Rogeri de Berneslay, Roberto filio Thomæ, Gerardo filio Thomæ, Ricardo de Cravena, et aliis.

Translation.

TRANSLATION.

Charter of John de cellario de Bretton, granting to Gerard de Berneslay, son of Averdus, and his heirs and assigns, two crimbles in the fields of Bretton, viz., those which belonged to his two assarts, to wit, Lamerod and Langlay, which he held of the Lord Prior of Bretton, which lay nigh unto the mill of Berneslay, and one crimble butted on the mill, and the other end on the water, and one end of one crimble butted on the Dearne, and the other end on the Bridge. To hold to him and his heirs in fee and inheritance, freely and quietly, paying thereout annually three pence in lieu of all service at the Annunciation of the Blessed Mary. For that grant the said Gerard gave to him two shillings as the price. WITNESSES: John son of Hugh de Bretton, Robert de Pul, Henry son of Roger de Berneslay, Robert son of Thomas, Gerard son of Thomas, Richard de Craven, and others.

John, son of Adam de Oldfeld.

CARTA JOHANNIS FILII ADAMI DE OLDFELD.

Sciant præsentes et futuri quod ego Johannes filius Adami de Oldfeld dedi concessi et hac presenti carta mea confirmavi pro

PEDIGREE OF THE FAMILY OF WOOD.

ARMS—*Azure*, three savage Men of the Wood passant in fess, each holding in his left hand a club, which rests on his left shoulder, all proper, and on his right hand a shield, *Argent* charged with a cross *Gules*. CREST—A Man of the Wood, as in the Arms.

George Wood of Monk Bretton, buried at Royston, 1589 === Ann.

George of Monk Bretton, Gent., died 1638 === Janet, daughter of Roger Swift of Rothwell. — John, second son.

Robert of Monk Bretton, Gent., son and heir, died 1676. === Jane, dau. of John Stocks, Alderman of Doncaster. — John of Smithies, from whom descended Sir George Wood, Baron of the Exchequer. — George. Stephen. William. — Esther. — Peter slain at the siege of Leipsick.

Ann, 1 W., dau. of John Fox of Smallfield. === Henry Wood, of Barnsley, Esq., 7th son, J.P., born 1645; d. May 4, 1720; buried at Barnsley. === Dorothy Woodhead of Woodseats, 2 W. — Elizabeth Simpson, 3 W., died Dec. 31, 1748; bur. at Barnsley. — John, d. y. — William of Masbro'. — John of Royston. — James, an attorney. — George. Robert. Isaac, d. y. — Douglas, Dorothy. d. y. Sarah. — Jane. Elizabeth.

George. Robert, d. y. — Mary, d. y. — Dorothy, marrd. John Cunliffe, County of Lancashire. — Henry, of Barnsley, Esq., eldest son and heir. — Mary-Dorothy, 1 W., daughter of Charles Palmer, D.D., Prebendary of York. — Francis Wood, of Barnsley, Esq., died 1775, aged 79. — Rebecca, 2 W. dau. of William Ellison of Barnsley; died 1784, aged 71. — Ellen, mar. George Wheatley of Roystone. — Jane, mur. Richard Mawood of Ardsley. — Elizabeth, mar... Cornwall of Hull.

Henry Wood, D.D., Rector of Hemsworth, died October 27, 1790. === Elizabeth, dau. of Charles Gore, of County Lincoln. — Sir Francis Wood of Barnsley, created Baronet Dec. 10, 1783; no issue. — Chas. Wood, Captain in the navy, killed in action in the East Indies, Oct. 9, 1782, aged 51. — Caroline, dau. of John Lacon Barker, of Ottley, Esq., mar. Jan. 6, 1770. — John, slain in Nova Scotia, 1760. — Elizabeth Maria-Dorothea, died unmarried.

Elizabeth Laura, d. y. — Sir Francis Lindley Wood, 2nd Bart., heir to his father and uncles; died Dec. 31, 1846; bur. at Hickleton. — Ann, daughter of Samuel Buck, Esq., of New Grange, near Leeds, married 1798. — Henry, second son, died s. p. — Caroline, married William Busfield, of Upwood, Esq. — Dorothy, mar. Charles Armstrong, Esq. — Elizabeth, married Edward O'Reilly, Esq.

Sir Charles Wood, of Hickleton Hall, Co. Yorkshire, M.P. for Halifax, and late First Lord of the Admiralty, 3rd Baronet. === Lady Mary Grey, dau. of Earl Grey of Howick, mar. July 30, 1829. — Samuel-Francis, d. s. p. — Ann, mar. John Childers, of Cantley, Esq.

Mary-Louisa, d. y. — Charles Lindley. — Emily-Charlotte. — Francis Lindley. — Henry-John Lindley. — Frederick-George Lindley. — Alice-Louisa. — Blanche.

DONATIONS TO THE MONKS. 81 Chap. V.

salute animæ meæ et patris mei et matris meæ et omnium ante- Ancient Charcessorum et hæredum meorum Deo et Ecclesiæ Sancti Johannis ters.
de Pontefracto et monachis ibidem Deo servientibus totam illam John, son of
terram quam Hugo frater meus tenuit de me in territorio de Adam de Oldfeld.
Berneslay et quam idem habuit in terra domini prioris de
Pontefract sursum reddidi et omnino de me et heredibus suis
quietos clamavi illos seliones qui jacent intra diversas culturas
qui fuerunt quondam Adami patris mei versus australem partem.
Tenend. et habend. præfatis monachis in puram et perpetuam
eleemosinam. Hanc vero donationem et concessionem ego
Johannes et heredes mei præfatis monachis contra omnes
homines warantizabimus in perpetuum. 𝕳iis 𝕿estibus —
Domino Willielmo de Bretton, Henrico de Seville, Hugone de
Berch, Ricardo de Cravena, Henrico filio Rogeri, et aliis.

TRANSLATION.

Translation.

Charter of John, son of Adam de Oldfield, granting, for the
salvation of his soul, and of his father and mother, and all his
ancestors and heirs, to the monks of Saint John of Pontefract,
all that land which Hugh his brother had held of him in the
territory of Barnsley, and surrendering that which the same
(person) had had in the land of the lord prior, and altogether
quit claiming those selions[1] which lay in divers fields, which were
formerly of his father Adam, towards the southern part, to hold
to the aforesaid monks in pure and perpetual alms. WITNESSES :
Domino William de Bretton, Henry de Seville, Hugh de Berch,
Richard de Craven, Henry son of Roger, and others.

CARTA JOHANNIS DE OLDFELD.

𝕾ciant presentes et futuri quod ego Johannes de Oldfeld dedi John de Oldconcessi et hac mea presenti carta confirmavi Hugoni fratri meo feld.
et heredibus suis vel cui assignare velit pro homagio et servicio
suo sex acras terræ in Oldfeld versus south. Tenendas et
habendas de me et de heredibus meis illi et heredibus suis vel
cui assignare voluerit in feudo et hereditate libere et quiete et
honorifice solvent. inde annuatim mihi et heredibus meis sex
denarios in die Sancti Martini pro omni servicio et demand.
Ego autem et heredes mei warantizabimus ei et heredibus suis
vel suis assignatis prædictam terram contra omnes homines.
𝕳iis 𝕿estibus—Roberto de Sepelay, Hugone de Berch, Rogero
fratre ejus, et aliis.

[1] Selion, a ridge of land between two furrows.

F

Chap. V.   82   HISTORY OF BARNSLEY.

Ancient Charters.

TRANSLATION.

Translation. Charter of John de Oldfeld, granting to Hugh his brother, and his heirs and assigns, for his homage and service, six acres of land in Oldfeld, towards the south, to hold in fee and inheritance, freely and quietly, paying thereout annually six pence on Saint Martin's day in lieu of all service. WITNESSES: Robert de Sepelay, Hugh de Berch, Roger his brother, and others.

Through the influence of the monks a charter for holding a market and fair at Barnsley was obtained in the middle of the thirteenth century from Henry III., while that king was residing at Clarendon (in Wiltshire), his favourite hunting seat.

Charter authorisng the holding of a market and fair at Barnsley.

HENRICUS Dei Gra. Rex Anglie Dns. Normand. Aquitan. et Com. Andegau Archiepis. Epis. Abbatbs. Priorbs. Comitbs. Baronbs. Justiciars.Viceomits. Ministrs. et omnibs. aliis Ballivis et fidels. suis salutm. Sciatis quod concessims. et hac psenti. carta nra. cfirmavims. p. nob. et hdbs. nris. Dilectis nob. in Xro. Pori. et cventui. de Pontefr. qd. ipsi et successores eor. in pptuum. heant. unum mcatum. singlis. septimanis p. diem mcuri. in Villa sua de Bnesl. et qd. heant. ibidem unam feriam singlis. annis durantem p. quatuor dies scil. in vigla. in die Sci. Michaels. et p. duos dies prxmo. sequentes cu. ombs. libertbs. et libs. csuetudinibus. ad hujusmodi mcatum. et feriam ptinentbs. nisi mcatum. illud et feria illa sint ad nocumentum vicinor. mcator. et vicinar. feriar. Quare volumus et firmr. pcipms. p. nobis et hdbs. nris. quod pdicti. Prior et Conventus et successores eor. in pptuum. heant. unum mcatum. singlis. septimanis p. diem Mercurii in Villa sua de Bnesl. Et qd. heant. ibidem unam feriam singlis. annis durantem per quatuor dies in vigilia in die Scti. Michaelis et p. duos dies pxmo. sequentes cum omnibs. libertbs. et libis. csuetudinibs. ad hujusmodi mcatum. et feriam ptientbs. nisi mcatum. illud et feria illa sint ad nocumentum vicinor. mcator. et vicinar. feriar. sicut pdctm. est. 𝕳𝖎𝖎𝖘 𝕿𝖊𝖘𝖇𝖘. —Willmo. de Valenc. fre. nro.,Willm. Lungesp,Willmo. de Cantilupo, Johe.Maunsell ppo., Hug. de Vinon, Robto. de Mustegros, Johe. de Lessincon, Bartholomeo Peach, Paulino Pevir, Henrico Mara, Matho. Bezell, Robto. Norreys, Rado. deWauncy, Johe. de Neville, et aliis. Data p. manu. nram. apud Clarendon. sexto die Febii. Anno regni nostri tricessimo ttio.

CHARTER FOR A MARKET AND FAIR. 83 Chap. V.

Ancient Charters.

TRANSLATION.

Translation.

Henry, by the grace of God, King of England, Lord of Ireland, Lord of Normandy, Aquitaine, and Earl of Anjou, to the Archbishops, Bishops, Abbots, Priors, Barons, Justiciaries, Sheriffs, Servants, and all others his Bailiffs and Lieges, greeting: Know ye, that we have granted, and by this our present confirmed, for us and our heirs, to our beloved in Christ the Prior and Convent of Pontefract, that they and their successors may have for ever one market every seven days on Wednesday in their town of Barnsley, and that they may have there one fair every year lasting for four days, viz., the eve of Saint Michael's[1] day and two days next thereafter, with all the liberties and free customs to a market and fair of this kind belonging, unless that market and that fair be to the hurt of the neighbouring markets and neighbouring fairs. Wherefore we will, and firmly order for us and our heirs, that the aforesaid Prior and Convent and their successors may have for ever one market, every seven days, on Wednesday, in their town of Barnsley, and that they may have there one fair every year lasting for four days, the eve of Saint Michael's day and two days next thereafter, with all the liberties and free customs to a market and fair of this kind belonging, unless that market and that fair be to the hurt of the neighbouring markets and the neighbouring fairs, as aforesaid. THESE BEING WITNESSES: William de Valence our brother, William Lungesp, William de Cantilupo, John Maunsell ppo.—, Hugh de Vinon, Robert de Mustegros, John de Lessincon, Bartholomew Peach, Paul Pevir, Henry Mara, Matthew Bezell,

[1] This makes four days, including Saint Michael's day. Barnsley, at this season of the year, appears to have been noted from time immemorial for the excellence of its goose pies. Mr. Henry Rayney of London, in a letter to Mr. Carrington of the Views, near Barnsley, dated 19th September, 1727, in the course of his remarks, says :—"Pray, buy me three goose pyes at Barnsley of a groat a piece, not those that has a quarter of a goose whole in them, but those that cut the goose in small pieces, as Timothy tells me, and one pye bigger; these I desire may be purchased on Mich. day, and sent up in a box by the carr., and I will return the money with thanks, or I will have no pyes. It being purely to shew people here what good things Yorkshire produces, and what sort of goose pyes is made, &c."—Two old franked directions of letters from London are still in existence, dated 1712 and 1730, addressed, " Mr. Carrington, at Views, by Barnsley Bagg, Yorkshire" (not, as we should now say, near Barnsley).

Chap. V. 84 HISTORY OF BARNSLEY.

Ancient Char-
ters.
Robert Norreys, Ralph de Wauncy, John de Neville, and others. Given under our hand at Clarendon, the sixth day of February, in the year of our reign the thirty-third.

William Lungesp, one of the witnesses to this charter, was son of the Earl of Salisbury, and left an only daughter and heiress, who married Henry de Laci.

1258. Edmund de Laci, constable of Chester, confirmed to the monks of Saint John of Pontefract, one cartload of dead wood, and also the town of Barnsley, with two oxgangs of land in Markesden, which they had of the gift of William de Vescy. Dated at Rowelle the day before the Ides of May.

According to the *Rotuli Hundredorum*, we find that the prior had fairs, a market, gallows,[1] and the assize [2] of bread and beer at Barnsley, which right had been exercised for twenty-six years, but the jury knew not by what warranty.

31st Edw. I. Charter of Free Warren was granted to the prior of Pontefract in his demesnes of Barnsley.

We have next five undated charters of Godfrey, one of the priors of Pontefract, which are supposed to have been executed towards the close of the thirteenth century. In some of these mention is made of the Town Head and Cross.

Godfrey the
Prior of Ponte-
fract.

CARTA GODFRIDI PRIORIS DE PONTEFRACTO.

UNIVERSIS Christi fidelibus præsens scriptum visuris vel audituris frater Godfridus Prior Monasterii Sancti Johannis de Pontefracto et ejusdem loci conventus salutem in Domino. Noverint nos ad firmam annuam in perpetuum demississe concessisse et hac presenti carta confirmasse Hugoni clerico de Vetera villa et hæredibus suis in perpetuum tres acras terræ arabilis in Wodeboyes quas Geraldus filius Thomæ de Berneslay quondam de nobis tenuit et unam acram et dimidiam quæ jacent inter terram Johannis de Bergh et pratum fratris Anglice

---

[1] The right of trying and convicting criminals, with power to inflict capital punishment.

[2] Power given to determine the weight and regulate the price of different commodities.

DONATIONS BY THE MONKS.

85   Chap. V.

Ancient Charters.

Frereheng. Insuper demisimus eidem unam culturam sicut jacet in terra quæ vocatur Motharp Smyiflat. Tenendas et habendas de nobis et successoribus nostris sibi et hæredibus suis libere quiete et pacifice cum omnibus asiamentis ad illas terras pertinentibus. Reddendo inde annuatim nobis et successoribus nostris sex solidos ad duos anni terminos medietatem ad Pentecost et aliam medietatem ad festum Sancti Martini in Hyeme. In cujus rei testimonium præsenti scripto sigillum nostrum apposuimus. 𝕳íís 𝕿estíbus—Alexandro Portbref, Willielmo ad Caput, Thoma de Keresford, Hugone ad Crucem, Ricardo Nades, et multis aliis.

Godfrey the Prior of Pontefract.

TRANSLATION.

Translation.

Charter of Godfrey, the Prior of Pontefract, and the convent of the same place, demising, as a yearly farm for ever, to Hugh the Clerk of Old Town, and his heirs for ever, three acres of arable land in Wodeboyes, which Gerard, son of Thomas de Barnsley, formerly held of the same monks, and one acre and a half situate between land of John de Bergh and the meadow of his brother, in English Frereheng. Moreover, demising to the same person one piece of cultivated ground, as the same lay in the land called Motharp Smyiflat. To hold freely and quietly, with all easements, rendering thereout yearly six shillings at two periods of the year, viz., half at Pentecost, and the other half at the feast of St. Martin in winter. WITNESSES : Alexander Portbref, Willielmo at the (Town) Head, Thomas de Keresford, Hugh at the Cross,[1] Richard Nades, and many others.

CARTA GODFRIDI PRIORIS DE PONTEFRACTO.

Godfrey the Prior of Pontefract.

UNIVERSIS præsentes literas visuris et audituris frater Godfridus Prior Monasterii Sancti Johannis de Pontefracto et ejusdem loci conventus salutem in Domino. Noverint nos demississe concessisse et hac præsenti carta confirmâsse Ricardo dicto Nades de Veteri Villa et hæredibus suis ad annuam firmam in perpetuum unam culturam quæ vocatur Brerirodes. Tenendas et habendas sibi et heredibus suis libere quiete et pacifice cum omnibus asiamentis ad dictam culturam pertinentibus. Reddendo inde annuatim nobis et successoribus nostris tres solidos ad duos anni terminos scilicet medietatem ad Penticost et aliam medietatem ad festum Sancti Martini in Hyeme. In cujus rei testimonium præsenti scripto sigillum nostrum commune apposuimus. 𝕳íís 𝕿estíbus—Thoma de Keresford, Willielmo ad Caput Villæ, Alexandro Portebref, Hugone ad Crucem, Hugone de Cumberword, Elia Serviente, Jordano Wilde, et aliis.

[1] Probably this refers to the Market Cross.

Chap. V.   86   HISTORY OF BARNSLEY.

Ancient Charters.

Godfrey the Prior of Pontefract.

TRANSLATION.

Charter of Godfrey, the Prior of Pontefract, and the convent of the same place, demising to Richard, called Nades, of Old Town, and his heirs, as a yearly farm for ever, one piece of cultivated land, called Brerirodes, to hold freely and quietly, with all the easements thereto belonging, rendering thereout three shillings at two periods of the year, viz., half at Pentecost, and half at the feast of St. Martin in Winter. WITNESSES : Thomas de Keresford, William at the Town Head, Alexander Portbref, Hugh at the Cross, Hugh de Cumberword, Elias Serviens, Jordan Wilde, and others.

The same.

CARTA GODFRIDI PRIORIS DE PONTEFRACTO.

UNIVERSIS presentes literas inspecturis frater Godfridus Prior Monasterii Sancti Johannis de Pontefracto et ejusdem loci conventus salutem in Domino sempiternam. Noverit Universitas vero nos demississe concessisse et hoc præsenti scripto nostro confirmâsse Evæ filiæ Sibillæ de Oldtona tres acras terræ arabilis in territorio nostro de Berneslay quarum una jacet de super montem de Bernesclif et una dimidia acra ad Lefyscros juxta terram Thomæ clerici et una dimidia acra abbutat super Colconne Welle et alia pars super Oldfeldflat et una dimidia acra abbutat super forestam de Kirketona cum duabus perticis predictis prope adjacentibus et ejusdem dimidie acre pertinentibus et una dimidia acra super Delacres juxta terram Alexandri Portberf et una dimidia acra apud Dicgeve juxta terram Thomæ clerici. Reddend. inde annuatim nobis et successoribus nostris decem et octo denarios medietatem ad Pentecost et aliam medietatem ad festum Sancti Martini pro omni servicio et demand. In cujus rei testimonium sigillum nostrum commune presentibus duximus apponendum. Hiis Testibus— Ricardo Nades de Oldtona, Hugone filio Hugonis de eadem, Willielmo ad caput Ville de Berneslay, Alexandro Portbref, Hugone ad Crucem, et aliis.

Translation.

TRANSLATION.

Charter of Godfrey, Prior of Pontefract, and the convent of the same place, demising to Eve, daughter of Sibil del Oldton, three acres of arable land in their territory of Barnsley, whereof one half acre lay on the hill called Bernesclif, and one half acre at Lefyscros, near to the land of Thomas the Clerk, and one half acre abutted on Colconne Well, and other part on Oldfeldflat, and one half acre abutted on the Forest of Kirketon, with two perches to the aforesaid near adjoining, and to the same half acre belonging, and one half acre on Delacres, near the

DONATIONS BY THE MONKS.

87   Chap. V.

Ancient Charters.

land of Alexander Portbref, and one half acre at Diegeve, near the land of Thomas the Clerk, rendering thercout yearly eighteen pence, half at Pentecost, and half at the feast of St. Martin, in lieu of all service. WITNESSES: Richard Nades of Old Town, Hugh son of Hugh of the same place, William of the Town Head of Barnsley, Alexander Portbref, Hugh at the Cross, and others.

CARTA GODFRIDI PRIORIS DE PONTEFRACTO.

Godfrey the Prior of Pontefract.

UNIVERSIS presentes literas inspecturis frater Godfridus Prior Monasterii Sancti Johannis Evangelisti de Pontefracto et ejusdem loci conventus salutem in Domino sempiternam. Noverit Universitas vero nos demississe concessisse et hoc presenti scripto nostro confirmâsse Willielmo forestario et hæredibus suis unum toftum in villa nostra de Berneslay cum tribus acris terræ in campis ejusdem cum pertinentibus et asiamentis tanto tenemento pertinentibus intra villam et extra illud scilicet toftum et illam terram quam Roberto Fullo quondam de nobis tenuit in eadem redden. inde annuatim nobis et successoribus nostris quatuor solidos ad duos anni terminos scilicet medietatem ad Pentecost et aliam medietatem ad festum Sancti Martini pro omni seculari servicio et demand. Saluis nobis sectis curiæ et molendinorum. In cujus rei testimonium, &c. &c.

TRANSLATION.

Translation.

Charter of Godfrey, Prior of Pontefract, and the convent of the same place, devising to William the Forester and his heirs, one toft in their town of Barnsley, with three acres of land in the fields thereof, with the appurtenances and easements to such a tenement belonging within and without the town, viz., that toft and land which Robert Fullo formerly held of them, rendering thereout annually four shillings at two periods of the year, viz., half at Pentecost, and half at Martinmas, in lieu of all service, saving to them the suits of the court and of the mills.

CARTA GODFRIDI PRIORIS DE PONTEFRACTO.

Godfrey the Prior of Pontefract.

UNIVERSIS presentes literas inspecturis visuris vel audituris frater Godfridus Prior Monasterii Sancti Johannis de Pontefracto et ejusdem loci conventus salutem in Domino. Noveritis nos demississe concessisse et hac presenti carta confirmâsse Matheo Caruisia de Bernesley et hæredibus suis in perpetuum unam de domibus nostris noviter constructis in vasto fori nostri de Berneslay illam scilicet quæ est superior et foro propinquior cum quatuor acris terræ et dimidia in territorio de Berneslay

Chap. V.   88   · HISTORY OF BARNSLEY.

Ancient Charters.

Godfrey the Prior of Pontefract.

quarum duæ acræ jacent super culturam nostram quæ vocatur Oldfeldflat versus veterem villam et una dimidia acra cujus unum caput abuttat super Longlandgerd versus occidens et aliud super terram Jordani Wilde versus oriens et una acra quæ abuttat super foveam molindini juxta terram Hugonis Molendinarii et ascendit juxta Mapelwelsibum et una acra quæ abuttat super Bernesclif ex parte occidentali et super gardinum Willielmi Copping ex parte orientali. Tenend. et habend. dicto Matheo et hæredibus suis in perpetuum libere quiete integre et in pace pro tribus solidis argenti et sex denariis solvend. annuatim ad duos anni terminos medietatem scilicet ad Pentecost et aliam medietatem ad festum Sancti Martini in Hyeme pro omnibus aliis serviciis et demand. Saluis nobis relevis et escaetis. In cujus rei testimonium, &c.

Translation.

TRANSLATION.

Charter of Godfrey, the Prior of Pontefract, and the convent of the same place, granting and confirming to Matthew Caruisia, of Barnsley, and his heirs, one of their houses newly constructed in their market-place of Barnsley, with four acres and a half of land in the territory of Barnsley, whereof two acres lay in their field called Oldfeldflat towards Old Town, and one half acre, whereof one end abutted upon Longlandgerd towards the west, and the other end on land of Jordan Wilde towards the east, and one acre which abutted on the mill next the land of Hugh the miller, and went up towards Mapelwelsibus (Mapplewell), and one acre which abutted on Bernesclif on the western side, and on the garden of William Copping towards the east. To hold to the said Matthew and his heirs for ever, freely and quietly, for three shillings and sixpence, to be paid at two periods of the year, one half at Pentecost, and the other half at the feast of St. Martin in winter, saving to them reliefs and escheats.

Among the witnesses to some of the last charters of the Prior of Pontefract we meet with a Keresforth and a Nades; the same surnames are also mentioned in the *Nonarum Inquisitiones*, an extract from which will not be out of place.

It appears that at a Parliament holden at Westminster, in the fourteenth year of the reign of Edward III. in England, and the first of his reign in France, a grant was made of a subsidy of the

NONARUM INQUISITIONES.

ninth and fifteenth. The prelates, earls, barons, and commons, for the good keeping of the realm, and in aid of the king's wars against Scotland, Gascony, &c., granted to him the ninth lamb, the ninth fleece, and the ninth sheaf, for two years next to come, and of cities and boroughs the ninth of their goods and chattels, and of merchants foreign that dwelt not in the cities and boroughs, and of people that dwelt in forests and wastes (except the poor Boraile people), they should be charged a fifteenth. Assessors and venditors were appointed to assess and sell the ninth and fifteenth. The following is copied from the record, in making which, inquisitions were taken on the oath of the parishioners in each parish.

Com. Ebor.

SILKESTON.

Tax, iiij., xx., vi.[li].

"Of which parish, to wit, Philip de Lyces, William de Keversforth, William de Nades, Peter de Stayburgh, John de Falthwayt, William Attewelle, Matthew Daygnell, John, son of Roger, Adam de Legh, William de Hethyley, Adam de Hawkeshirst, and Richard Mickelthwayt, to this jury, on their oath present, by an indenture between them and the prior and his brotherhood, made and interchangeably sealed, that the ninths of sheaves, of wool, and of lambs, of the whole of the said parish, are worth this year £36, and not more; that the revenue of the said church consists of a rent of 10 marks, of tithes of hay, oblations, and other small tithes, with 311 acres of land, which are worth 65 marks; they also present that there is not any merchant within the said parish, nor any person living otherwise than by agriculture."

John Annotson of Barnsley gave the monks leave to make a pool or mill-dam in his essart there, called Wytokebyl.

In the account contained in the *Valor Ecclesiasticus*, made *temp*. Hen VIII., of the possessions of the Mon-

Chap. V. 90   HISTORY OF BARNSLEY.

Valor Ecclesiasticus. astery of Pontefract, are the following entries which relate to Barnsley. Under the head of " Temporals," viz., consisting of rents and farms, &c., in divers townships, we find mentioned (*inter alia*) :—

> " Barnsley with £15, arising from the proceeds of the tolls of the fair and the markets there, and with ten shillings of the perquisites of the courts *(perquisita curiarum*[1]*)* there, £55 12s. 5d."

There are mentioned in the account of the above monastery or priory the following names amongst others :—

> " George Darcy, knight-seneschal of Barnsley ; Thomas Beamond, seneschal of Barnsley; William Twhait, receiver of the priory there ; Thomas Hegley, bailiff of Barnsley."

The subjoined account of early manor courts held at Barnsley is extracted from the Harleian MSS. :—

Minutes of Manor Courts.

1240. " At a court held at Barnsley, on the Monday next after the feast of Saint Peter, John le Barker appeared and produced a charter, by which he purchased a messuage with edifices, which John Mustard some time held in Barnsley."

1341. " Court held at Barnsley, on the Monday next before Palm Sunday, when the jury upon an inquisition say that Agnes de Galbergh did not put herself in her lifetime out of her tenements in Barnsley, but in the same died seised. It was therefore ordered to distrain the heirs of the said Agnes."

1341. " Court held at Barnsley, on Monday before the feast of Whitsuntide, at which Thomas, son and heir of Agnes de Galbergh, did fealty for tenements in Dodworth, Barnsley, and Oldton, in the county of York, and of one field in Barnsley, called Wod-

---

[1] " *Perquisita curiarum*" is also otherwise construed to mean the gains or proceeds of country estates or manors.

MANOR COURTS. 91 Chap. V.

house, with a cottage and garden in the same town *Minutes of* *Manor Courts.*
with the appurtenances."

At the same court—

"Fine between Maud, Countess of Cambridge; 1341.
Percival Cressacre, Esquire; James Cressacre,
Esquire; and John Bosvile of New Hall, Esquire;
and Isabel, his wife, deforciants of lands in Barnsley, the right of the same James," &c.

"Fine between Thomas Clifford, Knt.; William *Ibid.*
Mirfield, Esquire; and Percival Cressacre, Esquire,
plaintiffs; and William Bosvile, and Maud his wife,
deforciants of lands in Barnsley."

"Thomas, son of John de Dodworth,[1] and heir of *Ibid.*
Agnes de Galbergh, did fealty and acknowledged
that he held of the lord the moiety of one part,
called Dickerode, rendering by the year twelve
pence."

"William de Keresforth attended the same *Ibid.*
Court, and produced a certain charter, by which
he purchased of Marjoria Portbref, of Barnsley, one
messuage lying near the scale of the churchyard of
the church, &c. To hold to him and his heirs and
assigns."

"At a court at Barnsley, held on Monday the 23rd Edw. III.
4th day of March, Richard Bosvile of Edlington
came and did fealty for a tenement which he purchased of Dionysia Bosvile of Barnsley."

"Court held at Barnsley, on Monday the 14th *Ibid.*
day of March, at which time Adam de Holand took
of the lord three shops in the market of Barnsley,

---

[1] In a rental of the late monastery of Pontefract, made 11th
September, 36 Henry VIII., it is stated that the heirs of
Richard Dodworth held freely certain lands in Barnsley called
Dobrode.

Chap. V. 92   HISTORY OF BARNSLEY.

Minutes of Manor Courts. which Thomas de Dodworth previously held, rendering by the year four shillings."

Barnsley and Oldton. 1341. 23rd Edw. III. "At a great court held at Barnsley, on Wednesday next after the feast of Saint Michael, Thomas de Dodworth came and did fealty for the tenements which descended to him after the death of John his brother, and acknowledged that he held of the lord the moiety of one messuage and two acres and a half-perch of land in Barnsley by the service of eighteen pence per annum and suit of court, and as tenant agreed for to do so henceforth," &c.

At the same court—

" Dionysia de Bosvile had to do her fealty for one messuage and three acres of land in Barnsley, for which she rendered by the year three shillings."

" Richard, son of Christian de Oldeton, also came into court, and did his fealty for one messuage and three perches of land, rendering xvi pence and paying relief, at the same time owing suit of court."

" In the petition of William Dodworth, lands, &c. It was awarded that John Jenkynson and Ralph Jenkynson should have, to them and to the heirs of the same Ralph for ever, in recompense of their full and whole part or portion, certain houses or cottages, with all the lands and appurtenances to them belonging, situate in Barnsley."

" William Dodworth,[1] Esquire, defunct. The jurors say that the same William Dodworth, by his charter, dated at Dodworth, the 7th Feb., in the 3rd year of the now King, by the name of William Dodworth of Gawber Hall, in the parish of Darton,

---

[1] William Dodworth died seised of Oldton, 4th Henry VIII. This family was of the place bearing the same name, and bore for arms—Argent, three bugle horns sable.

PRIVATE GRANTS. 93 Chap. V.

Esquire, did enfeoffe Thomas Wortley, Knight, and Private Grants.
Thomas Wortley, his son and heir, and others, of
and in one messuage, 40 acres of land, 30 acres of
meadow, 12 acres of pasture, and 4 acres of wood,
with the appurtenances, in Barnsley and Oldton."

Private grants of property at Barnsley, from the
reign of Edward I. :—

"Geffery de Staynton gave to Thomas Clark, 1306.
called Bayliffe, two parts of a messuage, ten acres
of land and some meadow, and a certain fountain
in the aforesaid messuage, &c., in the town and
territory of Barnsley, in Wodehallecroft," &c.
Witnessed.

"Richard, son of Geffery de Berneslay, gave to 1320.
Thomas, called the Bayliffe of Barnsley, the third
part of one messuage in Barnsley, and of ten acres
of meadow, in a certain place called Wodehallecroft,
that he had by hereditary right after the death of
William his brother, which Ellen his mother was
endowed with." Witnessed.

"Henry de Rockley gave to John de Dodde- 1327.
worth, clerk, and his heirs, all his messuages, lands,
and tenements at Keresforth, in Barnsley, the day of
the making of these presents."

"Robert Whitacre, chaplain of Barnsley, gave 1248.
to William de Keresforth, and to Maud his wife,
and to Richard his son, all the lands and tenements
he had by the gift of the aforesaid William, in the
town and territory of Barnsley." Witnessed.

"John, the Prior of Saint John of Pontefract, 1387.
granted to Richard de Keresforth of Barnsley, for
the term of 160 years, one messuage, with seven
and a half acres of land, which said half acre lies in
territory of Barnsley." Witnessed.

"Thomas, son of Simon de More, gave to Richard,

Chap. V. 94 HISTORY OF BARNSLEY.

Private Grants. son of Thomas Bosyile, one messuage and eight acres of land in the town of Barnsley." No date.

10th Rich II. "John Dickinson of Horseley Woodhouse, and Agnes his wife, released to Richard de Keresforth all right which they had in one messuage at Barnsley." Witnessed.

1401. "John Humbie, prior of the monastery of Pontefract, gave to Richard de Keresforth of Barnsley, his heirs and assigns, five rode of land, particularly lying in the fields of Barnsley, in exchange for five rode of land of the aforesaid Richard in the same town." Witnessed, &c.

1411. "Joan, widow of John Holynworth of Barnsley, gave to Richard Arkin of the same place, and Alice his wife, lands and tenements in the town of Barnsley."

Among the charters in the possession of Edward Armytage of Keresford, Gent., 1629 :—

1416. "John, son of Richard Keresford of Barnsley, Thomas Chawmberlayn, and Thomas Chaworth, chaplain, grant to Thomas Cotryngton, and Isabel his wife, one messuage in Doncaster, situate in Marshgate. Witnesses: Richard Lytster, then Mayor of Doncaster, William Garbor, Thomas Mysyn, and others."

1426. "Christopher, son of John, Lord Talbot, and of Furnival and John-Harrington, gave to John de Keresforth and his heirs, all lands which they had by the gift of the same John in Keresforth and Barnsley." Witnessed, &c.

"Thomas, son of Simon Moore, gave to Richard, the son of Thomas Boysevile, land in Bernislay."

1434. "Thomas Phillip of Balby gave to John Keresforth of Barnsley and his heirs, one messuage, with

PRIVATE GRANTS. 95 Chap. V.

a garden lying thereto, situate in Old Barnsley, Private Grants. called Hudrede, lying near the lane leading from Oldton Greene to Wodehouse on the west side, but at the north head upon an essart late of Thomas Dodworth, called Wilmerstorth." Witnessed, &c.

"Thomas, son of John Maunsell of Notton, 22nd Hen. IV. rector of one moiety of the church of Claypole, in Lincolnshire, gave to John Talbot, Knight, son and heir of John Earl of Salop, and to Richard, the son of John Keresford, and to William Smith, all his lands in Barnsley." Witnessed.

"John Keresforth and Richard his son confirmed 1st Edw. IV. to Thomas Grippe, for the term of life, one service and chantry of Saint Mary of Barnsley."

"Richard Symmes and William Wuddehall gave 3rd Edw. IV. to John Tynker of Barnsley, draper, two messuages in the same town." Witnessed, &c.

Four of the annexed refer to the Rooke family, three of which may be found in the Chartulary of Monk Bretton :—

"William Holdam granted and confirmed to 22nd Hen. VII. John Roke of Barnsley, mercer, and Johanna his wife, all the lands and tenements, with their appurtenances, late belonging to Edward Holdam (his father), situate in the parish of Ruston (Roystone), to hold the same to the aforesaid John Roke and Johanna his wife, and their heirs lawfully begotten, of the chief lords of that fee, by the services therefore due and of right accustomed. If no lawful issue between the said John Roke and Johanna his wife, the said lands and tenements to descend to John Genne, junior, and Margaret his wife, and their heirs. Dated at Royston, 26th August, 22nd Henry VII."

"Richard Roke, son and heir of John Roke and 20th Hen VIII

Chap. V. *96*   HISTORY OF BARNSLEY.

Private Grants. Johanna his wife, quit claimed from him and his heirs, to John Hopkynson, his heirs and assigns, one messuage and ten acres of land, meadow and pasture, with the appurtenances, in Upper Cudworth. Dated 6th April, 20th Henry VIII."

Receipt of four marks for the aforesaid lands and tenements :—

21st Hen. VIII   " Know all men by these presents, that I, Richard Roke, have received and had on the day of the making these presents, of William, prior of the monastery of the Blessed Mary Magdalene of Monk Bretton, four marks sterling, in full payment and satisfaction of and for all my possession, right, title, claim, interest, and demand, which I, the aforesaid Richard, have had, have, or in anywise hereafter shall have, of or in one messuage, with the appurtenances, in Cudworth, in the county of York, late of Edward Holdam; as to which four marks I confess myself to be paid, and the aforesaid Prior thence to be discharged by these presents, sealed with my seal. Given the 26th day of July, in the year of Henry VIII. the 21st."[1]

" Feoffment from Richard Rooke of Barnsley, yeoman, to Percival Heape of 'Owldbarnesley,' yeoman, and Elizabeth his wife, for £87 3s. 4d., of a close of land called the Brereroydes,[1] in the town-

---

[1] We have seen mention of this property in the charter of Godfrey, one of the priors of Pontefract. The word " Royd" often occurs in the termination of the names of property about Barnsley. The Leeds historian supposes it to have originated from its having been roid land, which, in respect of its original barrenness, paid but two pence an acre, and was freed from the greave service and other taxes.

Rodd—Rode—Royd—an obsolete participle of " rid," meaning a " ridding," or forest grant. It sometimes occurs in the last form, as an addition to the name of an early proprietor, or

PEDIGREE OF THE ANCIENT FAMILY OF ROOKE OF BARNSLEY.

PRIVATE GRANTS. 97 Chap. V.

ship of Barnsley, sometime in the tenure of William *Private Grants.*
Woulfe, late of John Rooke (deceased), and then
of the said Richard Rooke, abutting on a certain
narrow way between the aforesaid close and other
lands of the said Richard Rooke on the west, on
two closes called the Little Ing and Longroyd,
late in the tenure of widow Rooke and widow
Thrist, on the north, and on lands of John Jenkinson on the east and south-east, to hold in as full
and ample a manner as the same Richard Rooke *31st March,*
held the same of Henry Swinden of Wisketroid, in *1616.*
the township of Wombwell, yeoman, by his indenture dated the 6th March then last past; and in as
full and ample a manner as the said Henry Swinden
held the same of Percival Hobson of Dodworth,
Thomas Copley of Tearshill (Tyers Hill), George
Wood of Monk Bretton, Richard Oxley of Dodworth, Henry Potter of Pilley, and John Longley
of Hudhill, in the said county, yeomen, by their
indenture dated 27th June last past; and in as full
and ample a manner as the said Percival Hobson
and others held the same of the Lord James, then
King of England, by letters patent under the great
seal of England, dated 30th November, in the 12th
year of the said King's reign; to be held of the
said King, as of his manor of East Greenwich, in
free and common socage. Witnesses: Thomas
Oxley, William Chappel, Nicholas Hawkesworth,
Richard Coldwell, Ralph Shepheard," &c.

Lands, called " Flesh Hall"[1] closes and " Abbot   *1665.*

to the names of the trees cleared, as Ack-royd, Hol-royd, &c.;
and Brier-royd as above, so denominated from the brier.

[1] " Flesh Hall closes"—what is the meaning of? In many places
where manorial courts were held certain officers were annually

G

Chap. V. 98 HISTORY OF BARNSLEY.

Private Grants. Royd," in Barnsley, were devised by the will of William Wordsworth of Falthwaite, in 1665, to his daughter Priscilla Rayney and her heirs. The former of them having descended to the families of Watkins of Silkstone, and Jackson of Doncaster, were by them sold in 1855 to Mr. George Pitt.

The subjoined charters are taken out of the Monk Bretton Chartulary, from which it will be seen that the monks of that house had also property at Barnsley, but this was not of any great extent :—

William Bretton. CARTA WILLIELMI BRETTON, THOMÆ BOTON, JOHANNI THOMSON, ET THOMÆ ROBYNSON, DE OMNIBUS MESSUAGIIS ET TERRIS IN BYRTTON ET KIRKBY.

Sciant presentes et futuri quod ego Willielmus Bretton de Ackworth dedi concessi et hac presenti carta mea confirmavi Thomæ Boton Johanni Tomson capellano et Thomæ Robynson **6th Edw. IV.** unum clausum vocatum Sighrode jacentem juxta pontem de Barnslay ac etiam altera omnia messuagia terras et tenementa mea prata boscos et pasturas infra parochias de Ruston et South Kirkby cum omnibus suis pertinentibus. Habend. et tenend. predictum clausum et omnia messuagia terras et tenementa prata boscos et pasturas cum suis pertinentibus prefato Thomæ Johanni et Thomæ heredibus et assignatis suis de capitalibus dominis feodorum illorum per servicia inde debita et de jure consueta. Et ego vero predictus Willielmus et heredes mei predictum clausum et omnia messuagia terras et tenementa prata boscos et pasturas cum suis pertinentibus prefato Thomæ Johanni et Thomæ et heredibus et assignatis suis contra omnes gentes warantizabimus et defendemus in perpetuum. Insuper noveritis me dictum Willielmum Bretton attornasse et loco meo posuisse

chosen, by whom were regulated the supply and quality of victuals, &c. Amonst these were viewers of flesh (carnarii), who exercised a superintendence over the butchers. Was there any place at Barnsley like a hall or public building where meat was exposed for sale or inspection, from whence the above lands derived their name?

ANCIENT CHARTERS.

99 Chap. V.

Ancient Charters.

dilectum in Christo Johannem Walker de Ruston et Ricardum Wilde de Barnyslay conjunctos et divisos meos fideles attornatos ad deliberandam pro me et in nomine meo predicto Thomæ Botòn Johanni Tomson capellano et Thomæ Robynson plenam et pacificam seisinam et in uno clauso vocato Sighrode ac etiam in omnibus terris et tenementis meis cum suis pertinentibus infra parochias de Ruston et South Kirkby secundum formam et effectum cartæ meæ &c. In cujus rei testimonium huic presenti carta sigillum meum apposui. *Hiis Testibus*—Johanne Clyfe, Johanne Person, Willielmo Rainald, et aliis. Data apud Ackworth quinto die Januarii, Anno Regis Edwardi quarti post conquestum Anglie sexto.

TRANSLATION.

Translation.

Charter of William Bretton, granting to Thomas Boton, John Thomson, chaplain, and Thomas Robinson, one close called Sighrode, lying near to the Bridge of Barnsley, with all his other messuages, lands, and tenements, meadows, woods, and pastures, in the parishes of Roystone and South Kirkby, with the appurtenances, to hold to the aforesaid Thomas, John, and Thomas, their heirs and assigns, of the chief lords of those fees, by the services therefore due, and of right accustomed; the aforesaid William declaring that he and his heirs would warrant the aforesaid to the said Thomas, John, and Thomas, their heirs and assigns for ever, and that he, the said William Bretton, had substituted and put in his place his beloved in Christ John Walker of Roystone and Richard Wilde of Barnsley, his joint and several attorneys, to deliver for him, and in his name, to the aforesaid Thomas Boton, John Thomson, chaplain, and Thomas Robinson, full and peaceable seisin, both in one close called Sighroyd, and also in all his lands and tenements within the parishes of Roystone and South Kirkby, according to the form and effect of his charter, &c. In testimony to which he affixed his seal. WITNESSES: John Clyfe, John Person, William Rainald, and others. Given at Ackworth, 5th January, 6th Edward IV.

CARTA JOHANNIS THOMSON, ET THOMÆ ROBYNSON, RICARDO PRIORI DICTI MONASTERII DE CERTIS ASSARTIS VOCATIS SIGHROYD ET TURVEYING.

1st Edw. IV.

Sciant presentes et futuri quod nos Johannes Thomson capellanus et Thomas Robynson demisimus et liberavimus concessi-

J. Thomson and T. Robinson.

Chap. V. 100   HISTORY OF BARNSLEY.

Ancient Charters. mus et hac presenti carta nostra confirmavimus Ricardo Ledes Priori domus Beate Marie Magdalene de Monkebretton unum clausum vocatum Sighroyd et unam parcellam prati vocatam Turveying jacentes juxta pontem de Barnyslay cum suis pertinentibus in Monkebretton que nupper habuimus et alia similiter cum Thoma Boton jam defuncto ex dono et concessione Willielmi Bretton. Habend. et tenend. predictum clausum et parcellam prati cum suis pertinentibus predicta Ricardo Ledes Priori et successoribus suis in perpetuum de capitalibus dominis feodorum illorum per servicia inde debita et de jure consueta. In cujus rei testimonium huic presenti cartæ nostræ sigilla nostra apposuimus. *His Testibus*—Willielmo Dodeworth, Ricardo Keresforth, Ricardo Symmes, et aliis. Data apud Monkbretton vicesimo die Maii Anno Edwardi quarti post conquestum septimo.

Translation.   TRANSLATION.

Charter of John Thomson, chaplain, and Thomas Robinson, by which they grant to Richard Ledes, Prior of the Blessed Mary Magdalene of Monk Bretton, one close of land called Sighroyd, and one parcel of meadow called Turveying, situate near to the Bridge of Barnsley, with their appurtenances, in Monk Bretton. WITNESSES: William Dodworth, Richard Keresforth, Richard Symmes, and others. Given at Monk Bretton the 20th day of May, 7th Edward IV.

14th Edw. IV. OBLIGACIO RICARDI BROUNE PRIORIS DE PONTEFRACTO DE COMPLETIONE DE SUPRA SCRIPTO ARBITRIO WILLIELMI BRADFORD ET ROBERTI CHALONER.

Bond of Richard Broune prior of Pontefract. NOVERIT UNIVERSIS per presentes nos Ricardus Broune Prior et Conventus Sancti Johannis Apostoli et Evangelisti de Pontefracto teneri et firmiter obligari Ricardo Ledes Priori et conventui domus Beate Marie Magdalene de Monkbretton in centum liberis sterling solvend. eisdem Ricardo Ledes Priori et Conventui et successoribus in festo paschæ proximo futuro sine dilatione ulteriore ad quam quidem solucionem bene et fideliter faciendam obligamus nos et successores nostros firmiter per presentes sigillo Conventus domus nostræ predictæ signatas. Data vicesimo quarto die mensis Septembris Anno Edwardi quarti post conquestum Anglie quarto decimo. Condicio hujus obligationis predictæ est quod si supra obligati Ricardus Broune

ANCIENT CHARTERS. 101 Chap. V.

Prior et Conventus ac Ricardus Keresford et Ricardus Symmes de Barnsylay steterint et compleverint et quisque illorum ex parte sua steterit et compleverit omnes et singulas ordinationes in dicto arbritrio contento in quibusdam scriptis indentatis per Willielmon Bradford et Robertum Chaloner arbitratores inter dictos Ricardum Broune Priorem et Conventum ac Ricardum Keresford et Ricardum Symmes et prescripto Ricardum Ledes Priorem et Conventum inde ferent elect factis et ordinatis et precipue de jure titulo et possessione omnium terrarum pratorum et tenementorum que nuper fuerunt Ricardi Wilde in Monkbretton et similiter de omnibus aliis articulis in dictis scriptis indentatis specificatis tunc presens obligatio pro nullo habebitur alioquin in suo robore permanebit et virtute.

Ancient Charters.

TRANSLATION.

Translation.

Know all men, now and hereafter, by these presents, that we, Richard Broune, Prior, and the Convent of Saint John the Apostle and Evangelist of Pontefract, are held and firmly bound unto Richard Ledes, Prior, and the Convent of the House of the Blessed Mary Magdalene of Monk Bretton, in £100 sterling, to be paid to the said Richard Ledes, Prior, and the Convent, and their successors, at the feast of the Passover next to come without further delay, for which payment, well and faithfully to be made, we bind ourselves and our successors firmly by these presents, sealed with the seal of the Convent of our aforesaid house. Dated 24th September, 14th Edward IV.

The condition of the aforesaid obligation is, that if the above-bounden Richard Broune, Prior, and the Convent, and Richard Keresforth and Richard Symmes of Barnyslay, shall have performed and fulfilled, and each of them on his part shall have performed and fulfilled, all and singular the ordinances in the said award, contained in certain writings indented by William Bradford and Robert Chaloner,[1] arbitrators between the said Richard Broune, Prior, and the Convent, Richard Keresford and Richard Symmes, and the aforesaid Richard Ledes, Prior, and the Convent, made and ordained, and especially concerning the right, title, and possession of all the lands, meadows, and tenements which were formerly of Richard Wilde, in Monk Bretton, and likewise concerning all the other articles in the said writings

[1] The award of Bradford and Chaloner will be given hereafter, when speaking of the Mills of Barnsley.

Chap. V. 102 HISTORY OF BARNSLEY.

Ancient Charters. indented specified, then the present obligation shall be void, otherwise shall remain in full force and virtue.

14th Edw. IV. CARTA RICARDI KERESFORD ET RICARDI SYMMES, JOHANNI GENNE, ET JOHANNI CALTHORNE DE OMNIBUS TERRIS ET TENEMENTIS REDDITIS ET SERVICIIS QUONDAM RICARDI WILDE.

Richard Keresforth and Richard Symmes. Sciant presentes et futuri quod nos Ricardus Keresford et Ricardus Symmes de Barnyslay concessimus liberavimus et hac presenti carta nostra confirmavimus Johanni Genne de Workesburgh et Johanni Calthorne de eadem omnia illa terras prata tenementa boscos pasturas redditus et servicia cum suis pertinentibus que nuper habuimus ex dono et feoffamento Ricardi Wilde in Monkbretton. Habend. et tenend. omnia predicta terras prata tenementa boscos pasturas redditus et servicia cum suis pertinentibus prefatis Johanni Genne et Johanni Calthorne heredibus et assignatis suis in perpetuum de capitalibus dominis feodorum illorum per servicia inde debita et de jure consueta. In cujus rei testimonium huic presenti cartæ nostræ sigilla nostra apposuimus. Hiis Testibus—Adeinero Burdett, Thoma Oxspring, Willielmo Gilberthorpe, et aliis. Data apud Monkbretton vicesimo die mensis Octobris Anno Edwardi quarti post conquestum quarto decimo.

Translation. TRANSLATION.

Charter of Richard Keresforth, and Richard Symmes, John Genne, and John Calthorne, concerning all the lands and tenements, rents and services, late of Richard Wilde :—

Know all men, now and hereafter, that we, Richard Keresforth and Richard Symmes of Barnsley, have granted, freed, and confirmed, by this our present charter, to John Genne of Worsbrough, and John Calthorne of the same place, all those lands, meadows, tenements, woods, pastures, rents, and services, with their appurtenances, which we heretofore had of the gift and feoffment of Richard Wilde in Monk Bretton. To have and to hold the same to the aforesaid John Genne and John Calthorne, their heirs and assigns for ever, of the chief lords of those fees, by the services therefore due, and of right accustomed. In witness whereof we have set our seals. WITNESSES : Adeinero Burdett, Thomas Oxspring, William Gilberthorpe, and others. Given at Monk Bretton, 20th October, 14th Edward IV.

ANCIENT CHARTERS. 103 Chap. V.

EXCAMBIUM INTER RICARDUM KERESFORTH THOMAM HALLE
ET RICARDUM SYMMES EX UNA PARTE ET WILLIELMUM
WYLDE EX ALIA PARTE DE CERTIS TERRIS ET TENEMENTIS
IN MONKBRETTON BARNSLEY ET DODDWORTH.

Ancient Charters.

38th Hen. VI.

Sciant presentes et futuri quod nos Ricardus filius Johannis Keresforth de Barnyslay Thomas Halle de Pontefracto et Ricardus Symmes de Barnyslay dedimus concessimus et hac presenti carta nostra indentata confirmavimus Ricardo Wilde de Monkbretton heredibus et assignatis suis omnia terras et tenementa prata boscos et pasturas cum omnibus pertinentibus que nuper habuimus ex dono et concessione Nicholai Halle Prioris domus Sancti Johannis Apostoli et Evangelisti de Pontefracto et ejusdem loci conventus in Barnyslay et Doddworth in excambium pro uno messuagio cum edificiis suis cum crofts adjacenti et cum omnibus terris tenementis pratis boscis et pasturis cum pertinentibus que predictus Ricardus Wilde habuit jure hereditarie post decessum Willielmi Wilde patris ejus in Monkbretton predictas. Habend. et tenend. omnia predicta terras tenementa prata boscos et pasturas cum suis pertinentibus predicto Ricardo Wilde heredibus et assignatis suis in excambium pro omnibus terris et tenementis cum suis pertinentibus que predictus Ricardus Wilde habuit in Monkbretton predicta de Priore et Conventu Sancti Johannis Apostoli et Evangelisti de Pontefract per servicia debita et de jure consueta. Et nos vero predictus Ricardus filius Johannis Thomas et Ricardus et heredes nostri omnia predicta terras tenementa prata boscos et pasturas cum suis pertinentibus predicto Ricardo Wilde heredibns et assignatis suis in excambium contra omnes gentes warantizabimus. Pretera ego predictus Ricardus Wilde de Monkbretton dedi concessi et hac presenti carta mea indentata confirmavi Magistro Thomæ Mannyng secreta. Domini Regis Thomæ Halle Ricardo Keresforth et Rico. Symmes heredibus et assignatis suis unum messuagium cum edificiis cum croftis adjacentibus et cum omnibus terris et tenementis prata boscis et pasturis cum suis pertinentibus que habui jure hereditario post decessum Willielmi Wilde patris mei in Monkbretton predicta in excambium pro omnibus terris et tenementis prata boscis et pasturis cum suis pertinentibus que predicti Ricardus filius Johannis Thomas Halle et Ricardus Symmes nuper habuerunt ex dono et feoffamento Nicolai Prioris domus Sancti Johannis Apostoli et Evangelisti de Pontefract et ejusdem loci Conventus libere et in pace de capitali domino feodi illius per servicia inde debita et de jure consueta.

Excambium between R. Keresforth, &c. and W. Wylde.

Chap. V.   104   HISTORY OF BARNSLEY.

Ancient Char- Et ego vero predictus Ricardus Wilde et heredes mei omnia
ters. predicta messuagia cum edificiis cum croftis adjacentibus et cum
omnibus terris tenementis pratis boscis et pasturis cum pertinentibus suis in excambium predictis Magistro Thomæ Mannyng
Thomæ Halle Ricardo Keresforth et Ricardo Symmes heredibus
et assignatis suis in excambium contra omnes gentes warantizabimus. In cujus rei testimonium hiis cartis indentatis presentibus sigilla sua alternatim apposuerunt. 𝕳𝕚𝕚𝕤 𝕿𝕖𝕤𝕥𝕚𝕓𝕦𝕤—
Willielmo Skergill, Willielmo Oxspring, Johanne Keresford,
Johanne Tynker, et aliis.

Data apud Barnysley et Monkbretton duodecimo die Maii
Anno regni Regis Henrici sexti post conquestum Anglie tri-
cesimo octavo.

TRANSLATION.

Translation. Exchange between Richard Keresforth, Thomas Hall, and
Richard Symmes, of the one part, and William Wylde of the
other part, of certain lands and tenements in Monk Bretton,
Barnsley, and Dodworth :—

Know all men, now and hereafter, that we, Richard, son of
John Keresforth of Barnsley, Thomas Hall of Pontefract, and
Richard Symmes of Barnsley, have given, granted, and by this
our present charter indented confirmed, to Richard Wylde of
Monk Bretton, his heirs and assigns, all the lands and tenements, meadows, woods, and pastures, with their appurtenances,
which we heretofore had of the gift and grant of Nicholas Hall,
Prior of the house of Saint John the Apostle and Evangelist of
Pontefract, and the Convent of the same place, in Barnsley and
Dodworth, in exchange for one messuage, with its buildings,
with the croft adjoining, and with all the lands, tenements,
meadows, woods, and pastures, with the appurtenances, which
the aforesaid Richard Wylde had of hereditary right after the
decease of William Wylde his father in Monk Bretton aforesaid.
To have and to hold the same to the aforesaid Richard Wylde,
and his assigns, in exchange for all the lands and tenements,
with their appurtenances, which the said Richard Wylde had in
Monk Bretton aforesaid, of the Prior and Convent of Saint John
the Apostle and Evangelist of Pontefract, by the services due
and of right accustomed. And we, the aforesaid Richard son
of John, Thomas, and Richard, and our heirs, the aforesaid
lands, tenements, woods, meadows, and pastures, with their ap-

ANCIENT CHARTERS. 105 Chap. V.

purtenances, to the aforesaid Richard Wylde, his heirs and *Ancient Charters.*
assigns, in exchange, will warrant against all men. Moreover I,
the aforesaid Richard Wylde of Monk Bretton, have given,
granted, and by this my present charter indented have confirmed, to Master Thomas Mannyng, Secretary of our lord the
King, Thomas Háll, Richard Keresforth, Richard Symmes, their
heirs and assigns, one messuage, with the buildings and crofts
adjoining, and with all the lands and tenements, woods and
pastures, with their appurtenances, which I had by hereditary
right after the decease of William Wylde (my father), in Monk
Bretton aforesaid, in exchange for all the lands and tenements,
meadows, woods, and pastures, with their appurtenances, which
the aforesaid Richard the son of John, Thomas Hall, and Richard
Symmes heretofore had of the gift and feoffment of Nicholas,
Prior of the house of Saint John the Apostle and Evangelist of
Pontefract, and the Convent of the same place, freely and quietly,
of the chief lord of that fee, by the services therefore due and of
right accustomed. And I, the aforesaid Richard Wylde, and
my heirs, the aforesaid, with the appurtenances, in exchange to
the aforesaid Master Thomas Mannyng, Thomas Hall, Richard
Keresforth, and Richard Symmes, their heirs and assigns, against
all men will warrant. In witness whereof we have set our seals.
WITNESSES: William Skergill, William Oxspring, John Keresforth, John Tynker, and others.

Given at Barnsley and Monk Bretton, 12th May, 38th
Henry VI.

The monks held the manor of Barnsley for near *Manor of Barnsley.*
four centuries. Upon the dissolution of the priory
of Saint John of Pontefract, the manors of Barnsley
and Dodworth came to the crown ; and when Bernard's survey of lands in Yorkshire held of the
Duchy of Lancaster, was made, 19th Elizabeth,
A.D. 1577, it was returned that they were then in
the hands of the Queen by reason of the dissolution
of the said priory. Afterwards the manor of
Barnsley was granted in fee by King William III.
to William Bentinck, Earl of Portland, whose grandson, William, the second Duke of Portland, sold it in
1735 to Thomas Osborne, the fourth Duke of Leeds,

Chap. V.   106   HISTORY OF BARNSLEY.

Manor of Barnsley.

in whose descendants it continued till the year 1836, when it was devised by the will of the sixth Duke to his son-in-law, Sackville Walter Lane Fox, Esquire, who is the present lord of Barnsley.

William Thwaites of Barnsley, Gent., appears to have held the tithes in 1590, when they passed to Downing and Rant, who held the same at a yearly rent of £8. They were next sold to Isaac Waterhouse, and by him bequeathed to his sons Isaac and Daniel, and after passing through various hands, the tithes came into the possession of Mr. Marsden, who dying in 1776, they were sold to the Duke of Leeds, who, at the time of the enclosure, received allotments of common in lieu thereof, and a perpetual rent-charge per acre and upon buildings. The payments in lieu of tithe were disposed of by the fifth Duke to the late Jonas Clarke, and are now received by his representatives.

Tourns.

TOURNS.

I have before given some account of Manorial Courts held at Barnsley. The business of these last-named courts, which every lord of a manor had within the precinct of his manor, was to inquire of matters concerning the lord and tenant in their civil capacity only—as of the death of tenants since the previous court, of alienations, surrenders, encroachments, trespasses, escheats, and such like. The tourn, as held by the sheriff, was the King's Court of Record for criminal causes and redressing of common grievances within a county, and was held twice a year, once within a month after Easter and another time within a month after Michaelmas. Every person

THE SENESCHAL'S TOURN.

107 Chap. V.

Tourns.

above the age of twelve years (except peers, clergy-men, and tenants in ancient demesne) were bound to appear at the tourn to inquire of grievances, and to take the oath of allegiance. The Court Leet had the same jurisdiction within a particular precinct, as the Sheriff's Tourn had in a county.

The tourns hereafter described would seem to have been held by the seneschal of the honour of Pontefract, of which the wapentake of Staincross, including Barnsley, formed a part; and to have had a similar jurisdiction to those held by the sheriff.

Tourn[1] (or court) of the liberty of Staincross held at Barnsley, May 4th :—

" Inquisition taken on the oath of Thomas Chamberlayn and other twelve jurors. They say that William Fleming, an inhabitant of Woolley, came into the ground of Robert Rockley, Knight, in the parish of Darton, and there felled, took, and carried away, against the will of the aforesaid Robert or his servants, one oak of the value of xl pence, being not a little hurt and grievance to the said Robert; therefore it is commanded that he be attached to answer to the lord of the matters presented concerning him, who afterwards made answer thereto, and puts himself on the favour of the lord (or court), whose fine is xii pence."

Minutes of Tourns. 1st Hen. IV.

Tourn, &c., held at Barnsley, 12th April :—

" The jurors say that the township of Woolley have repaired the King's highway within the town there, for which they were fined in the penalty of x. shillings at the last tourn; therefore they may be excused from the said fine 'sine die.'

8th Hen. IV.

[1] These extracts are taken from Parchment Court Rolls in the possession of Godfrey Wentworth, Esq. of Woolley.

Chap. V. 108 HISTORY OF BARNSLEY.

Minutes of Tourns. "They also say that John Blackbourne and John Cusseworth have cleansed their ditches there, for which they were fined vi*s*. viij*d*.; therefore they are excused from the said fine ' sine die.' "

Tourn, &c., held at Barnsley, 13th April:—

10th Hen. IV. " The jurors say that John Notingham, about the last feast of the Passover, assaulted John Himsworth, against the peace; therefore let him be attached."

Tourn, &c., held at Barnsley, 2nd April:—

11th Hen. IV. " The jurors say that David, rector of a moiety of the church of Hoyland, in the 5th Henry IV., entered Woolley church, and there broke a certain chest and took thereout money, oblations, and tithes, and carried the same away, against the peace; therefore, &c., attached."

Tourn held at Barnsley, 11th May:—

12th Hen. IV. " The jurors say that Thomas Jagger of Kexbrough, who hid xxxiii*s*. iiij*d*. in money at Kexbrough under the ground, on Monday next after the feast of Saint Edward last past, the said sum of money was feloniously stolen by John Silcocke the younger, and which (sum) belonged to our lord the King by right of his liberty of the honour of Pontefract, as the goods of felons and fugitives, and afterwards it came into the hands of Robert Rockley of Woolley, *de quibus onerat. feodar*."

Tourn held at Barnsley, 18th April:—

2nd Hen. V. " The jurors say that William Tottie, constable of Woolley, has not attended this tourn; he is therefore fined iij*s*. vij*d*."

Tourn held at Barnsley, on Wednesday in the seven days of the Passover:—

18th Hen. VI. " The jurors say that Edward Godyson of Wort-

THE SENESCHAL'S TOURN. 109 Chap. V.

Minutes of Tourns.

ley, William Odes of the same place, William Shepperde of Stayneburgh, William Hinchliffe of Woolley, and others, *brass lez helpales*,[1] and took somewhat too excessive gain (or profit), against the statute; therefore, &c., attached.

18th Hen. IV.

"They also say that William Hinchliffe of Woolley and Robert Wright of Hemsworth, are common players at forbidden games, viz., dice, tables, and others, against the statute; therefore, &c., attached.

"The jury also present that William Tottie of Woolley has turned the course of the water at Clarellbusk from the right and ancient course into an unjust course, to the grievous harm, &c., and contempt of the lord; therefore, &c., attached."

Tourn held at Barnsley, 15th April:—

"The jurors say that William Hinchliffe[2] of Woolley, on the feast of Saint Stephen, made a rescue from William Wood, constable of Woolley, and would not be arrested; therefore, &c., attached."

11th Hen. VI.

Tourn held at Barnsley, 13th April:—

"The jurors say that John Barneby, tenant of the land late of Achilles Bosvylle and Robert Johnson of Woolley, owe their suit; therefore, &c., attached.

17th Hen. VI.

"They also say that William Hinchliffe of Woolley, Thomas Ravenfield, in seven days of the Passover last past, *brass lez helpales*, against the statute; therefore, &c., attached."

---

[1] This probably means "brewed ale." Du Cange says that "brassare" signifies "to brew."

[2] These Woolley people appear to have been desperate rogues, especially William Hinchliffe.

Chap. V. 110 HISTORY OF BARNSLEY.

Minutes of Tourns.

20th Hen. VI.

Tourn held at Barnsley, 3rd April:—

" Inquisition taken there on the oath of John Whetley. The jurors say that William Highley of Notton, on the x December, in the . . . year of the reign of Henry VI., at Notton, assaulted John Forster in a violent affray, and against the peace ; therefore, &c., attached. And Robert Handcocke (vij*d.*) of Dodworth, Roger Burgege of Barnsley ; therefore, &c., attached.

" They also say that Hugh Glover has amended the highway which he obstructed in the wood of Notton, as in the penalty of xl*d.* assessed on him ; therefore, &c., exonerated."

Tourn held at Barnsley, 27th April :—

25th Hen. VI.

" William Hinchliffe of Woolley answered here in court concerning the offences presented against him, as appears, &c. He puts himself on the favour (mercy) of the lord, whose fine is by the seneschal, as above."

Tourn held at Barnsley the last day of March:—

34th Hen. VI.

" The jurors say that William Hinchliffe of Woolley, Margaret Hiffe, William Bradley, and Robert Bradley, all of the same place, last year, within the township of Woolley, *brass lez helpales*, and sold, contrary to the statute; therefore, &c., attached."

Tourn held at Barnsley, 12th April:—

36th Hen. VI.

" The jurors say that William Hinchliffe of Woolley, at different times, *brass lez helpales*, and sold, against the statute ; therefore, &c., attached."

Tourn held at Barnsley, on the feast of Saint George the Martyr :—

38th Hen. VI.

" The jurors say that John Hunt of Woolley, and John Sekarre of the same place, are common players at (speras) dice and other unlawful games, against the statute ; therefore, &c., attached."

THE SENESCHAL'S TOURN.   111   Chap. V.

Tourn held at Barnsley, 17th October:—

"Thomas Wortley (xx*d.*), Knight; Richard Woodruffe (xij*d.*), Esquire; and divers others, who owe suit to this tourn (or court), came by their attorneys, and arranged their fines separately with the lord; the aforesaid suit is to be relaxed to them, in manner and form, &c."

Tourn held at Barnsley, 3rd October:—

"Thomas Wortley (xx*d.*), Knt., Richard Woodruffe, Knt., and others, who owe suit to this court, came here by their attorneys, and arranged their fines separately with the lord; the aforesaid suit is to be relaxed to them in manner and form before noted."

Tourn held at Barnsley, 18th April:—

"The jurors say that the township of Woolley have not sufficient stakes; therefore the said township, &c."

Tourn held at Barnsley, 12th October:—

"The jurors say that Robert Hobson of Cawthorne, John Popeley of Woolley, &c., answered here in court concerning divers offences presented against them, and are not able to justify themselves, but therefore put themselves on the favour of the lord, whose fines are settled by the seneschal, viz., each of them for himself, as above."

Tourn held at Barnsley, 11th April:—

"The jurors say that William Hinchliffe should be punished because he repaired not his hedges within the field of Woolley and the field of Notton by the day prefixed; therefore he incurs the same fine, viz., vi*s.* viij*d.*"

Tourn held at Barnsley, 7th April:—

"The jurors say that John Richardson of

Minutes of Tourns.

12th Hen.VII.

13th Hen.VII.

15th Hen.VII.

18th Hen.VII.

19th Hen.VII.

22nd Hen.VII.

Chap. V. 112   HISTORY OF BARNSLEY.

Minutes of Tourns. Woolley is to be punished as ordered at the last tourn, because he did not turn the course of the water into the right channel at Townegrene in Woolley; therefore he incurs the same penalty, viz., xvi*d*."

Tourn held at Barnsley, 24th . . . :—

23rd Hen.VII. "The jurors say that Roger Marshall (xij*d*.), who *brass lez helpales* to be sold, entertains players at forbidden games; therefore he in iiij*d*. as above. Also, John Wilcocke (xij*d*.) of Darton, John Prynce (xij*d*.) of the same place, Thomas Wheatley (viij*d*.) of Woolley, John Bradley (viij*d*.) of the same place, William Hunt (viij*d*.) of the same place, answered here in tourn concerning divers offences against them presented, and are not able to clear themselves from the same, and therefore put themselves on the mercy of the lord, whose fines are settled by the seneschal, viz., each of them for himself in the sum set over his head."

Tourn held at Barnsley, 3rd April:—

7th Hen. VIII. "The jurors say on oath that Robert Waterton (viij*d*.), Knight, Richard Woodruffe (viij*d*.), Knight, and others, owe suit to this tourn, and have not come, but made default; therefore each of them for himself in iiij*d*. as set over their heads."

Tourn held at Barnsley in seven days of the Passover:—

20th Hen.VIII "The jurors say on their oath that Thomas Wodrove (vi*d*.), Esquire, Lord Monteagle (vi*d*.), and others, owe suit to this tourn, and have not come; therefore each of them for himself in iiij*d*. as above."

Tourn held at Barnsley, on the Wednesday next after the feast of Saint Michael the Archangel:—

THE SENESCHAL'S TOURN.   113   Chap. V.

"Robert Griffin was elected constable of Wool- Minutes of
ley, and made default; therefore he incurs a fine   Tourns.
of iiij*d*.   27th Hen.VIII

" They also say that Richard Whetley (viij*d*.),
and Richard Crawshaw (viij*d*.), obstructed the way
leading from the town of Woolley into the town of
Wakefield, which ought to be used by the inhabitants of Woolley, from the feast of Saint Michael the
Archangel until the end of the purification of the
Blessed Mary, and likewise in harvest; therefore
each of them, &c., as above."

Tourn held at Barnsley, 28th March:—

" The jurors say on their oath that Thomas,   1st Mary.
Lord Mounteagle (xij*d*.), Francis Woderove (xij*d*.),
and others, owe suit to this tourn, and have not
come; therefore each of them for himself as set
above."

. Tourn held at Barnsley, Wednesday next after
the feast of the Passover:—

" The jurors say that John Hutchonson (iv*d*.) 4th and 5th
and John Crawshaie (iv*d*.) have not suffered the Philip & Mary.
water to have its right course at Woolley; therefore, &c., attached."

Tourn held at Barnsley, 23rd April:—

" Inquisition taken there on the oath of Amer 3rd Elizabeth.
Burdeheade, Esquire, and other xii jurors, who on
their oath say that Lord William Mounteagle owes
suit of court, and has not come, but made default;
therefore in ij*s*.   Also, John Lord Darcy (viij*d*.) for
the like; Robert Rockley for the like, ij*s*.; also,
Francis Woodruffe, Esquire, for the like, viij*d*."

Subjoined is an extract from a second account
of courts held at Barnsley.   It is headed as follows:—

Chap. V. 114 HISTORY OF BARNSLEY.

Minutes of Tourns.

"Elizabeth, by the grace of God, of England, France, and Ireland, Queen, Defender of the Faith, to all to whom these presents shall come, greeting:

"We have looked upon certain separate rolls of divers separate courts of our ancestors: Henry, formerly King of England, the Sixth; Henry, formerly King of England, the Seventh; and of our most noble father, Henry, late King of England, the Eighth; and of our sister Mary, late Queen of England; within our honour of Pontefract, parcel of our duchy of Lancaster, in our county of York, in which several rolls stand inrolled and recorded amongst other things, as follows," viz. :—

Tourn held at Barnsley, 15th April:—

11th Hen. VI. "Inquisition, &c., by the oath of John Whetley. The jurors say that the township of Notton have repaired their stocks, as in the penalty of xs. assessed on them; therefore they are exonerated."

Tourn held at Barnsley, 20th April:—

13th Hen. VI. "Inquisition by the oath of John Whetley. The jurors say that John Forster of Notton, senior, William Shepley, and John Forster of the same place, junior, *brass lez helpales*, and sold, and took excessive gain, against the statute; therefore, &c., attached."

Tourn held at Barnsley, 13th April:—

4th Hen. VI. "They say that Roger Gill of Woolley, John Forster, son of John Forster of Notton, William Pennynge, John Bene, William Righley, and John Forster, senior, of the same place, *brass lez helpales*, and sold and took excessive profit, against the ordinance of the statute; therefore, &c., attached.

"They also say that John Birkley of Carlton, on the 20th February last, at Notton, assaulted Hugh Glover, and struck him and drew blood; therefore, &c., attached.

THE SENESCHAL'S TOURN. 115 Chap. V.

Minutes of Tourns.

"They also say that he obstructed the highway with his wood growing there; therefore a fine of xl*d.* is assessed on him, that he should amend the same by next tourn."

Tourn held at Barnsley, in seven days of the Passover:—

"The jurors say that William Hinchlife of Woolley, John Marshall of Notton, *brass lez helpales*, and took excessive gain, contrary to the statute; therefore, &c., attached." *18th Hen. VI.*

Tourn held at Barnsley, after the feast of the Passover:—

"The jurors say that John Forster, senior, and John Forster, both of Notton, *brass lez helpales*, and took excessive gain, contrary to the statute; therefore, &c., attached." *19th Hen. VI.*

Tourn held at Barnsley, in seven days of the Passover:—

"Inquisition on the oath of John Whetley. The jurors say that William Hinchliffe of Woolley, William Campsall of the same place, John Forster of Notton, Simon Jackson of the same place, *brass lez helpales*, against the statute; therefore, &c., attached." *25th Hen. VI.*

The following notice appears of a tourn held at Fieldkirk:—

"The jurors say that Alice, wife of William Highley of Notton, and Simon Jackson of the same place, are common scolds against the peace, that Simon is a foul-mouthed rascal, and Alice a common stealer and carryer away of cocks, hens, sheaves, and other small things; therefore, &c., attached."

Tourn held at Barnsley, in seven days of the Passover.:—

Chap. V. 116 HISTORY OF BARNSLEY.

Minutes of Tourns.

26th Hen. VI.

" Inquisition on the oath of John Wheteley. The jurors say that John Wodrove (iiij*d.*) of Notton owes suit to this tourn, and came not; therefore on the mercy of the lord."

Tourn held at Barnsley, 17th October :—

12th Hen VII.

" Inquisition on the oath of Christopher Beaumont. The jurors say that Richard Woderuffe (xij*d.*), Knight, owes suit to this tourn, and came hither by his attorneys *et fec. finem*[1] with the lord, for suit of court to be relaxed to him until the feast of Saint Michael the Archangel, unless anything should happen in the meantime, by reason whereof the lord should have present need of him.

" They also present that Richard Fixby (iij*d.*) of Notton, had been commanded by the constable to come to this tourn, and came not; therefore on the mercy of the lord."

Tourn held at Barnsley, 3rd October :—

14th Hen.VII.

" The jurors say that Richard Wodrove (xij*d.*), Knight, owes suit to this tourn, and came by his attorney, &c."

Tourn held at Barnsley, 1st October :—

16th Hen.VII.

" The jurors say that Richard Wodrove owes suit to this tourn, and came by his attorney, &c."

Tourn held at Barnsley, 12th October :—

18th Hen.VII.

" The jurors say that Richard Wodrove owes suit to this tourn, and came by his attorney."

Tourn held at Barnsley, 7th April :—

22nd Hen.VII.

" Inquisition taken on the oath of Alexander Boswell, &c. The jurors say that Ralph Dighton (xij*d.*) of Notton, and Richard Robinson (xij*d.*) of Woolley, answered in tourn, concerning divers offences presented against them, and are not able

[1] Arranged.

THE SENESCHAL'S TOURN. 117 Chap. V.

to deny the same, but put themselves on the mercy of the lord, whose fines *admittuntur* by the seneschal, viz., each of them as set over their heads." *Minutes of Tourns.*

Tourn held at Barnsley, 7th October :—

"The jurors say that Richard Wodrove (xij*d.*) owes suit to this tourn, and came by his attorney." 22nd Hen. VII.

Tourn held at Barnsley :—

"The jurors say that William Benkes (vi*d.*) of Woolley, and Lawrence Haighe (vi*d.*) of Haighe, are common hen stealers *(pullorum latrones)*; therefore, &c., attached. 2nd Hen. VIII.

"They also present that Lawrence Haighe of Haighe, son of Thomas Haighe, with force and arms assaulted John Cawood, both within and without the churchyard of Woolley.

"They likewise say that John Popley of Woolley drew blood of Henry Greve."

Tourn held at Barnsley :—

"The jurors say that Richard Wodrove owes suit, &c." 6th Hen. VIII.

Tourn held at Barnsley :—

"The jurors say that Richard Wodrove, Knt., owes suit, &c." 7th Hen. VIII.

Tourn held at Barnsley, 3rd April :—

"The jurors say that Richard Woderofe (xij*d.*), Knight, owes suit to this court, and came not, but made default; therefore he on the mercy, &c." 7th Hen. VIII.

Tourn held at Barnsley, Wednesday after the feast of Saint Michael :—

"Inquisition on the oath of Thomas Mokeson, &c. The jurors say that the township of Notton should suffer the penalty enjoined on them for that they did not mend the gate called Buryate; therefore they incur the penalty." 8th Hen. VIII.

Tourn held at Barnsley, Wednesday after the feast of Saint Lucy:—

"The jurors say that Richard Wodrove (xij*d.*) owes suit, and came not to this court; it is therefore ordered that he be attached."

Tourn held at Barnsley, Wednesday next after the feast of Saint Michael the Archangel:—

"Inquisition on the oath of Thomas Woderove and Roger Rockley, Esquires," &c.

Tourn held at Barnsley, on Friday next after the feast of Saint Michael the Archangel:—

"The jurors say that Richard Webster (iiij*d.*) of Woolley should be punished, for that he fastened animals in the sowed fields; therefore he in iiij*d.* as above.

"They also say on oath that John Gill (vj*d.*), constable of Roleston, and Richard Webster (vj*d.*) of Woolley, owe suit to this tourn, and have not come; therefore each of them as affixed."

Tourn held at Barnsley, Wednesday in seven days of the Passover:—

"The jurors say by information of the constable and four men of Woolley that John Hinchliffe (iv*d.*), Robert Dighton (iv*d.*), Richard Addie (iv*d.*), and John Adamson (iv*d.*) should be punished as enjoined at the last tourn, because they had not made their fences sufficient; therefore they incur a penalty as above."

Tourn held at Barnsley, after the feast of Saint Michael:—

"The jurors say that Thomas Wodrove (iiij*d.*), Esquire, owes suit to this court, and hath not come; therefore, &c."

Tourn held at Barnsley, after the feast of Saint Michael:—

THE SENESCHAL'S TOURN. 119 Chap. V.

" Robert Griffyn (iiij*d.*) was elected constable of 27thHen.VIII. Woolley, and made default; therefore he in a fine as affixed above."

Tourn held at Barnsley :—

" The jurors say that Richard Wodrove, Esquire, 32ndHen.VIII owes suit, &c.

" They also present that Robert Lunde, constable of Woolley, has made default, inasmuch as he does not keep the watch of our lord the King; therefore he is at the mercy of the lord."

Tourn held at Barnsley, 28th March :—

"Inquisition on the oath of Nicholas Whetley, 1st Mary. &c. The jurors say that Francis Wodrove (iiij*d.*) owes suit to this tourn, and has not come; therefore he is at the mercy of the lord."

" All and singular which things, at the request of Richard Wroe, alias Roe, we have caused to be exemplified. WITNESS: The most noble Gilbert, Earl of Shrewsbury (Salop), Knight of the most illustrious Order of the Garter, and one of the lords of our Privy Council, our chief seneschal of our honour aforesaid, under the seal of his office of seneschal and of the seneschalsie of the honour aforesaid, at Pontefract aforesaid, the 7th day of July, in the 44th year of our reign.

" Compared with the several rolls of the aforesaid courts remaining in the treasury of the Castle of Pontefract, in the custody of the aforesaid Earl, constable of our lady the Queen, of the aforesaid castle,

" By me,

" ROBERT SOMERSCALES,

" Sub-seneschal of the aforesaid Earl of the

" Honour aforesaid, 1602."

120 HISTORY OF BARNSLEY.

Chap. VI.

The Sough Dike.

CHAPTER VI.

THE SOUGH DIKE.

By this name is known a small stream running through the centre of the town, supplying the mills, and acting as the main drain into which all the town sewerage empties itself; from this latter circumstance it no doubt derives its appellation. It is referred to in the year 1636 by its present name, and widow Hinchliffe is described as having at that time resided near it. Formerly its filthy and turbid waters flowed uncovered close to the main street, which circumstance gave strangers a very disagreeable impression of the town.

The spring-head of this stream is at Whinny Nook, a place situate between Pogmore and the Dodworth Road Before the water reaches the town it is perfectly clear, but during its further course, dye-houses, calenders, and sewers complete its defilement. Previously to the introduction of steam power into Barnsley, and the increase of collieries, the quantity of water flowing in the Dike was much greater than at present. We have seen that the monks of Pontefract had mills at Barnsley; in this they followed the example of the lords of other manors, it being a custom in the middle ages for the chief lord to erect mills for the accommodation of his neighbourhood, but on the express condition that the whole of the inhabitants

REMAINS OF AN ANCIENT MILL. 121 Chap. VI.

thereof should grind their corn there, in order that he might receive some adequate remuneration for the expense he had incurred. Barnsley Mills.

The question now arises as to where the mills of Barnsley stood. An eminent antiquarian of the seventeenth century informs us, that their situation was upon the bridge below the town, on which bridge, in the year 1670, were the words—

"Sanctae Mariae."

He also states that they were leased to the Wortleys, and by them to Thomas Edmunds, in 1648.

With these facts before us, I think we may fix the situation of the mills above mentioned as having been upon the Dearne, at the Old Mill.

But there is also proof of a mill having stood on the smaller stream before mentioned. About twenty years ago, while Messrs. Day and Twibell's workmen were excavating in a field near to the Pontefract Road, and opposite the Oak Well toll-bar, they laid bare the foundations of an ancient mill, the water course of which was entire, and the stone work in an excellent state of preservation— a millstone, some bones, part of the water wheel and smaller wheels, were found. From the appearance of the wheel race, the water wheel would seem to have been about ten feet in diameter.

Is this the site and remains of the mill which Ralph de Caprecuria gave to the monks of Pontefract at the time he made a donation of the town of Barnsley?

The monks of Bretton had property adjoining that of the monastery of Pontefract, as appears from an award between the priors of those houses:

HISTORY OF BARNSLEY.

Chap. VI. 122

Property of the Monks of Bretton.

13th Edw. IV.

Arbitrium Willielmi Bradford et Roberti Chaloner inter Priores de Pontefract et Monkbretton de certis terris tenementis et redditibus in Monkbretton quondam Ricardi Wilde ac de aisamento molendini de Barnyslay.

To all Crysten people to whome this present wrytyng indented shall come, we, William Bradford and Robert Chaloner, gretteynge:

Knawe ye that wereas divers clames, ryghtes, and titles off landes and tenements, some tyme in the haldynge and possession of Richard Wilde in Monkbretton, and also clames, chalenges, and demandes of certen rentes late hade and moved betwixte Richard Ledes, prior off Monastery off Sent Mary Magdalene off Monkbretton, of the one partie, and Richard Browne, prior off the Monasterie of Sent John Apostle and Evangeliste of Pomfret, Richard Keresford, and Richard Symmes of Barnyslay on the other partie, were put to the ordenance, deme, and award off hus the aforesaid William and Robert. And we, the said William and Robert, takyng upon hus ye said deme, ordenance, and awarde, the xii day of June, in ye xiii yere of the raigne of Kynge Edward the IV., att Hymesworth, ordaines, demes, and awards in these premises in manner and forme followinge; that is to say: that ye sayd Richard Ledes, prior of the monastary aforsayd, shall hafe to hym and to hys successores for evermore, all the aforesaid landes and rents, the whiche were the forsaid Richard Wilde in Monkbretton, withouten any vexacion, perturbacion, or interruption of the said Richard Browne, prior, and convent of Pomfret and thare successors, and of Richard Keresford and Richard Symmes, thare heirs and assigns, or any other by theme or in thare name, also the said Richard, prior of Pomfret, and convent, Richard Keresford and Richard Symmes sall delyver, or else make to be delyveryd, to the foresaid Richard, prior of Monkbretton, all such charters, evidens, and monuments as thay, or any othor by thame, hafe, that are concerning the foresaid lands and tenements. Also the said Richard, prior, and convent of Pomfrette, Richard Keresford, and Richard Symmes, sall suffer or recover to be hade agaynes thame, or ther feffes of the forenamyd lands and tenements maide by the assent of the said Richard, prior of Monkbretton, after whiche recovere and possession therein, hade in such forme as ye said William and the said Richard, prior, and convent of Pomfrette, sall under their common seall release all such rights, titles, and possessions as thay haffe in all the

BRADFORD'S AND CHALONER'S AWARD.

Property of the Monks of Bretton.

13th Edw. IV.

foresaid lands and tenements, and also the foresaid Richard Keresford and Richard Symmes, and thare feoffes, sall release unto yᵉ foresaid Richard, prior of Monkbretton, and to his successores for evermore, all such right, title, and clame as thay hafe in the forenamyd lands and tenements, for the wiche recovere and releases in forme afore rehersyd on the partie off the sayd Richard, prior off Pomfrette, Richard Keresford, and Richard Symmes, to be fulfyllyd and performed, we, the said William and Robert, arbiters, ordains, deems, and awards that the said Richard, prior of Monkbretton, sall pay, or make to be payd, unto the aforesaid Richard, prior of Pomfrette, Richard Keresford, and Richard Symmes, or to any of thame, xlv markes of money, and on that the foresaid Richard, prior of Monkbretton, under their common sealle, sall release unto the said Richard, prior of Pomfrette, Richard Keresford, and Richard Symmes all manner of rerage of rentes to hym dewe of all yᵉ forenamyd lands and tenements. And over that we, the said William and Robert, arbritors, ordains, and deems, and awards that yᵉ said Richard, prior, and convent of Monkbretton, shall make, or do to be maid, under thar common seale, a sufficient and a lawful grant and giffte unto the foresaid Richard, prior, and convent off Pomfrette, and to thare successores for evermore, of licence and liberty within certain cloyses, called be the names of Normanroid, Pageroid, or else by what other name tha be callyd, as thay lye upon the south est parte off Barnyslay Brygge, and next ajoyneynge unto the said Brigge, the which cloises are parcell of yᵉ forenamyd lands and tenements, for attachement, keepeinge, preserynge, and makeynge off newe of a were and milnedame for yᵉ corne milne of Barnyslay, with fre entre and issue with all manner of carriage leddyng stone, tymbre, tynsell, or any other stuffe for makyng, repellynge, or amendinge of the said werre and milnedam as oftetymes as they are nedfull to be maked, repellyd, or amended, with sufficient licence for the said tymbre, stone, tynsel, and other stuffe necessarie for the said werre, to rest and abyde within the foresaid cloises dureyng the tyme of the foresaides warkes withoute fraude and malice engyne, and if it happen that by creating and werynge of the water, the festynygne of the said werre and milnedame to be worne outte, yᵗ then itt fall, itt shall be lawfull unto yᵉ foresaid Richard, prior, and convent of Pomfrette, and to their successores, for to knytte, attache, festen, and make of new another new werre and milnedame in any other parcell of

Chap. VI. 124 HISTORY OF BARNSLEY.

Property of the Monks of Bretton.

grounde within the forenamed cloyses where it is to thame moste necessari, and behoveth for the will and profitt of thare foresaid milne, paying therefore yearly unto the·said Richard,

13th Edw. IV.

prior, and convent of Monkbretton, and to their successores for evermore, a rose floure in the fest of nativite of Sent John Baptist, iffe itt be askyd, the said grant and licence to be made also sufficiently as the councell judged of ye said Richard, prior of Pomfrette, can be reason thynke, ordaine, and advise, and by the oversight of hus, the foresaid William and Robert, arbitors, at the costage of the said Richard; prior of Pomfrette, provideth alway that if any articule, clause, or matter be comprehended in this oure award, the which necessari for the kepeng abidynge and everlasting of the same, to be amended, or added, or admnyshed, y^t we, the said William and Robert, arbitors, ordains, deems, and awards the foresaid clausys, articules, or make to be amended and corrected by us, ye said William and Robert, at any tyme hereafter when it sall happen to be perceived and finden, and y^t the said Richard, prior of Monkbretton, and his successors, on there partie, and Richard, prior of Pomfrette, and his successors on there partie, shall consent thame to kepe and perform the same severally on another partie; and for the more suretie hereof we, ye said William and Robert, ordains, deems, and awards that ye said Richard, prior, and convent of Pomfrette, and Richard, prior, and convent of Monkbretton, shall severally be bounden under there comon seales, thay and thare successors, in sevrall obligations, either of thame to other, to kepe, fulfyll, and perform all the clauses, articles comprehended withyn oure award. In witness whereoff to this oure awarde, we, ye said William and Robert hafe, put our sealles, the xxii day of Septembre, ye yeare and place aforerehearsyd.

Ancient Streets.

ANCIENT STREETS.

The oldest parts of the town are Church Street, anciently called Kirkgate, Shambles Street, formerly known as Westgate, and the Market Place. The two former are mentioned in deeds centuries ago.

On one of the houses in Shambles Street was

ANCIENT STREETS. 125 Chap. VI.

Ancient
Streets.

formerly an inscription, which, from the style of spelling, was probably of good antiquity:

> *" Before thou sleepe,*
> *Call thou to minde*
> *What thou hast done this day,*
> *And if thy conscience be oppressed,*
> *To God for mercye praye."*

Here still exist some ancient buildings, which exhibit traces of their former consequence, and show this to have been the best part of the town. The Fentons, who now hold property in this street, formerly resided in a house which is still standing, in the front whereof may be seen their arms, together with those of West on an escutcheon.[1] One of the Fentons, while travelling through Spain a few years ago, along with his sister, was brutally murdered by robbers.

The name of Kirkstile appears in the will of Edmund Brookhouse, dated 1493, and that of Kirkgate in records of the seventeenth century. The site of Peas Hills is an old enclosure, and is supposed to have taken its name from grain of that description formerly being extensively grown there.

Wilson's Piece—so called from John Wilson, a nephew of the founder of the linen trade, to whom about twenty acres of common were allotted at the time of the enclosure, in 1777—is chiefly inhabited by hand-loom weavers. Here is a school in connection with the Establishment; and a church, dedicated to Saint John, is in course of erection.

---

[1] Fenton—Argent a cross gules between four fleur-de-lis sable. West—Argent a fess dancette between three leopards' heads sable.

Chap. VI.

Ancient Streets.

The May-day Green is a large piece of ground where the fruit and vegetable market is held. A May-pole is said to have formerly existed on this spot, which accounts for the name. Bull and bear baitings formerly took place there. These proceedings were abhorred by the more respectable inhabitants of the town; though none of them had courage to attempt to put a stop to them, until the late Mr. James Cocker tried the following stratagem: Going into the midst of the crowd during the performance, he inquired whose property the bear was, but receiving no reply, he took a pistol, apparently with the intention of shooting the animal; he had no sooner done this, than a man stepped forward and begged of him not to kill the bear;[1] said he was his property, and he would take the animal away, and never use him in Barnsley again. This had the desired effect, and no other exhibitions of this nature ever after took place on May-day Green.

[1] Bull and bear baitings do not appear to have been the only entertainments of the people. It seems that there had been races at Barnsley previous to 1738, for in the "Leeds Mercury," of September 5th in that year, is an advertisement announcing these amusements for the 21st and 22nd of September, on the usual course. On the first day a stake of £5 5s., in three heats, was to be run for; and on the second, one of £10 10s., with the like heats. There were to be ordinaries at Mr. Thomas Bradford's and Mr. Francis Roper's, and an assembly each night at the Free School. These races, it appears, were after a time discontinued. An attempt was made to restore them in the year 1851, and races were held for a few years in succession, but from some cause or other the sport was again abandoned, much to the dissatisfaction of many of the inhabitants of the town and neighbourhood.

THE MOOT HALL. 127 Chap. VI.

There is a monument recording the time when *Gas introduced* gas was introduced into this town by the following inscription thereon :—

This
Column
was presented to the
Town of Barnsley,
by Mr. John Malam of
London, Civil Engineer and
Contractor for Lighting
the Town with Gas,
A.D. 1821.

Barnsley has been much improved during the last thirty years, many old buildings having been removed, and some elegant and substantial ones erected; the streets have also been widened, and the shops in neatness are superior to those in some larger towns.

A notice of the public buildings, past and present, will not be out of place, which I give in the order of their seniority, commencing with the

Public Buildings.

MOOT HALL.

Moot Hall.

A description of this edifice, though long since removed, will no doubt be read with interest. Its site was in the centre of the Market Hill; it was pulled down about the year 1820. Like some of the adjoining buildings, it had the appearance of great antiquity; but the period of its erection is involved in obscurity. Amongst the town's accounts of the year 1622 appears this entry :—

Payde for they Moulthall dore keaye and yᵉ locke
mendinge to John Roolin - - - - - - viij*d.*

The upper story of this place comprised one large room, entered by a flight of unsightly steps,

Chap. VI.   128   HISTORY OF BARNSLEY.

Moot Hall. which projected into the street opposite to the shop now occupied by Mr. Henry Elstone, grocer. Up to about the year 1795 the quarter sessions were held here, and had been from as early as the reign of James I. Annexed is a copy of a document pertaining thereto, the heading of which is in Latin :—

Barnsley Sessions. 20th James I. At a General Session of the Peace, held at Barnsley, in the West Riding of the county of York, on the 9th day of January, in the year of the reign of our Lord James, by the grace of God, of England, France and Ireland King, Defender of the Faith, the 20th, and of Scotland the 56th, before Thomas Wentworth, Knight and Baronet; John Jackson, Knight; Godfrey Rodes, Knight; Thomas Wentworth of Elmsall, Esquire ; William West, Esquire ; John Ermsditch, Esquire; and Francis Burdett, Esquire, Justices.

Upon the hearinge of a difference amongst the inhabitants of Woolley, upon the complaynt of the constables thereof, y^t sundry persons refuse to pay unto him their rates and assess^{mts} due for the common service of the countrye, this court doth thincke fittinge, and thereupon doth order, that the inhabitants theire shall from hencefurth contynue payment of all rates and assess^{mts} within themselves, according to ancyent agreement and custom heretofore used amongst them, which beinge in writinge under theire handes and shewed to this court, the Justices here present doth ratify and confirm, requiringe the constables for the tyme beinge, that if any inhabitant refuse to pay, accordingly to convey him or them soe refusing before some of his Maties Justices of Peace neare thereunto, to enter securitie for their appearance at the next sessions to answer theire contempt in the premises.

(Signed)   .   RADCLYFFE.

Subjoined are particulars of some trials which took place here during the seventeenth century, and also other matters in connection with Barnsley Sessions :—

At Barnsley Sessions, 12th October :—
A man was indicted for shootinge at pigeons, and witness swore he saw ye p^{tle} shoote and psul (pistol) smoke as they flye,

BARNSLEY SESSIONS. 129 Chap. VI.

Barnsley Sessions.

and six pigeons killed. Y⁰ jurie found y⁰ fact, and y⁰ court sentence him to fine xv*d*., according to y⁰ 33rd Henry viij. But upon better consideration, and . . . . a respite of judgment, and . . ` . . . . of y⁰ pᵗˡᵉ till better examination of y⁰ case, as not beinge satisfied in judgment yᵗ he by yᵗ shote was soe fynable, neither could be punished by 1*s*. 3*d*. fine, because yᵗ there statute requires two witnesses; y⁰ clarke has order therefore to staye judgement.

At Rotherham Sessions it was ordered to require an accouᵗ, amongst others, of publique receipt of y⁰ country's money to y⁰ treasurers for laime soldiers since 1664. Mr. Reilly wrote a l're to the sessions at Barnesley, y⁰ 16th October, after . . . . concerninge much discontent, yᵗ he should be questioned after so longe a tyme after his beinge in yᵗ office. After giving a certᵗ to Sʳ John Goodricke and Hen. Fairfax, he handed his bookes to his successor. . . . .

Thomas Clayton of Clayton Hall, at Barnsley Sessions, 16th October, 1667, was indicted for baribrie. The grand jury found y⁰ indictment. Thomas Clayton, in person, treating one of y⁰ jurors yᵗ he would have him, they all appear at y⁰ . . . barr, y⁰ jurors complain of it. This, by Sʳ Willia. Adams opinio., was judged a true marke of baribrie, soe ordered (none contradicting) to be entered amongst theire notes in theire booke.

. . . . takes a goose, and carries hit a good bit, perceivinge some companie to come yᵗ he . thought discovered him, he threw y⁰ goose oure an hedge yᵗ quicke not at all hurt notwʰstandinge, and he beinge proved by witnesses to be in his possession, it was put to y⁰ jury whether they thought, yᵗ beinge soe in his possession, he took it feloniousle and wᵗʰ a felonious intent, if soe it was felonie, if not, but done in rallarie or soe, it was but a trespasse; so likewise it was judged of, a copy yᵗ was to . . . . . some.

Thomas Clayton of Clayton Hall prefers an information before my Lᵈ Chief Justice of England agᵗ Will. Spencer of Cannon Hall, to have broken y⁰ recoknizance for y⁰ good behaviour . . . . . . a manslaughter of a joyner in High Hoylande. Clayton gets a warrant from Tho. Stringer, Esq., to bring five or six . . . . . . before him or some other justices, to examine as material witnesses to prove y⁰ said breach, but the sessions at Barnsley commencinge y⁰ 16th October, 1667, they offered to bee examined there, but y⁰ court refused to examine them upon y⁰ cause dependinge before my Lᵈ Chief Justice, but

I

HISTORY OF BARNSLEY.

Chap. VI.

Barnsley Sessions.

thought it more proper they should preferre an indictment of breach of peace or good behaviour . . . . . order to a tryal before yᵉ justices at yᵉ sessions to have them examined, or bynde them over to give evidence there. After this beinge come of yᵉ bench into yᵉ . . . . where justices usually by divers marke warren moved me to examine those witness, thoe beinge alone, which havinge been soe . . . . before I . . . . . . p'haps as might appear to them . . . .

The papers from which the above are taken are so mutilated, that it is impossible to give the whole of what has been comprised therein.

Poachers.

At Barnsley Sessions, on the 10th October, 1671 :—

Matthew Prince, high constable of the Wapentake of Staincross, had orders given from the justices to require all constables to find out who used or kept bows, guns, greyhounds, setting dogs, ferrets, coney dogs, lurchers, hare nets, hare pipes, snares or engines for destroying game, contrary to the statute, other than those persons who had property or inheritance of his own or wife's right to the value of one hundred pounds per annum, or the son and heir apparent of an esquire or other person of a higher degree, or the owners of forests, parks, or warrens, and to discover what ordinary or mean persons kept or used any nets, angle hair, or spear ; or to lay in waters pots, nets, fish hooks, or other engines to take away fish by any means without leave of the lord or owner of such water, and to give the names of such persons at the next quarter sessions to be held at Barnsley, in order that proceedings might be taken against them,

From this it would seem that there were many poachers about Barnsley in the latter part of the seventeenth century ; we may attribute this to the poverty which then existed.

The town also appears, from the following document, to have been noted for the number of its vagrants, which may be referred to the same cause as the prevalence of poaching :—

BARNSLEY SESSIONS.

131   Chap. VI.

To all Christian people to whom these presents shall come, greeting:

Barnsley Sessions—vagrant poor.

Whereas, at the special sessions of the peace held at Barnsley, the 10th day of March, in the seven and twentieth year of his now Majesty's reign, before John Wentworth, Henry Edmunds, and Jasper Blythman, Esqs., his Majesty's Justices of the Peace for the West Riding of the county of York, divers and sundry persons made complaint that they were oppressed by the poore of Barnsley, whereof great numbers wandered begging; whereupon the principal inhabitants of the town of Barnsley being present, did likewise complain that the number of the poore was so many, that of themselves they were not able to maintain, relieve, or raise a stock for to employ the poore without the assistance of the hundred. All which being fully made appear, an order was made at the speciale sessions of the peace, which was confirmed by an order of the general quarter sessions of the Peace held at Pontefract, according to an Act of Parliament, in the three and fortieth yeare of Elizabeth, wherein, amongst other things, itt is enacted, that if the Justices of the Peace doe perceive that the inhabitants of any parish is not able to raise a stock for to sett the poore on worke, that them, the said Justices, shall and may tax, rate, assesse any other of the parishes, or out of any parish within the hundred wherein the parish is, by which order, and in pursuance of the said act, the several inhabitants of all and every the towns within the wapentake of Staincross, according to the book of rates, were taxed and assessed to pay unto the overseers of the town of Barnsley monthly their several taxations and assessments, which in the whole hundred did amount to ten pounds one shilling and a penny a month, which taxation continued for the space of four years, until such time as many of the poore children were placed as apprentices, and some stock over and besides what maintained the poore was raised, which is now accounted for by several overseers when by the Justices of the Peace called to an account, but the said assessment being thought grievous and burthensome by the inhabitants of the said wapentake, they being unwilling to have itt continued upon them any longer, being in many places sore charged with poore of their own, the said Justices thought fitt to put a period to it. Now, at the conclusion thereof, John Wentworth of Woolley, in the said county of York, Esq., although he was during the time that the said taxation continued a contributor with the rest of the inhabitants of Woolley towards the raising of the said stock, yett hee out of his meere

Chap. VI. **132** **HISTORY OF BARNSLEY.**

Barnsley Sessions.

goodwill, and out of a Christian charity, as likewise to encourage industry and to prevent idleness and begging, than which nothing can be more destructive to the Government, has given for ever, for the raising and advancing of the stock to employ the poore of Barnsley, the sum of fifty pounds, which wee, the inhabitants, do most thankfully receive, and promise to employ the same, and as much as in us lyeth to endeavour for the future to prevent the wandering abroad of our poore in the country so loosely as they have done. Witness our hands, this first day of November, in the one and thirtieth yeare of the raigne of our Soveraign Lord, King Charles the Second, anno Domini, 1679.

> JOHN ARMITAGE.
> HENY. WOOD.
> WM. BAGULEY.
> FRAS. USHER.
> JOHN OXLEY.
> SAML. WILDMAN.
> J. ROOKE.

The wrytinge from the inhabitants of Barnsley upon the receipt of £50 given by mee towards raising of a stocke for the use of the poore thereof.

About eighty years ago one John Bedford was charged at Barnsley Sessions with entering Royston Church, and taking away the communion plate, which he hid in the lane leading to Carlton; for this he is said to have been publicly whipped at three market towns on their respective market days. He had previously done penance in the same church for bastardy.

John Wright of Thurnscoe was tried here for stealing a cover from a winnowing machine. He was sentenced to be flogged round the Moot Hall.

Moot Hall Clock.

The town's business was transacted in the upper room of the Moot Hall. [1] A clock with two dials was placed in the north-west corner of the building. Edmund Rogers, in 1646, amongst other bequests, gave ten pounds towards the procuring a

---

[1] One of the cellars under this building served as a prison.

THE MOOT HALL. 133 Chap. VI.

clock for the benefit of the public, and the subjoined particulars relate to its being placed in the Moot Hall :—

Moot Hall Clock.

DISBOURSEMENT FOR THE CLOCK IN THE MOULT HALL.

Monies laid out about the settinge upe of the Clocke in the Moult Hall, August, Anno Domini, 1649.

	s.	d.
Imp. to Symon Stones that brought yᵉ clocke, sett it upe, and stayde with it four daies and four nights	vij	—
For Richard Shearwood for nayles . . .	iij	—
„ Robert Denton for nayles	—	viij
„ Boards and other timber	iij	—
„ Lead to the plummer	v	x
„ Eight pound of ironn	j	iiij
„ The wrights for theire worke . . .	xx	—
„ Drinke to them	ij	—
„ Binds and Crooks	—	vj
„ Gudgings and plats	—	xij
„ Other two peniworth of nayles . . .	—	ij
„ A locke for yᵉ clocke doore	—	iiij

There has evidently been much more informa-tion comprised in this document, but in consequence of its being much mutilated, the above is all that can be deciphered.

Under the clock on the west side of the building was a pillory, which fell into disuse about eighty years ago. A little lower down the hill, and on the same side of the edifice, were some stocks, which were used until a later period.

Pillory and Stocks.

The lower story of the Moot Hall comprised several divisions, and the one opposite to where Mr. Travis now has his shop, was used by the venders of butter, eggs, and poultry on the market day, and at other times served as a repository for stalls and other requisites of the market ; the other compart-

Chap. VI. 134   HISTORY OF BARNSLEY.

Shops in Moot Hall.

ments were used as shops, and appear to have served for that purpose as early as 1660, being then tenanted by Richard Thwaites and Thomas Exley. It appears from Keresforth's deed relating to the Grammar School, that there was an annual rent charged upon these shops towards the support of the master. In the succeeding century, and about the year 1750, one of them was tenanted by Joseph Smith, a bookseller, respecting whom I have seen a curious advertisement, of which the annexed is a copy :—

Joseph Smith, bookseller, in Barnsley, and at his shop in Baxter Gate, Doncaster, selleth all sorts of books, in divinity, history, law, mathematicks, musick, classicks, and all other school books, Bibles, and Common Prayers, gilt and plain, of all sizes, with all sorts and sundry wares, as paper and paper boxes of all sorts, shop books, ledgers, rul'd and unrul'd, likewise all sorts of Justices' warrants, &c., and paper hangings for rooms, imboss'd paper, gilt, marble, and other papers, likewise maps and curious prints of all sorts, with pens, pencils, slates, wax, wafers, spectacle cases and reading glasses, stamp't parchment and paper of all sizes, Daffy's, Houghton, and Bateman's drops, with Godfrey's cordial, Scot's and Hill's British oil, women's hats, children's toys, musical instruments, with several other things. Any person may have their old books, prayers, or any other sort new bound, either gilt or plain, likewise any gentleman may have any gilt-back and lettered after the newest fashion by Thomas Smith.

Redy money for any parcel or library of books.

Thomas Cockshott married Smith's daughter and succeeded to the business; he was one of the last residents under the Moot Hall.

On the demolition of this building the clock was sold to Mr. Porter of Park House, who removed it to his residence; he also purchased the bell, which was used for some time at his coal wharf, Hoyle Mill, and at the completion of the Tower of Monk

PUBLIC BUILDINGS. 135 Chap. VI.

Public Buildings.

Bretton church, was taken and placed therein, and now fulfils a holier mission. It has the inscription—" T. Hylton, Wath, 1786." This person is said to have stood high as a bell founder.

THE OLD WORKHOUSE,

now used for offices, stands on the site of Brookhouse's Almshouses, and was erected at a cost of upwards of £90, in accordance with the wishes of a majority of the townspeople, at a meeting held at the Moot Hall, on the 22nd of November, 1735; the object of which was to provide for the employment and maintenance of the poor of Barnsley. The plan was prepared by John Bower, and the expense defrayed by the inhabitants.

THE COURT HOUSE,

which is situate in St. Mary's Gate, nigh to the building last mentioned, is in the Grecian style of architecture, and was constructed in the year 1833, at a cost of £1,300, defrayed by subscription and poor rate. Petty sessions are held here: the acting magistrates being Lord Wharncliffe, the Hon. Col. Monckton, John Spencer Stanhope, Godfrey Wentworth, Walter Spencer Stanhope, Wentworth Blacket Beaumont, Vincent Corbett, and Thomas Taylor, Esquires, the Hon. James Frederic Stuart Wortley, and the Rev. Wm. Wordsworth.

Barnsley is included in the thirteenth circuit of County Courts under the new Act; the sittings of this court are held in the Court House. William Walker, Esquire, is judge; Mr. William Shepherd, registrar; Mr. James Milner, clerk; and Mr. Charles Bailey, high bailiff. The Trade Protection Society's office is in the Bank Yard, and Mr. Henry Nichol-

Chap. VI. 136 HISTORY OF BARNSLEY.

Public Buildings.

son, collector. At a short distance from the Court House is

THE NEW LOCK-UP,

to which is attached a residence for the superintendent of the County Constabulary in this district. Previously to the year 1856, the town's police were under the direction of the Local Board of Health. A building, formerly known as the

ODDFELLOWS' HALL,

situated in Pitt Street, is of the Ionic order, and was erected for the use of the society whose name it bears, from plans prepared by Mr. Hindle, at a cost of £1,100, raised in shares of £1 each. The first stone was laid by Mr. G. H. Smith on the 18th of July, 1836. This structure did not long serve for the purpose intended. In consequence of the embarrassed state of the society it was ultimately sold by auction, and is now used as a furniture warehouse.

THE CORN-EXCHANGE AND MARKET HOUSE,

of which an engraving has been given in a former part of the work, is a useful building, in the Grecian style, situate on Market Hill, at a short distance from the site of the Moot Hall. The foundation stone was laid by Mr. Edward Parker on the 26th of May, 1851. Mr. Whitworth furnished the design for this necessary structure, which was erected at a cost of £3,865 12s. 2d., raised partly by subscription and partly by £5 shares. The upper story is used on the market day by farmers and others connected with agricultural pur-

PUBLIC BUILDINGS.

137 Chap. VI.

Public
Buildings.

suits, and is also occasionally occupied for concerts and other amusements, for which it is well adapted. The lower part serves for the accommodation of the venders of butter, poultry, &c. The

COMMERCIAL BUILDINGS,

in Church Street, forming a handsome pile of the Ionic order, were erected in 1837 from a plan prepared by Mr. Hindle, at a cost of £1,500, raised by a company of proprietors in £25 shares. The length of the west front is forty feet, and that of the south front forty-eight feet. One of the lower rooms, fronting the main street, is used as a Post-office, and the other is occupied as the library of the Mechanics' Institution. The Commercial News Room and the Reading Room of the Mechanics' Institution are on the upper story. The postmaster (Mr. Thomas Lister) resides in the back part of the building.

THE UNION WORKHOUSE

is a commodious and handsome structure, situate on a slight eminence on the Gawber Road. The following townships are comprised in the Barnsley Poor-Law Union:—Ardsley, Barugh, Billingley, Carlton, Cudworth, Darfield, Darton, Dodworth, Nether Hoyland, Monk Bretton, Notton, Stain-brough, Wombwell, Woolley, and Worsbrough. The guardians meet every alternate Tuesday at the Union House. Mr. John Tyas is clerk to the guardians; Messrs. Charles Lorimer and George W. Atkinson, relieving officers; John Wright, master of the workhouse; and Mary Ann Wright, matron.

Chap. VI. 138 HISTORY OF BARNSLEY.

*Railway
Stations.*

RAILWAY STATIONS.[1]

Barnsley has every advantage of railway accommodation: a branch of the Lancashire and Yorkshire Railway, joining the main line at Horbury, was opened in 1850, affording direct communication with Wakefield and Leeds. The South Yorkshire Railway, running from Barnsley to Doncaster, was opened in 1851, and the line to Sheffield in 1853. In 1856 a branch of the Manchester, Sheffield, and Lincolnshire Railway was completed. All the railways run into one station, but passengers are booked on the latter railway at a small temporary station on the west side of the town.

The station at which passengers are booked for the South Yorkshire and Lancashire and Yorkshire lines is a miserable-looking structure at the bottom of Regent Street, possessing little or no accommodation for passengers; and should a stranger merely pass through this building, without entering the town, he will at once conclude from appearances that the place has a good claim to the title of "Black Barnsley." The road is on a par with the station in wet weather, being almost impassable.

Banks.

BANKS.

It is generally understood that there were scarcely any country banks formed in England previously to 1780. As a system, the business of country banking, as we know it now, hardly existed then.

The leading mercer, grocer, or woollen draper usually acted as the local banker. People deposited their cash with him, and with his assistance pro-

---

[1] The nearest station to Barnsley, on the Midland line, is at Cudworth, a distance of about three miles.

BANKS. 139 Chap. VI.

Banks.

cured change for notes or bills. Remittances to distant parts of the country were frequently made in specie either by private messengers[1] or the public carrier.[2] During the thirty years subsequent to 1780 nearly all the private country banks of issue that were ever opened for business in England were formed.

In an old directory, published in the latter part of the last century, there is mention made of one Foljambe Wood, woollen draper[3] and banker, who is stated to draw on Mr. William Bent, No. 55, Paternoster Row, London. This seems to have been the first banker in Barnsley of which we have any record. From some deeds, he appears to have purchased, in 1782, the Angel Inn at Barnsley, upon the site of which he erected two houses, which were afterwards occupied by himself and Mr. John Dickenson, grocer. In 1796 he was made a bank-

---

[1] In the Doncaster town accounts, 1648-9 :—

	£	s.	d.
Paide for a bage that money was sent in to London to pay the fee farme	0	0	4
Paid Will. Armitage, Esq. (Recorder), to pay the fee farme	75	11	1½
Paide Mr. Ayre for carriage the fee farme rent to London	0	13	0

[2] The "Leeds Mercury," of Feb. 14, 1737-8, has the following :—"On Friday morning early, the Newcastle waggon coming to London was stopp'd on the road near Baldock, in Hertfordshire, by three highwaymen, well mounted and armed, who plundered the waggon, and took away £500 in specie."

[3] Mr. Henry Rayney of Covent Garden, London, writing to Mr. Carrington of the Views, near Barnsley, 17th of August, 1725, says :—" When I saw you last I tould you I was at this time a little pinch'd, and being, it is so long since the assizes at York, I hope now you may be at leasure to procure a bill, wch I desire may not be of a long date, nor upon a woollen draper, for I have known the trouble of them, but rather upon a goldsmith, &c. No doubt but some at my Lord Stafford's can supply you."

Chap. VI.

Banks.

rupt, as a linen manufacturer and banker. He afterwards removed to Ackworth, where, with Esther his wife, he was residing, 15th of October, 1796.

Afterwards Messrs. Beckett and Clarke opened a bank in Church Street, which eventually passed into the possession of a company known as the Wakefield and Barnsley Union Bank. Their London bankers are Glyn and Co. A beautiful and more spacious structure is in course of erection, also in Church Street. Mr. James Frudd is manager.

The Barnsley Banking Company was first established in 1832, and is in a prosperous state; a larger building is being erected; their present place of business is on Market Hill. Manager, Mr. Samuel Linley. London bankers, Barnett and Co.

The Savings' Bank, which is situated in Church Street, was established in the year 1829, and now holds investments amounting to upwards of £63,000, belonging to private individuals and friendly societies of the neighbourhood. Mr. Edward Lancaster is manager.

Local Acts.

THE WATERWORKS AND BOARD OF HEALTH ACTS.

Barnsley is supplied with water partly by the water carriers, and partly from the waterworks, which are now under the control of the Local Board of Health. The Waterworks Company's Act was obtained in 1837, and the capital consisted of 700 shares of £10 each; a clause in the act fixing the capital of the company at £7,000, and the amount of borrowed money at £2,500. The pool at Smithies is supplied from the river Dearne, and the water is forced into a reservoir on Jordan Hill, which furnishes the town with the necessary element.

LITERARY SOCIETIES. 141 Chap. VI.

Local Acts. The Board of Health Act was applied to the town in 1854, though not without some opposition, as many of the inhabitants looked on its introduction with suspicion. The meetings of the board are held in the Court House, and the jurisdiction extends within the circuit of 1,200 yards from the site of the Moot Hall.

Of the other acts which relate to the place, may be mentioned one for lighting, watching, and improving the town of Barnsley.

THE MECHANICS' AND FRANKLIN INSTITUTES.

Institutes. The Barnsley Mechanics' Institute and Literary Society first originated in the year 1837; but for want of support, the objects of the founders could not be carried out, and were for a time abandoned. In 1848, a few individuals, seeing the advantages which would be derived from an institution of this nature, were desirous to establish one if possible. The affair being taken up with spirit was successful, and the institution is now in a flourishing condition—the members numbering upwards of 300. The library contains upwards of 1,300 volumes, and the reading-room is well supplied with newspapers and periodicals; in addition to which, lectures are delivered on popular subjects in the Mechanics' Hall, a building formerly used as a theatre, but now occupied by this institution. Mr. William Harvey is president; Dr. Jackson and Mr. William Harrison Peacock, vice-presidents; Mr. Thomas Allen, treasurer; Mr. J. A. Smith is the only secretary at present—a vacancy having occurred by the death of Mr. Thomas Ross, a much respected and valuable officer of this society.

Chap. VI. 142   HISTORY OF BARNSLEY.

Institutes.

Another institution, possessing similar advantages to the Mechanics', was formed by Messrs. John Burland, John Kenworthy, and John Garlick, in 1843, but had no reading-room till the year 1854, when this necessary want was with some little difficulty supplied, and the number of members reached to 354, but have since decreased considerably, there being now only 197 on the books. The reading-room is well supplied with newspapers and periodicals, and the library numbers 700 volumes. Mr. Edward Parker is president; Messrs. Thomas Lister and William Lawton, vice-presidents; Mr. William Darnbrough, treasurer; and Mr. John Wood, secretary.

Family of Hallifax.

THE FAMILY OF HALLIFAX

were originally of the town bearing the same name, the surname, according to family tradition, having been assumed by Robert Waterhouse, rector of Springthorpe, county of Lincoln, whose grandson, John, settled at Barnsley in the beginning of the eighteenth century, where he followed the business of a clockmaker. Many articles of his manufacture may be met with in the neighbourhood. From the inscription on his tombstone in St. Mary's churchyard, a copy of which is given below, it would appear that he was of an ingenious turn of mind:—

" In memory of Mr. John Hallifax of this town, whose abilities and virtue few in these times have attained. His art and industry were such as his ingenious inventions will be a lasting monument of his merit, such as recommended him to the favour and esteem of all good men that knew him. He departed this life, Sept. 25, 1750."

What his inventions were I have not been able to ascertain; they probably related to his business.

THE FAMILY OF HALLIFAX. 143

He had a numerous family; amongst them was Thomas, whom we may justly consider to have been one of the most eminent men this town has produced.

Thomas Hallifax was originally apprenticed to a grocer at Barnsley, but before his indentures were fully expired, he exchanged that situation for one in the metropolis, where, by unremitting industry, he acquired an ample fortune. In 1762 he was a partner with Sir Richard Glyn as a banker, at No. 18, Birchin Lane. He was elected alderman of Aldersgate ward in 1766, in succession to Mr. Nelson. He served the office of sheriff in 1768-9; and that of Lord Mayor in 1777; received the honour of knighthood, 1778;.was a member of the Goldsmiths' Company, in whose hall his arms are set up, and M.P. for Aylesbury, 1784; he married the eldest daughter of Thomas Savile, Esq. of Enfield, by whom he had two sons. He died intestate, although supposed to have accumulated £100,000, and was buried in the family vault of the Saviles in Enfield churchyard, nearly opposite to the south entrance of the church, under a plain altar monument of white stone, enclosed with iron rails, which bears the following inscription :—

" In the vault under this tomb lie ,the remains of Thomas Savile, Esq., late of Clayhill in this parish, who departed this life the 23rd of April, 1767, aged fifteen years. Also, are deposited the remains of Dame Margaret Hallifax, wife of the Right Honourable Sir Thomas Hallifax, Knight, late Lord Mayor of the city of London, who departed this life the 17th of November, 1777, aged twenty-eight years. She was the eldest daughter of John Savile, Esq. of this parish, and has left issue two sons, Thomas, borne on the 9th of February, 1774, and the youngest, named Savile, borne on the 6th of November, 1777. Also are deposited the remains of John Savile, Esq., late of Clayhill in this parish, and father of the above, who departed this life the 8th of April, 1778, aged sixty-six years. Also of

Chap. VI. 144 HISTORY OF BARNSLEY.

Family of Hallifax.

Sir Thomas Hallifax, Knight, member of Parliament for the borough of Alesbury, in Buckinghamshire, Alderman of London, and of Gordon House in this parish, who departed from us on the 7th day of February, in the year of our Lord 1789, in the 58th[1] year of his age.

He was interred the Tuesday after his death in great funeral pomp; the hearse was decorated with escutcheons, and attended by seven mourning coaches, and eight private coaches, besides his own chariot. The pall was supported by Aldermen Lewes, Le Mesurier, Pickett, Clarke, Wright, and Hopkins; Deputy Harding, a relation by marriage, walked as chief mourner, followed by Sir Thomas's two sons.

The following appeared in the " Gentleman's Magazine," March 7, 1789:—

" Died at Kenilworth, county Warwick, Mrs. Hallifax, wife of John Hallifax, Esq., brother to the late Sir Thomas Hallifax of Birchin Lane."

Beevor Hall.

BEEVOR HALL

is a handsome mansion in the Elizabethan style, embosomed in trees and surrounded with pleasure grounds, near to the course of the Barnsley stream, and about half a mile- distant from the town.

The animal known as the beaver may possibly have frequented this place in early times, to which circumstance the origin of the name may be referred. In a deed, without date, which appears to have been executed in the reign of Elizabeth, it is written Beverhole; and the place is again noticed in a bond of the seventeenth century, the obligatory part of which may probably interest some of my readers:

[1] Sir Thomas is stated to have died at the age of 58. This is evidently a mistake.

PEDIGREE OF HALLIFAX.[1]

ARMS—*Or*, on a pile engrailed *Sable*, between two fountains proper, three cross crosslets of the field.
CREST—On a wreath of the colours, a Moorcock per bend sinister, *Sable* and *Gules*, combed and wattled of the last, gorged with a Ducal Coronet *Or*; on the breast a cross crosslet as in the Arms. (Granted 11th December, 1788, to John Hallifax, Esq., of Kenilworth, Co. Warwick.)

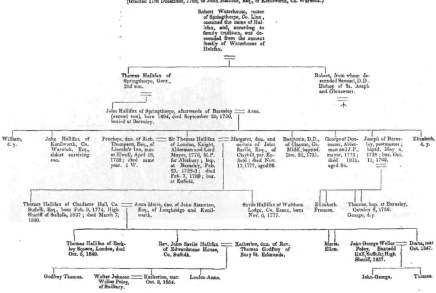

[1] The Hallifax's new quarter the Arms of Savile with those of Waterhouse, having twice married heiresses of that family.

BEEVOR HALL.   145   Chap. VI.

Beevor Hall.
————
Bond, 1622.

𝔑𝔬𝔟𝔢𝔯𝔦𝔫𝔱 𝔘𝔫𝔦𝔟𝔢𝔯𝔰𝔦 per presentes nos Rogerum Bureges de
Beverhouse in com. Ebor. Wollenweaver et Willimum. Barquith
de Barnsley in com. prædicto husbandman teneri et firmiter
obligari Franncisco Wortley de Wortley in com. prædicto Mil. et
Baronit. et Franncisco Burdet de Burthwait Armiger. In quatuor
libris bonœ et legalis monetœ Angliœ solvend. eidem Franncisco
Wortley aut Franncisco Burdet aut suis certis atturnatibus heredibus executoribus administratoribus aut assignatis suis ad quam
qudem. solutionem bene et fideliter faciend. Obligamus nos et
utrunque nostrum per se pro toto et in solidem conjunctam et divi-
sem heredes executores administratores et assignatos nostros firmiter per præsentes sigillis nostris sigillat. Dat. ultimo die
mensis Septembris anno Regni dni. nri. Jacobi Dei Gra. Angliœ,
Franciœ et Hiberniœ Regis vicessimo fidei defensoris et Scotiœ
quinquagesimo sexto.

The bond was conditioned for payment of fortye shillynges
to the s^d F. Wortley and F. Burdett, and four shillinges to the
overseers of the poore of Barnsley, and was

Witnessed by	Signed by	
	Roger	
his mark		
WILLIAM *M* MEDLEY.	BURGES.	L. S.
JOHN × HEPWORTH.	his mark	
JAB. DONFORD.	WILLIAM ⧣ BARQUITH.	L. S.
RICH. DONFORD.		

Family of Burges.

The family of Burges, of which several memorials may be seen in St. Mary's churchyard, was
early seated at Barnsley. It became extinct towards the latter part of the last century. Jonathan
was the last who had any issue; he died in the year
1749, leaving a son of the same name (a mercer at
Barnsley), George, who died young, Tobias, and
William. He had two daughters, one of whom,
Alice, married Thomas Watson of Bolton-upon-
Dearne, in 1771, and the other, Elizabeth, was wife
of Joseph Sanderson of Roystone.

About a century ago, John Lupton, a custom
weaver, and some relation to the Listers, had a shop
of several looms at Beevor, where he likewise
carried on bleaching, which could not be of much

K

HISTORY OF BARNSLEY.

Chap. VI.

Beevor.

extent, as the linen trade was then in its infancy. William Jackson afterwards purchased this property, erected the hall, and, in conjunction with James Lister, carried on business on an extensive scale, as will be seen by the following account of linen and cotton yarns and pieces bleached there under the superintendence of William Buckley their manager, extending over a period of twenty-five years, viz., from January 1, 1814, to December 31, 1838:—

Year.	Pieces of Linen.	Bundles of Cotton.	Bundles of Linen Yarn.	Packs of 240 Lbs.	Lbs.
1814	1,427	504	60,326	3,300	76
1815	3,441	950	74,412	4,541	141
1816	4,247	..	64,542	4,092	134
1817	7,235	..	90,342	6,084	42
1818	7,838	..	102,080	6,067	26
1819	9,059	464	98,995	6,269	125
1820	9,551	2,097	131,119	8,328	93
1821	9,640	667	160,646	9,648	193
1822	17,312	1,430	174,117	10,471	106
1823	13,399	1,817	158,354	9,570	111
1824	17,790	1,790	191,045	11,021	168
1825	19,351	1,266	186,441	10,441	164
1826	22,431	81	150,954	8,265	200
1827	16,498	541	166,669	8,591	206
1828	9,189	2,029	180,525	9,308	148
1829	9,761	2,021	120,374	6,135	131
1830	11,667	2,876	132,258	6,279	5
1831	11,898	1,471	117,491	5,281	11
1832	14,030	2,507	101,424	4,959	95
1833	17,883	4,119	130,427	5,663	7
1834	19,492	2,859	133,991	5,221	76
1835	16,343	1,902	153,725	5,378	97
1836	17,739	2,491	162,352	5,426	24
1837	14,434	834	78,195	3,023	200
1838	15,393	30	110,746	3,888	24
	317,048	34,746	3,231,554	167,259	203
	Cotton added..		34,746	1,447	180
	Total		3,266,300	168,707	143

THE HAMLET OF POGMORE.

147   Chap. VI.

On the death of William Jackson this estate
descended to his son Edward, who, dying in 1841,
bequeathed it to his wife, which caused expensive
law proceedings to be instituted by some of his
family; and after several years of litigation, a com-
promise was effected, Beevor sold, and George Jackson' of Barnsley became the purchaser. In consequence of the prevalence of smoke and dirt caused
by the rapid increase of the town, the place no
longer serves for bleach works.

Beevor.

POGMORE,

Pogmore.

now so well known throughout England from the
annual publication of the almanac bearing its
name, has its appellation from the nature of the soil,
and lies about a mile to the north-west of the town.
It. is inhabited chiefly by weavers and colliers.
There is mention of a family of the same name, but
it does not appear that the Pogmores had property
here.

William Pogmore ══ . . . .
|
Adam.

The hamlet of Pogmore can lay claim to high
antiquity, being mentioned in a charter of Walter,
one of the priors of Pontefract, about the reign of
John:—

Sciant presentes et futuri quod ego Walterus prior de Pontefract et ejusdem loci conventus dedimus concessimus et presenti carta nostra confirmavimus Ricardo Palmario fil. Galfridi
de Berneslay decem acras terræ de essartis in territorio de
Berneslay in loco quodam vocato Poggemor tenendas et habendas
sibi et heredibus suis de nobis libere et quiete in feodo et

Charter of
Walter, Prior
of Pontefract.

HISTORY OF BARNSLEY.

Chap. VI. 148

Pogmore.

Charter of Walter, Prior of Pontefract.

hereditate reddentibus inde nobis annuatim tres solidos pro omni servicio medietatem ad Pentecost et medietatem ad festum Sancti Martini occasione autem hujus tenementi idem Ricardus vel heredes sui nullam exigent communam in boscis nostris aut terris de Berneslay quam possimus dare aut vendere in essartis libere ubicunque volumus sine impedimento vel contradictione prefati Ricardi et heredum suorum et ne ipse Ricardus vel heredes sui in perpetuum contra tenorem hujus carta venire possint presenti quam penes nos retinemus sigillum suum pro se et heredibus suis apposuit. Ḥiis Testibus — Gilberto de Notton, Roberto de Berch, Jeremia de Thornhil, Rogero de Derton, Radulpho de Rupe, Ricardo de Marton, et aliis.

Translation.

TRANSLATION.

Know all men, now and hereafter, that we, Walter prior of Pontefract and the convent of the same place, have given, granted, and by our present charter confirmed, to Richard Palmer, son of Galfred de Berneslay, ten acres of land of essarts in the territory of Barneslay, in the place which is called Poggemor, to be held and had to him and his heirs of us, freely and quietly, in fee and inheritance, paying therefore to us yearly three shillings for all service, a moiety at Pentecost and a moiety at the feast of St. Martin. Nevertheless, on account of this tenement the same Richard or his heirs shall demand no common in our woods or lands of Berneslay, which we are able to give or sell in essarts freely to whoever we will without hindrance or objection by the aforesaid Richard and his heirs. WITNESSES: Gilbert de Notton, Robert de Berch, Jeremiah de Thornhill, Roger de Derton, Ralph de Rupe, Richard de Marton, and others.

Johnstone, writing in the year 1670, says, that "Pogmore consists of some farm houses in the township of Barnsley, part of it belonging to the heirs of Mr. William Wordsworth of Falthwaite, and some part to Mr. Hollingworth of Cheshire. The Ellisons (a family of gentry, whose descent is given in connection with the Rookes), resided here during the latter part of the seventeenth century."

THE OLD TOWN. 149 Chap. VI.

THE OLD TOWN.

Old Town.

In a bleak and exposed situation to the north-west of the town, at a short distance from Pogmore, may be seen a number of ancient houses constituting this hamlet, where, it is supposed, stood the Vill of *Berneslai*, mentioned in Domesday Book. We find the name is differently written in old charters, in which it occurs as Holdtona, Altona, and Oldton.

The more modern Barnsley, if it may be so termed, must have exceeded that of the Old Town in point of importance and population as early as the thirteenth century; this is evident from the site of the chapel, from the market and fair having been held there from time immemorial, and from the great number of benefactions to the monks, particulars of which have before been given.

KERESFORTH

Keresforth.

appears, along with Barnsley, in the Conqueror's survey; and was, at the period that record was prepared, of equal importance, if not, indeed, the most important of the two places.

There is nothing to lead us to suppose that this hamlet was included in the grant of Ralph to the house of St. John of Pontefract. It early became the seat of a family whose surname was derived from the place; and from the frequent mention of the Keresforths as witnesses and principals to early charters, it is evident that they were of some importance at the time those documents were prepared.

Chap. VI. 150 HISTORY OF BARNSLEY.

Keresforth.   Roger de Keresford attests a deed of the time of Henry III., and Thomas de Keresford appears as a witness to a charter executed about the year 1280.

In a list[1] of the names and arms of such knights and gentlemen of the county of York as served King Edward I. in Scotland and elsewhere, I find mentioned, amongst others:—

> " Keresford—Ar. a fesse battelie bet. 3 Butterflies, S."
> " Thwayts—B. a fesse bet. 3 Starrs of 6 points, Or."
> " Fleminge of Wath—Barrie of 6 A. and B. in chief 3 Mascles G."

As many grants have been recorded which relate to this family, it will suffice to add the following:

1369.   Richard de Keresforth is witness to a charter of Thomas Bailly of Barnsley, parson of the church of Hickleton, who gives to Dionysia, who was wife of Walter Page of Kexbrough, lands at that place. Dated at Kexbrough, the 19th Sunday after the feast of the pure and blessed Mary.

1417.   By deed, bearing date at Wigfall, in Worsbrough, on the feast of St. James the Apostle, Robert de Loyne of Worsbrough, grants to Richard Keresforth of Barnsley, and Thomas Evison, lands in Worsbrough. Witnesses: Sir Robert de Rockley, Knight, Robert his son, Robert Moncke, and Richard de Hill.

25th Hen. VI.   I have seen an indenture respecting property at Keresforth made between Thomas Wentworth of Doncaster, Esq., on the one part, and William Oxspring, Esq., and Richard Symmes on the other part, whereby the said Thomas agrees to let to farm, to the said William and Richard, and their assigns,

---

[1] Harl. MSS. 1487.

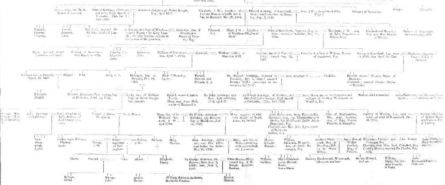

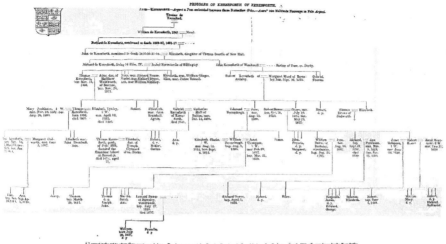

KERESFORTH. 151 Chap. VI.

Keresforth.

all the lands and tenements, rents, meadows, and pastures, with the appurtenances, which he had in Keresforth in Barnsley aforesaid, which formerly belonged to Sir William Dronsfield, Knight. To hold from the feast of St. Martin in winter then next ensuing for the term of twenty years, at a rent of sixteen shillings, payable at the feast of Pentecost and St. Martin in winter in two equal parts, with power to distrain in case of non-payment. Witnesses: Edward Haghton, Henry Croft, John Keresford, and Robert Fog.

This estate was for some time in the possession of the Cutlers, and afterwards belonged to Mr. Garnet, who disposed of it to the Armitages, who resided here at an ancient mansion known as Toad Hole, *alias* Keresforth Hall.[1] Part of this property, together with that held by the Keresforths, now belongs to Frederic William Thomas Vernon Wentworth, Esq. of Stainbrough.

Annexed is a pedigree of the family of Armitage, which is of great antiquity—the first on record being John Armitage of Wrigbowls, living in the time of Stephen.

THE CIVIL WARS — GARRISON AT BARNSLEY — AND ACCOUNT OF SOME EVENTS WHICH TOOK PLACE DURING THE SEVENTEENTH CENTURY.

Civil Wars. Garrison at Barnsley.

At the commencement of the Civil Wars the Earl of Newcastle, who was selected by his royal master to take the command of the Army of the North, established garrisons at Barnsley, Wakefield, and other places. Doncaster adhered to the King's

---

[1] About the year 1720, after an expensive lawsuit of twenty-two years, this estate was divided between John Armitage of Barnsley and William Collier of the same place. Armitage sold his share to the Earl of Strafford.

Chap. VI. 152   HISTORY OF BARNSLEY.

Civil Wars. party, while Rotherham and Sheffield took an opposite course. In the old castle at the latter place, a Parliamentary force was lodged, but in the year 1643, the Earl marching into this part, and the Sheffield garrison not being able to stand against him, fled into Derbyshire, and its place was supplied with a party of Royalists under Sir William Savile, who being otherwise engaged, empowered Major Beaumont to act in his stead. The Castle of Tickhill was entrusted to Major Monckton, and Sir Thomas Fane was made governor of Doncaster. The defeat of the royal army at the battle of Marston Moor was fatal to the King in this part; the Earl of Newcastle quitted the kingdom, when all the forces in South Yorkshire submitted to Major-General Crawford, who acted under the orders of the Earl of Manchester.

Soldiers were located at Barnsley as early as the year 1633. The subjoined account is taken from documents which relate to their drill, accoutrements, &c. :—

	s.	d.
Payde for they charge of trayning sogers at Ringstone Hill [1]	iiij	—

[1] Ringstone Hill appears to have been a place to which the militia also resorted for drill in after times. The high constable, in an order to the constables of Barnsley and other places, says, —" You are likewise to give notice to all p'sons charged with foote and armes within your constableries, belonging to Sr Thomas Osborne, that their souldiers appear at Ringstone Hill upon the twenty-sixte day of October by nine of the clocke in the forenoone, before Maior (Major) John Beverley, mustermaster for this county, to be mustered, or otherwise sende sixpence for each foot souldier, to be payde to the sayde mustermaster according to Act of Parliament, and by so doing theire appearance at this time may be excused. And you are to informe all principall bearers within your constabuleries that

THE CIVIL WARS. 153 Chap. VI.

	s.	d.
Payde Bagshaw for mendinge of muskets . . .	—	—
Layde downe for trayne sogers at Ringstone Hill .	xxx	ij
Payde Petter Sadler for dressing armer . . .	—	xvj
For half a lb. of gunpowder	—	viij

Soldiers' Drill, &c.

The military and inhabitants do not appear to have been on a friendly footing, for in August, 1641, a disturbance took place between the two parties, which resulted in the death of Gervase White, a cavalry officer. At the head of this fray was a person named Benton, who was committed to York on the 27th of the same month, but of his ultimate fate there is no account. The force stationed at Barnsley went to drill occasionally at Stainbrough; this would probably be at the request of Sir Gervase Cutler, who was a great Royalist, and took an active part in the defence of Pontefract Castle. He fell a martyr to his loyalty, and died before the surrender of that stronghold.

With respect to the training of soldiers at Stainbrough, the following is recorded :—

	s.	d.
For wages for soldyers when they went to traine .	iiij	—
And for carrieyinge theire armes to Stainber . .	—	vi
To Charles Hill for gunpother	—	x
And for match	—	ij
To the captaine for traineing	—	xvj

On the 1st of May, 1643, the following soldiers were buried at Barnsley: — "Thomas Carliel, William Dobson, and Luke Garfett."

In 1654, it was customary at Barnsley to pub-

Banns of Marriage.

they are desired to lay up and keepe the caps and coats provided for theire souldiers, yᵗ they may not be used at any other times than they are summoned to appeare with theire armes ; hereof you are not to faile, as you will answer the contrary. Dated the 17th October, 1665.—P. me, JOHN ADAMS."

Chap. VI.   154   HISTORY OF BARNSLEY.

lish banns of marriage in the market place for three successive market days.

Some bailiffs entered the premises of one John Elliot of Barnsley; he resisted, and was killed in the struggle. This took place in the month of August, 1670.

EXTRACTS FROM THE CHURCHWARDENS', OVERSEERS', AND CONSTABLES' ACCOUNTS OF THE SEVENTEENTH CENTURY.

Ancient Town's Accounts.

Disburses by me, Richard Oxley, since I came to be church-warden, and this laid forth at after 1622 :—

	s.	d.
Imprimis at Rotherham	iij	vi
For mendinge the locke of the church dore . .	—	iij
For fetcheinge of three loades of stones of the com-mon, and for two men's charges for helpeinge to leade them, and for leadeinge of j load of sand .	iij	—
Bestowed in wine of Mr. Micklethwayt, a preacher and beinge a stranger	—	x
For nayles, and for last nayles, and braggs for rails to the church yates	j	—
To Mr. Harberte, beinge pte of iijs. iiijd. bestowed on him, is	j	—
To Mr. Lawe, beinge pte of iijs. iiijd. which was given him	j	—
To Mr. Neweton, beinge halfe of iiijs. which was given him	ij	—
Payd to glaziers	j	ij
To the ringers the first daye	j	—
To the ringers the second time	j	ij
To a Welchman that had a passe to London to a brother of his there	—	ij
For a sacke of lime for the church . . .	j	v
Payd to Mr. Bamforth, chiefe constable, at twice .	ix	—
Payd to John Leake	—	vj
Bestowed on Mr. Rookes, preacher, in wine . .	—	x
To a marchant that had under sealle what losses hee had received by the Turkish pyratts . .	—	vj

The xxvij daye of October, 1622, was Mary Bartell and Margarett Norton, taken at Barnesley as wanderers, and punished accordinge to the statute.

TOWN'S ACCOUNTS. 155 Chap. VI.

Ancient Church-warden's Accounts.

Payde for dressinge of armor . . . . . — xij
Disbursed to Thomas Bagshaw for shaftinge the
   towne halberts, and for the pikes dressinge, and
   for nayles . . . . ij vii
Padè to John Ellis for carrieing of the croner's war-
   rant to three several townes . . . . — iiij
Payde to Mr. Burdet, beinge croner at Percifull
   Thrists, and to the jurye about Wells boye . . ij ix
In charges about Bartholomew Anderson, when he
   should have gone to the Castle of Yorke for his
   keepinge . . . . ij —
Given to one John Starr, a souldyer, wch had a passe — ij
Given the same daye to William Roggers for goinge
   with six wanderers to Ardsley . . . . — ij
And to Mr. Garnett for makinge them a pass . . — iiij
To Richard White for whipeinge (whipping) them
   accordinge to law . . . . . . — ij
For conveyinge five souldyers and a corporal, which
   lodged at Robert Bower's house, to Burton . . — vj
Given to Henrie Pettie, by Mr. Rockleye's order,
   and for the carrieinge of him awaye . . . iiij iiij
Given the same daye to one Abraham Kaye, a laime
   soudyer wch had a passe . . . . . — iij
Given to three souldyers and one woman which had
   a passe . . . . — viij
Given to a poore gentlewoman wch had a passe and
   two children . . . . — vj
Laide downe to Peter Robinson for his attendance
   about the graite, and for getting staples and nayles
   made for the same . . . . . . — vij
More for Peter Robinson for attending the commissioners and the troupers . . . . . — vj
To him more for attending the clarke of the market . . . . — viij
Given to one Antho. Robinson and William Berrine,
   two laime men wch had a lawfull passe . . — iiij
Given to one Mrs. Clifford, a minister's wife, which
   had a passe, and two small children travelling towards Ireland . . . . — ii

There is no date affixed to the above.

Chap. VI.   156   . HISTORY OF BARNSLEY.

Ancient Constable's Accounts.

Money layde downe by Edwarde Oxley for his constubbshipe, the 4th of December, 1632 :—

	s.	d.
Imp. They 6th of January pad. the high constubb .	—	—
They 8th of March	v	vj
The 19th April payd hym mor	iij	—
P^d they high constubb, by a warrant from my Lord Darcy, for thonend they 12 of December . .	ij	—
Leady downe for John Smythe for charges of keepinge of . . . . Yorke	v	—
Given to John Nuttye, an old man 60 years of age, who we sent by passe to Selbye	—	ij
Given to William White, who we sent by passe to Snayth	—	ij
Pade for keepinge of Sowden boy in the grate with meate and drinke 7 days	j	vj
Pade for carrieng of him to the House of Correction	—	viij
Gave Marye Carter, who stoole a silver spoone from Jarvis Donford of Barnsley, and was sent to the House of Correction, for which carriage and general charges while she remainde with me . .	—	xij
Given to one Robert Robley of Newcastle, travelling to London by passe and letter of testimoniale .	—	iiij
Given to one Dorman Thirlfield of Bilbraye, in the kingdom of Irelande, havinge been at his Majestie for letters of packet to my Lord Deputie of Ireland, given to his reliefe in his travel . . .	—	iiij
Given to one Mary Brown of Bilbraye, in the kingdom of Ireland, having been at his Majesty's .	—	iiij
Given to a souldyer	—	ij
Given to one John Davis, havinge served in the low countrye, and was to travil to Grayridge, in Westmorland	—	ij
Given to one Catherine Brown and Ellen Brown, whose husbands where taken captive in Turkey, having taken from them by the Turks a ship called the Trinitie, belonging to in Ireland, to the value of £13	—	iiij
Given to Edward Wood for whiping of three wanderers sent to their dwelling place by Sir George Plint and Mr. Rockley	—	iiij

Feb. 16, 1633.

TOWN'S ACCOUNTS.

157 · Chap. VI.

Ancient Constable's Accounts.

	s.	d.
Given to a pore man, his wife, and a child, who were to travil into Cumberland, for reliefe towards his losses sustained by shipreck, towards their lodgings	—	iiij
Given to three souldiers whose certificat wher scene and allowed by Sir John Jackson[1] and Mr. West .	—	iij
Given to a souldier who wer to travile to Ratchdill .	—	ij
Given to two poore men who had licence from the Lord Deputie of Ireland to seek after one Dudley, who had received of them a sum of money for his Ma$^{tie's}$ use, and he failed therein in the payment thereof to their undoeing	—	iiij
Given to Margaret Jager, who we sent by pass to . . . . . in Duesburie p'ish, towards her lodginge	—	iij
Given for wipeinge of two wandering persons, who were sent by pass to their dwellynge, the one of them sent to Almondburie, and the other to the countie of Derbie, and for their passe . . .	—	iiij
Paid to James Losh for the halfe parte of roofing .	j	iij
Paid to Thomas Bagshaw for dressing one of the town halbards	—	x
More for oil for rubbing of them	—	j
Given to a poore man, his wife, and a child, being sent by passe from Wesbro towards Richmond	—	iij
Paid for two boards and nayles for mendinge of the grate	—	xj
Paid for a bill of indictment against Thomas Charlesworth	—	xij
Paid for a horse goinge to Bargh with a cripple and her brother, who were sent by pass to Cumberland, and given to them ij d.	—	vj
Given to one James Hamblton coming forth of Ireland and traviling to his Matie, under two justices of peace hands in Ireland, who had his house and barns with al his goods burnt by rebels in Ireland, to the value of £500, besides had his wlfe, 1 childe,		

[1] Sir John Jackson was treasurer for lame soldiers, and represented Pontefract in Parliament, being elected in the years 1624, 1625, 1626, and 1629.

Chap. VI. 158 **HISTORY OF BARNSLEY.**

Ancient Constable's Accounts.

s. d.

and 2 servants burnt to ashes, wth fearfull act the rebels did to him in regard he was high constable in Ireland, and by comision from the Lord President had lattlie before that tyme taken six rebels of their companie who had burnt the sheriff's house. and the sheriffe himselfe, and after burnt the minister's house and killed the minister . — xij

Given to one William Croham, who had a wife and 5 small children, latlie lived in . . . . . in Irelan, being a pettie constable there, having received a warrant from the Lord President for the apprehension of certain rebels, who, according to the sence thereof, gote some companie and apprehended thre of them, and carried them to the jaile, and the rest of their confederats on August xx^th, 1633. In the evening, this constable bene at the generall sessions, and his wife at his mother's, cam onto his house, set it on fire, and burnt all his dwelling houses and goods, to the vallew of £400, as appears by certificate under the hands of three justices of peace in Ireland . . . — vj

Given to Edward Stewart, Gent., and his wife, who were travling towards London, whose dwelling were in Scotland, and being hie cunstable for the hundreth by commission arrested thre rebels, and carrieing them to the jaile, the rest of their confederats cam to this high constable's house in the neightime, burnt his house and houseing wth other goods, to the vallew of nyne score pounds, and in the same fier burnt this high constable's mother-in-law and two of his servants to ashes, they being in the same house, as appears under thre justices of the peace hands in Scotland . . . . . — vj

Given to Jane Jackson and Frances Jackson, who had grette losse by fyer, to value of £100 . . — vj

Payde Christopher Kingstone for goinge wth me to Rockley 2 days . . . . — vj

Given to a gent. that came from Boheamea wich could speak nothing but Layttin . . . — xij

For keepeinge Rickery that was taken upon suspeckt at Pogmore 4 dayes . . . . , . — xij

TOWN'S ACCOUNTS. 159 Chap. VI.

	s.	d.
Given to a gent. who served under Marquis Hambleton	—	iiij
Payde for they charges of thre men and ther horses for goinge to Hallyfax about Queen's B.	xxx	iij
Given to Michell Wourmwell and Michell Houtton, robed by Donkyrk	—	iiij

Ancient Constable's Accounts.

Richard Haslam, churchwarden, payde to the high constable at Barnsley sessions	ij	iij
Layde downe for a letter of request for one Francis Colleyer of Ponteffract Park, who had his house borned	—	xij
Rec. of collecktors for repayre of allmes howses	viij	viij
And I bestowed of allmes howses	xj	ij

Churchwarden's Accounts. 1634.

Payd to the post mester the 12th of Jully	xiij	iiij
Payd for the charges of man's meyt and horse meyt, and for the carts that went to Pomfret	x	—
Payd to the high constabb at Pomfryt Sheshons	ij	iij
Payd to Edmund Rogers for shay rent	—	—
Spent when Dockter Edsell came to towne	—	viij
Leayde downe to Randle to by him a sheayrt wth	—	vj

1635.

Martyn Clarke's, constubb, bill :—

Constable's Accounts. 1636.

Layde dowe to the high constabb, in p^{te}, for 2 warrants, for bridge and for gunpowder	xv	—
For a head piece wch came from Yorke	iij	iiij
For dressinge towne harnish	iiij	ij
To Ralph Ryton for bringing the towne pike from Yorke	—	vj
To John Truelove for bread and drinke and lodgeinge for 3 lame souldyers which had a passe	—	vj
Given to a poore gentlewoman, her name was Ellen Wade, with 5 small children, which had a passe	—	xij
Paide to George Swinden for mendinge the pinfould locke, and for nailes about the dore	—	vj
Given to one Edward Sikes which had a passe	—	ij
And for a horse for carrieing him to Bargh	—	iiij
Given to Henry Colyer for bidding the watch	—	viij
For my charges goinge to Penistone for the payeing of the second two entire subsidies to Edward Hinchliffe, col.	j	vj
And for a horse and a quittance	—	iiij

Chap. VI. 160 · HISTORY OF BARNSLEY.

	s.	d.

Ancient Constable's Accounts.

Given to one Mr. Vawham, servant of a foot company under the command of Sr Thomas Glenham, with a poore woman, his wife and a childe . . — ix

A bill of disboursement for the towne of Barnsley for the yeare of our Lord God, 1643 :—

	s.	d.

Imp. Fór my charges for myself and my horse to Bawtry conserning the Kinge's carriges . . . v iij

My charges for goinge to Worsbroughe about the death of George Woodhead . . . . iij jx

Layd downe for preferring an inditement and p'secuting against one Mr. White's death a souldier to Francis Scamaden . . . . . vj —

Churchwarden's Accounts.

Account of what money I have dysbursed this yeare for my office of churchwarden :—

	s.	d.

Imp. two lockes for registre chyst . . . . — xij

It cost me about mesuringe glas . . . — xviij

Payde for a spayde for church . . . . — xv

Payde Jervis Wright more for glas . . . — xviij

Payde for gatheringe oft leaydes and in churchyeard — vj

P{d} John Burges for worke about bellhouse . . v —

P{d} ringers the 5 of November . . . . vij —

They 2nd of December payd for the mynister's dyners at Mr. Dannielles . . . . . iij —

P{d} John Burges when he layde flages . . — xiij

Lent Mr. Wyld when he went to London . . jx —

Spent about goinge to Brerely about joustices . — xij

Payde neller wife . . . . — ij

	xxxij	—

Allowing me for last yeare . . . . xlij —

Rec. of this by Robert Bower by a fagot of styl, price is . . . . xxxiv —

Rest is due to me for last yeare . . . viij —

Constable's Account.

Constable's Account :—

	s.	d.

Spent goinge to joustices with Francis Tomson to Mr. Darcy Wentworth . . . . . — viij

ANCIENT TOWN ACCOUNTS. 161 Chap. VI.

Church-
wardens'
Accounts.

Charges laid out by Robert Bridghouse, one of the churchwardens for this present yeare, 1647 :—

	£	s.	d.
Maij yᵉ 17, given to two men that came with lettʳ of request from justices . . .	00	01	00
July 30, for charges layd out at the taking upe of yᵉ third bell that the bras might bee taken out and a newe one cast	00	00	08
July, att Routherham sessions, to yᵉ high coun- stabb. for yᵉ one halfe of yᵉ money pennson to Yorke	00	03	04
Given to William Ribchester wife in their ex- tremitye	00	01	00
Payd John Bradley for head robbs, September yᵉ 8ᵗʰ	00	09	04
Given to Thomas Kinchin att the request of some well-affected people, in a letter of re- quest, Septembr 22ⁿᵈ, 1647 . . .	00	01	06
Laid forth to Thomas Bagshawe for casting yᵉ bras to ley yᵉ bell in, with cost at yᵉ preesing of it, September 27, 1647	00	11	02
Given to a poore woman, with a lettʳ of re- quest, September 28, 1647 . . .	00	00	06
For charges to a poore minister in his lodgeing and diet	00	01	06
The thirde of November, given to some Irrish people	00	00	06
For staiveing yᵉ church ladder . . .	00	00	10½
For ringing yᵉ fift of November . . .	00	10	06
For a quart of wine, given to Mr. Burton yᵉ day he preached at oʳ church	00	00	08
Payd to Thomas Bagshawe for mendᵍ yᵉ clocke making a barre to yᵉ axeltree of yᵉ finger .	00	03	00
For an hower glasse	00	01	00
Payde to a Scotsman called Montgomery who had a passe	00	01	00
Payd to one John Massie, a souldier that cam with a letter of request	—	—	—
Payd for a bell rope, which cost . . .	00	03	04
Payd in charges of yᵉ officer on Thursday in Easter week	00	01	06
Payd to Thomas Oxley for wine att Ester, being yᵉ sacramᵗ wine	00	18	02½

L

Chap. VI. 162 HISTORY OF BARNSLEY.

Church-
wardens'
Accounts.

	£	s.	d.
Payd to Garvis Donford for his bill of charges at Easter	00	19	08
Payd Thomas Bagshawe, bill at Easter . .	00	05	10
Payd to Richard Hodgson wife for whiping of Dogges	00	02	00
Payd to Mr. Wild for his writting of oʳ accounts at Easter	00	02	00
Payd to Crawshawe for a bell stringe . .	00	04	02
Payd to Francis Follhirlee, a souldier . .	00	01	02
Payde yᵉ high counstubb. for qurter . .	00	04	06
Payd to yᵉ high counstubb. at yᵉ last cessions at Duncaster	02	02	00
Charges yᵉ 25 day of November . . .	00	04	10
Payd yᵉ Clarke for covring of 3 greaves .	00	01	00
Payd to Crawshawe for mendinge the bell strings	00	03	08
Given to an Irishman, whose wiffe lye in of child-bearing at Wilson's	00	02	00
Payd Robert Wood, bill	00	11	02
Payd to Thomas Chappell for a wine coppe fʳ church	00	02	04
Payd to young Dollerffe for mendinge yᵉ greater dore	00	02	08
Payd to Mr. Wilde for writtying att Easter and given to yᵉ poor	00	05	00

Accounts of James Allen, churchwarden, 1679 :—

	s.	d.
Impᵐⁱˢ to a letter of request from Royston . . .	iij	vj
At yᵉ visitations	xj	vj
Swearing yᵉ churchwardens and delivering in the presentments to Mr. Holmes	vij	ij
At yᵉ procesion	viij	—
To yᵉ ringers, May yᵉ 29	vj	viij
To yᵉ archbishop	v	—
Richᵈ Uttley's letter of request . . .	ij	—
To a poore minister	iij	vj
For wine at Michaelmas	jx	—
For wine at Christmas	vij	jv

MINERALS AND MANUFACTURES.   163   Chap. VI.

IRON AND COAL.   Iron.

It appears early to have been known that iron ore existed in this neighbourhood. Adam *filii Rogeri dispensatoris de Berneslay* mentions, amongst other lands which he gives to the monks at Bernsley, *(" quinque acræ de essarto juxta Forgiam Radulfi clerici"),* "five acres of essart near the forge of Ralph the clerk." The forge here mentioned might, however, be nothing more than a smith's shop. This deed belongs to the twelfth century.

In another record, of the year 1284, the tithe of iron mines is noticed. The quantity necessary at this early period must have been little, comparatively speaking, if the then requirements of the population be taken into consideration.

With respect to another valuable mineral (coal),   Coal. which now forms such an important addition to the traffic, and to which the present prosperous state of the town and neighbourhood is in a great measure attributable; this cannot claim as high antiquity in regard to its discovery. Subjoined is an extract from a court roll of a court held at Darton in the 1st Hen. V., and though this does not refer to Barnsley, still it may not be out of place:—*" Item dicunt quod Johannes Dodeson (iiijd.), Johannes Frith (iiijd.), Johannes Betram (iiijd.), Thomas (iiijd.) frater ejus sine licencia domini et Adam Lawton (iiijd.), perquisiverunt carbones infra vastum domini Ideo quisque eorum in mia. Item present. quod Willielmus West perquisivit carbones infra vastum domini Ideo ipse in mia."*

From this it appears that John Dodeson, John Frith, John Betram, Thomas his brother, and Adam Lawton sought for coals at Darton beneath the lord's waste without his (the lord's) consent, for which

Chap. VI. 164 HISTORY OF BARNSLEY.

Coal.

they were fined as in the sums set against their names. The jurors also found that William West sought for coals under the lord's waste.

In another record of a court held at the same place, A.D. 1624, they also present Michael Wentworth, Esq. (xxxixs. xid.),[1] because he did not fill up nor cover the old coal pits by him dug on the commons of Darton township, as he was enjoined by penalty at the last tourn imposed on him, to the great danger of the passers by there.

There appears no mention of coal having been got at Barnsley previous to the middle of the seventeenth century. This was no doubt attributable to the plentiful supply of wood with which the neighbourhood formerly abounded. Not that the inhabitants were so long ignorant of the existence of this mineral or of its value, but wood being more easily procured, and our ancestors not having the advantages of the mechanical contrivances by which coal is now so readily won, we can at once excuse them from putting forth great efforts for its acquisition. Consequently it was only obtained where it lay near the surface; and when it became necessary, from the increase of the population, to burn coal, means were found to obtain it. In 1650, it appears to have been pretty generally used at Barnsley. A lease of coal, under a close of land called Coal Pit Close, part of Keresforth farm, was granted in 1693 to Abraham Rock for one year, at the rent of £17; mines of coal under this land having been granted unto the lessors by William Beaumont of Darton, yeoman, in 1675.

[1] This was probably the highest penalty which could be inflicted for the offence.

MINERALS AND MANUFACTURES. 165 Chap. VI.

Coal.

By reason of the prevalence of gas in coal mines, explosions frequently occur, which are sometimes attended with great sacrifice of life. It appears that our ancestors suffered from accidents of this nature, for an explosion of fire-damp took place in a coal pit at Barnsley on the 11th of July, 1672, which resulted in the death of one James Townend.

In 1716, the trustees of the Shaw lands leased the same to John Shippen for a period of four years, to sink a coal pit, he paying annually the sum of twenty-five pounds.

There has been a great alteration in the price of coal. In 1745 it realised one shilling per ton; in the year 1789 two shillings and six pence were paid for the same quantity; while at the present day the prices, at the pit, for house coal, range from six to seven shillings per ton. The bed from which these coals are taken is of a thickness of nine feet and upwards of mineable coal, and at a depth of from one to two hundred yards from the surface of the ground. The yield of the mines at Barnsley and the neighbourhood is immense, many thousand tons being daily taken therefrom; the greater part of which is sent off by railway and boat.

Though a charter for a market and fair to be held at Barnsley had been granted, A.D. 1249, it appears from the *Nonarum Inquisitiones*, of the reign of Edward III. (upwards of a century after), that there was no merchant at Barnsley, nor any person in the parish of Silkstone engaged otherwise than in agricultural pursuits.

THE WIRE TRADE

Wire Trade.

is said to be of great antiquity here. We are informed that upwards of two centuries ago Barnsley excelled every other place in the kingdom for the

Chap. VI. 166   HISTORY OF BARNSLEY.

Wire Trade. manufacture of this article, which was mainly attributable to the ingenuity of the workmen, combined with the material used, from which two sorts were made, viz., hard wire, which served for the teeth of cotton and wool cards and fish hooks; and the softer description, used for stocking-frame needles. William Bower of Barnsley, wiredrawer, and Thomas Marshall of Barnsley, yeoman, are mentioned in a deed of the year 1620. Bower was carrying on the business in 1650. Of others engaged in the wire trade in the middle of the seventeenth century, may be mentioned Leonard Bower, Richard Ashton, Godfrey Ashton, Simon Parker, Thomas Tinker, Thomas Booth, and Edward Brooksbank. At the head of these firms was William Bower, whose mother was a Keresforth, as will be seen by the pedigree of that family.

Toward the close of the eighteenth century the wire trade began to exhibit signs of decay. The following were the principal manufacturers in 1789:—William Ellis, John and Thomas Hill, Thomas Liddall, sen., Thomas Liddall, jun., Godfrey Mason, John Mason, Thomas Mason, and John Rushforth. There is now only one manufactory of this article in the town.

Tradesmen's Tokens.

BARNSLEY TRADESMEN'S TOKENS.

Obverse.—THOMAS BROWNLEY IN * The Ironmongers'[1] Arms, between T. B. E.

Reverse.—BARNSLEY. IN. YORKSHEER * In the field, HIS HALF-PENY.

[1] Argent on a chevron gules, three swivels or (the middle one paleways, the other two with the line of the chevron) between three steel gads, azure.

MANUFACTURES. 167 Chap. VI.

Tradesmen's
Tokens.

Obverse.—HENRY. GRENE. IN * The Grocers'[1] Arms.
Reverse.—BARNESLEY. IIIS. HALF-PENY * In the field H.^G·M.

Obverse.—IOHN. SMITH. IN. BARNSLEY * . . . .
Reverse.—HIS. HALFPENY. 1666 * In the field. I.^S·R.

Obverse.—FRNCIS. VSHER. OF * ½ beneath a Talbot passant.
Reverse.—BARNSLYE. MERCER * In the field F.^V·H.

Obverse.—PAYABLE AT JACKSON AND LISTERS WAREHOUSE.
BARNSLEY * PENNY TOKEN.
Reverse.—In the field, a weaver working at his loom.

LINEN MANUFACTURE.

Linen Trade.

The present prosperous state of the town is in a great measure attributable to the linen manufacture, which was introduced in the year 1744 by William Wilson from Cheshire, a member of the Society of Friends. The business must have in creased rapidly, for we find that in the year 1789 the following firms had sprung into existence:— John Wilson (nephew of the founder), John Greenwood, Pickering and Jenkinson, Joseph Beckett, Nath. Dearman, Edward Taylor, and George Scales. At that period 500 looms were at work. The goods then produced were of a coarse description, such as sheetings, ducks, towels, &c.

About the year 1810 the manufacturers turned their attention to the making of finer and more expensive fabrics, comprising broad sheetings, damask, diapers, and huckabacks; and the production here surpassed those of Scotch and Irish make, by reason of the superior quality of the yarns. The Barnsley ducks were formerly used for smock frocks. This article, however, is partially superseded by the drabbet, which is cheaper and much

[1] Argent a chevron gules between nine cloves sable, three, three, and three.

Chap. VI. 168 HISTORY OF BARNSLEY.

Linen Trade. more suitable for the purpose. Goods of the latter description are now woven by power, as the small remuneration obtained for the making of this article by hand would not support the poor weaver and his family. Plain drills afterwards constituted another addition to the trade, and about thirty years ago some of the larger houses began to manufacture fancy drills, in which an extensive business is done by four of the leading firms, by whom they are exported to the Italian, Spanish, American, and other foreign markets. The manufacture of fancy woollens has recently been added by Messrs. Charles Tee and Son.

The value of the goods annually manufactured at Barnsley is estimated at from one to two million pounds sterling. There are about four thousand hand-looms in operation in the vicinity, and near one thousand power-looms. The goods now made embrace almost every variety.

Bleaching has also been carried on at Barnsley and in the neighbourhood for more than a century, and furnishes work for several hundred persons.

Weavers' Strikes. In common with all other trades in which a large number of the same class of workmen are brought together, the linen business has at various periods undergone some serious stoppages by reason of disagreements between the manufacturers and their weavers respecting wages.. The weavers struck for an advance on the 28th of September, 1818, but after a space of three months returned to their employment on the old terms. On the 1st of May, 1823, they again left off work in consequence of the masters having taken from them a perquisite known as the "fent," consisting of one yard of cloth

MANUFACTURES. 169 Chap. VI.

Weavers'
Strikes.

at the end of each warp, which had been allowed to the workman. But the most serious and protracted of these unfortunate occurrences was originated by the manufacturers attempting a reduction of wages in June, 1829. This strike continued for five months, during which time many acts of violence were committed in the town and neighbourhood. On the 14th of October a large mob went to Keresforth, the residence of Mr. Thomas Jackson, one of the principal manufacturers, and after breaking the windows and furniture, set the house on fire. Mr. Jackson appears to have been the object of their revenge; and though he and Mrs. Jackson were both[1] in the house during these proceedings, they fortunately had time to find a hiding place to elude the infuriated multitude.

Some soldiers were sent for, but before they arrived at Keresforth the rioters had left, and were met on their return to Barnsley by the military, when some of the principal ringleaders were taken into custody, committed to take their trial at the ensuing York assizes, and two of them were sentenced to fourteen years' transportation, which was afterwards commuted to seven years.

[1] Mr. and Mrs. Jackson were secreted in a closet, and had with them a small dog, which was with great difficulty kept from barking. Had they been discovered, no doubt they would have been murdered.

Chap. VII.   170   HISTORY OF BARNSLEY.

CHAPTER VII.

Silkstone
Church and
Barnsley
Chapel.

THE CHURCH OF SILKSTONE AND CHAPEL OF
BARNSLEY.

Where the religious houses possessed property, we find that it sometimes fell to their lot to make provision for the spiritual wants of the inhabitants of the place. It has already appeared that the town of Barnsley was given to the monks of Pontefract about the middle of the twelfth century. From there being no mention made of a chapel in the charter of Ralph de Caprecuria, nor yet in the confirmation deed of Jordan his son, it is probable that no place of this description existed here at that time; its erection may be referred to within a few years after the monks came into possession.

The earliest account of a chapel occurs in Pope Celestine's Bull confirming the donations to the monastery of Pontefract, mentioning *(inter alia)* the church of Silkstone, the church of Bernesleye, with the chapels, &c., to the same churches belonging. Also the "vills*(inter alia)*of Bernesleia and Dodwrde" with the appurtenances. It has been asserted that the monks found a chapel here; but there is nothing in the deeds before mentioned to bear out that supposition, for in grants of property to religious houses of the same extent as that acquired at Barnsley,

SILKSTONE CHURCH AND BARNSLEY CHAPEL. 171 Chap. VII.

Silkstone Church.

there has invariably been some mention made in the charter of the donor respecting the church or chapel, if such really existed.

The step taken by the monks in this direction would no doubt be an acceptable one to the inhabitants of the town, if the great distance from the parish church, to which they had previously to resort for religious instruction, be taken into consideration. The same house had acquired the mother church at least half a century before the town of Barnsley passed into their possession. Swein, the son of Ailric, was the benefactor. Subjoined is a translation of the charter which refers to that transaction, together with the confirmatory one of Adam. Copies of these rare documents are in the Pontefract Chartulary, in the possession of Mr. Wentworth:—

Charter of Swein the son of Ailric.

"To our perpetual father, Thurstan the archbishop, and to all the sons of Holy Church, Swein the son of Ailric sends greeting:

" I will that all men know, now and hereafter, that I, in remission of all my sins and for the salvation of my soul, and of all my ancestors who have passed from this world, and for the souls of my heirs, have given, by this my charter and seal, to the church of Saint John of Pontefract, and the monks who serve God there, the church of Silkstone and six bovates of land in the same vill, and with all things which belong to the same ; and the chapel of Cawthorne, with two bovates of land in the same vill, with two parts of all the tithes of my lordship, viz., of sheaves, in pure and perpetual alms, so that in the aforesaid church and chapel

Silkstone Church.

Chap. VII. 172 HISTORY OF BARNSLEY.

Charter of Swein the son of Ailric.

I have retained nothing to myself or any of my heirs; and if any who hold of me any alms in fee, wish to have the same made free, I grant it. To these gifts I call God to witness, and these men are witnesses — Godwyn, priest and parson of Darfield; Ulf, priest and parson of Adwick; Dolfin de Ulflay; Saxi de Horbiri, and many others."

Adam, son of Swein, who founded the priory of Bretton, confirmed this gift, as appears by a deed in the Chartulary of Pontefract, of which the following is a translation :—

Charter of Adam son of Swein.

"Know all men, present and to come, that I, Adam the son of Swein, the son of Ailric, for the love of God and for the salvation of my soul, and of my father and of my mother, and of all my ancestors and heirs, have given, granted, and by this my present charter have confirmed, to the church of Saint John the Evangelist at Pontefract, and the monks serving God there, in pure and perpetual alms, without any reservation to me or my

Silkstone Church.

heirs, the church of Silkstone, with six bovates of land, with the appurtenances in the same vill, adjacent to the same church, which my father gave to them, in pure and perpetual alms, with the chapels, and lands, and tithes, and with everything thereto belonging; and likewise the chapel of my father at Cawthorne, which my said father had heretofore given to them, with two bovates of land, and the appurtenances, in the same vill, and with two parts of all the tithes of the dominions of my father, which are expressed by the certain names—Cawthorne, Kexbrough, Gunthwaite, Peniston, Wors-

SILKSTONE CHURCH AND BARNSLEY CHAPEL. 173 Chap. VII.

brough, Carlton, Newhill, Brierley, Walton, Mensthorp, Wrangbrook, Middleton, viz., of sheaves, and with everything thereto appertaining. Moreover, I, Adam the son of Swein, devote, and from the feast of Hilary have granted, given, set over, and by this my present charter have confirmed, and have procured to be confirmed by our lord King Henry, to the aforesaid church of Saint John of Pontefract, and to the monks serving God there, that house of the Blessed Mary Magdalene of Lunda, which I have founded on my patrimony for the purposes of religion, with all the lands to the aforesaid house belonging, viz., Bretton, Newhall, Raynebergh, Lyntwayt, and whatsoever in Brainton, and whatsoever I have in Dirnam and Staynclyf, as far as Meresbrick and the mill of Dyrne, and Lunda in Cumberlanda, and the chapel of the Blessed Apostle Andrew near to Culcait, with all their appurtenances, to the use of the holy monks of Pontefract, who in the aforesaid house shall regularly serve God for ever, for the souls of my father and my mother, and for the salvation of my soul, and of all my ancestors and heirs, as a holy monastical institution of the order of Cluny and of their mother church of Pontefract. Adam, now prior of Pontefract, when he shall have departed from thence into the house of Lunda, shall continue custos and prior during all the time of his life with the monks of Pontefract sent there. On every vacancy the prior and monks of Pontefract shall substitute others who are fit in his place to regularly celebrate Divine service; nevertheless, the aforesaid house of Lunda shall render to its mother church of Pontefract every year, and for ever, one

Charter of Adam the son of Swein.

Lunda or Monk Bretton Priory.

Chap. VII.   174   HISTORY OF BARNSLEY.

Charter of Adam the son of Swein. mark of silver for an acknowledgment. I have also granted, given, and by this my present charter confirmed, to the aforesaid church of Saint John of Pontefract, and to the monks serving God there, sixty acres of my land in Calthorn, in pure and perpetual alms, &c. These being witnesses," &c.

Appropriation of the Church of Silkstone and its Chapels to Pontefract Priory. The church of Silkstone was appropriated to the priory of Pontefract in the year 1284, as appears by a document in the Chartulary of that house, which is to the following effect :—

" The ordination of the church of Silkstone made by William, Archbishop of York, at Thorpe, near York, in the eve of Palm Sunday.

" In the name of God, in the same year, the prior and convent of Pontefract, of the order of Cluny, by the right aforesaid, also of Silkstone, appear to me here, and also all right which they might have in the above-mentioned church, with all its rights and appurtenances, to our ordination have conceded, subjected, and submitted purely, simply, and absolutely.

" WE, WILLIAM, by Divine permission, Archbishop of York, Primate of England, by the grace of Holy God, deliberation having been had more sufficiently in council aforesaid, have thus directed and faithfully ordained, that in the church of Silk-

Vicarage of Silkstone. stone there shall be a holy perpetual vicarage of collation, of which we institute ourselves and our successors for ever. The holy vicarage shall consist of the under written, to wit, that whensoever the same vicar, by us or our successors, shall be instituted, he may have all the demesne lands, cultures, and meadows, with all their rights and

SILKSTONE CHURCH AND BARNSLEY CHAPEL. 175 Chap. VII.

appurtenances, and whether in pasture, grazing land, plains, or moors, with other advantages. The same vicar may have all that farm house the dwelling of the rector, with the granges, woods (or thickets) sheepfolds, fish ponds, warrens, and all their appurtenances. So also, the same vicar may have all the tithes of all sheaves of the towns of Silkstone and of Hoyland, with the tithes of the parish of Silkstone with its chapels, except the tithes of the farm of the aforesaid prior and convent of Pontefract at Barnsley. So also he may have the tithes of all the mills of the whole of the above-mentioned parish with its chapels, except the mills of the aforesaid prior and convent at Barnsley. So also the same vicar may have the lands and rents, with all their rights and appurtenances, of all the tenements of the church of Silkstone with its chapels, except the tenements at Barnsley, with their lands, to the rectory of the church of Silkstone formerly belonging. So also, he may have the tithes of iron mines, and all other personal tithes, pensions, with all tithes of wool and lambs, foals, pigs, calves, and brood geese, hens, eggs, white line and hemp, and all mortuaries, both quick and dead, with all other kinds of oblations, principal and others whatsoever, and all other obventions at the altar of the church of Silkstone, with its chapels, whensoever and in whatsoever name, with their appurtenances; all which things above mentioned we have perpetually assigned to the said vicarage, and to every vicar there by us or our successors, with full right to be instituted.

"Also, we have ordained, and in ordaining we have appointed, that the aforesaid prior and convent of Pontefract, and their successors for ever,

Chap. VII. 176   HISTORY OF BARNSLEY.

Silkstone Church and its Chapels.

shall have the church of Silkstone, with its chapels, and whatever to the same church and chapels belong, in perpetuity, except the vicarage and its portions or endowments as above mentioned and distinguished, which church of Silkstone, with its chapels, we have appropriated for the same for ever. So we have ordered that the same vicar himself, of the church of Silkstone and its chapels, by himself and other sufficient ministers in due and accustomed number, shall make safe all the books, ornaments, and lights of the church, which he shall provide, and shall sustain all things necessary for the reparation of the church and chancel of the church, and the chapels unto it belonging, and the extraordinary burthens shall be divided between the vicar and the prior; and the ordinary burthen shall be borne by the vicar, who shall answer for the archdeacon's procuration, which the said vicar shall sustain and support."

Rectory of Silkstone.

The annexed are particulars of the rectory of Silkstone, as the same appear in the Chartulary of Pontefract :—

	s.	d.
Tithes of Calthorne per annum .	xxx	—
Doddewrde	xv	vj
Staynbrugh	xvi	vj
Thurgerland	xvij	vj
Westbretton	—	—
Bernesley	xxiv	vj
Wrangbrocke and Brerelay	ij	vj½
Wirkesburg	xxv	—
Karleton .	x	—
Walton .	xxiv	—
Penigston	x	iiij
Newhall .	viij	—
Cumberwrd	x	—

CHURCH OF SILKSTONE. 177 Chap. VII.

			s.	d.	
Stanlowe	. . . . . .	.	iij	vj	Rectory.
Mottrum .	. . . . . .	.	xx	—	
The tenants of the church in Bernesley	.	.	ij	vj	

While speaking of the church of Silkstone,[1] an account of some arms and inscriptions which formerly existed there, may not be out of place. These notes were taken in the year 1629 : —

Arms and Inscriptions.

North Quire.

WODEROVE—Argent, a chevron between three crosses, gules.

EVERINGHAM—Quarterly, argent and gules, a bend, gules.

WADISLEY—Argent, a cross, sable. In the sinister quarter a martlet, gules.

A man with a shield of arms upon him, viz. :—

EVERINGHAM—Quarterly, or and gules, a bend, gules.

Behind him six sons, with a woman and three daughters behind her; under written—

"𝔓𝔯𝔞𝔭 𝔭𝔢 𝔣𝔬𝔯 𝔱𝔥𝔢 𝔰𝔬𝔲𝔩𝔰 𝔬𝔣 𝔥𝔢𝔫𝔯𝔭 𝔈𝔟𝔢𝔯𝔦𝔫𝔤𝔥𝔞𝔪 𝔞𝔫𝔡 𝔬𝔣 𝔐𝔞𝔯𝔧𝔬𝔯𝔦𝔞 𝔚𝔞𝔡𝔦𝔰𝔩𝔢𝔭 𝔥𝔦𝔰 𝔴𝔦𝔣𝔢, 𝔡𝔞𝔲𝔤𝔥𝔱𝔢𝔯 𝔞𝔫𝔡 𝔥𝔢𝔦𝔯 𝔬𝔣 𝔍𝔬𝔥𝔫 𝔚𝔞𝔡𝔦𝔰𝔩𝔢𝔭."

Cut on a Pew in the same Quire.

EVERINGHAM OF STAINBROUGH — Quarterly, argent and gules, a bend, gules.

WADISLEY—Argent, a cross sable; a martlet gules, in the sinister quarter.

On the same Pew.

EVERINGHAM—Party, per pale; quarterly, argent and gules; paled with Burton; argent, a bend wavy, gules.

In the Middle Quire Window.

DARCY—Azure, three cinquefoils between seven cross crosslets, argent.

[1] Agnes, the widow of John de St. Quintin, Knight, was buried in the quire of the church of Silkstone, near the sepulchre of John Wassard, sometime her husband, *Anno* 1404.

Chap. VII. 178   HISTORY OF BARNSLEY.

Arms and Inscriptions.

DRONFIELD—Paly of six . . . & . . . on a bend 3 mullets, or.
CLARELL—Gules, six martlets, argent.

In the South Quire.

BRANDON, DUKE OF SUFFOLK — Barry of eight, argent and gules; a lion rampant, or; over all on the honour point a ducal coronet.

In the South Window.

"𝔓𝔯𝔞𝔶 𝔶𝔢 𝔣𝔬𝔯 𝔱𝔥𝔢 𝔤𝔬𝔬𝔡 𝔰𝔱𝔞𝔱𝔢 𝔬𝔣 𝔑𝔦𝔠𝔥𝔬𝔩𝔞𝔰 𝔑𝔦𝔠𝔬𝔩𝔰, 𝔞𝔫𝔡 𝔈𝔩𝔦𝔷𝔞𝔟𝔢𝔱𝔥 𝔥𝔦𝔰 𝔴𝔦𝔣𝔢, 𝔫𝔬𝔴 𝔯𝔢𝔠𝔢𝔦𝔳𝔢𝔯 𝔬𝔣 𝔅𝔞𝔯𝔫𝔦𝔰𝔩𝔞𝔶 𝔞𝔫𝔡 𝔬𝔣 𝔱𝔥𝔢 𝔠𝔥𝔞𝔭𝔯𝔩 𝔬𝔣 𝔠𝔬𝔴𝔱𝔥𝔬𝔯𝔫𝔢, 𝔴𝔥𝔬 𝔠𝔞𝔲𝔰𝔢𝔡 𝔱𝔥𝔦𝔰 𝔴𝔦𝔫𝔡𝔬𝔴 𝔱𝔬 𝔟𝔢 𝔪𝔞𝔡𝔢 𝔦𝔫 𝔱𝔥𝔢 𝔶𝔢𝔞𝔯𝔢 𝔬𝔣 𝔬𝔲𝔯 𝔏𝔬𝔯𝔡 𝔪 . . . ."

South Aisle of the Church.

"𝔓𝔯𝔞𝔶 𝔶𝔢 𝔣𝔬𝔯 𝔱𝔥𝔢 𝔰𝔬𝔴𝔩𝔢𝔰 𝔬𝔣 𝔍𝔬𝔥𝔫 𝔇𝔢𝔫𝔱𝔬𝔫, 𝔞𝔫𝔡 𝔍𝔲𝔩𝔶𝔞𝔫𝔢 𝔥𝔦𝔰 𝔴𝔦𝔣𝔢, 𝔴𝔥𝔬 𝔪𝔞𝔡𝔢 𝔱𝔥𝔦𝔰 𝔴𝔦𝔫𝔡𝔬𝔴 𝔦𝔫 𝔱𝔥𝔢 𝔶𝔢𝔞𝔯𝔢 𝔬𝔣 𝔬𝔲𝔯 𝔏𝔬𝔯𝔡 mccccrvii."

"𝔓𝔯𝔞𝔶 𝔣𝔬𝔯 𝔱𝔥𝔢 𝔤𝔬𝔬𝔡 𝔰𝔱𝔞𝔱𝔶𝔰 𝔬𝔣 𝔱𝔥𝔢 𝔱𝔬𝔴𝔫𝔰𝔥𝔦𝔭 𝔬𝔣 𝔗𝔥𝔬𝔯𝔤𝔬𝔯𝔩𝔞𝔫𝔡. 𝔱𝔥𝔢 𝔣𝔬𝔲𝔫𝔡𝔢𝔯𝔰 𝔥𝔢𝔯𝔢𝔬𝔣."

In the Bellhouse Window.

BARNBY—Argent, on a lion rampant, tail quevye, gules, four escallops of the first.

EVERINGHAM—Quarterly, argent and gules; a bend, gules.

KERESFORTH—Argent, a fess embattled, between three butterflies, gules.

North Window.

"𝔓𝔯𝔞𝔶𝔢 𝔶𝔢 𝔣𝔬𝔯 𝔱𝔥𝔢 𝔤𝔬𝔬𝔡 𝔰𝔱𝔞𝔱𝔢 𝔬𝔣 𝔱𝔥𝔢 𝔱𝔬𝔴𝔫𝔰𝔥𝔦𝔭 𝔬𝔣 𝔥𝔬𝔭𝔩𝔞𝔫𝔡𝔰𝔴𝔞𝔶𝔫𝔢."

"𝔓𝔯𝔞𝔶𝔢 𝔶𝔢 𝔣𝔬𝔯 𝔱𝔥𝔢 𝔰𝔬𝔲𝔩𝔢𝔰 𝔬𝔣 𝔍𝔬𝔥𝔫 𝔊𝔞𝔩𝔟𝔢𝔯 𝔞𝔫𝔡 𝔄𝔤𝔫𝔢𝔰 𝔥𝔦𝔰 𝔴𝔦𝔣𝔢."

"𝔓𝔯𝔞𝔶𝔢 𝔶𝔢 𝔣𝔬𝔯 𝔱𝔥𝔢 𝔰𝔬𝔲𝔩𝔢𝔰 𝔬𝔣 𝔕𝔦𝔠𝔥𝔞𝔯𝔡 𝔗𝔥𝔲𝔯garland, 𝔞𝔫𝔡 𝔬𝔣 𝔍𝔬𝔫𝔢 𝔥𝔦𝔰 𝔴𝔦𝔣𝔢, 𝔞𝔫𝔡 𝔬𝔣 𝔱𝔥𝔢𝔦𝔯 𝔰𝔬𝔫𝔰, 𝔴𝔥𝔬 𝔪𝔞𝔡𝔢 𝔱𝔥𝔦𝔰 𝔴𝔦𝔫𝔡𝔬𝔴."

CHURCH OF SILKSTONE. 179 Chap. VII.

THE REGISTER OF SILKSTONE.

The Register

" In a codicil, made Kal. Nov. at the command of the lord, and of King Henry VIII., supreme lord of the Church of England, in the yeare of grace 1538, by John Nicols, vicar of Silkstone."

Amongst the entries was the following:—

" The prior of Pontefract submitted his churches of Sylkeston and Cattewyk to the ordinance of the archbishop," &c.

VICARAGE AND CHANTRIES OF SILKSTONE AND CAWTHORNE.

Vicarage and Chantries.

Previous to the Reformation, it was customary for persons to found and endow chantries in churches, the object of which was to support priests to offer up prayers at the altars for the health of the founder and his family. It appears from the *Valor Ecclesiasticus* of Hen. VIII. that one of this class existed in the church of Silkstone, and another in the chapel of Cawthorne. There is also the following notice of the vicarage of Silkstone:—

YORKSHIRE.

Silkstone, vicarage of the church there.

Silkstone Vicarage.

Master John Nicholes vicar there incumbent; and the rectory of the same appropriated to the house or monastery of St. John the Evangelist of Pontifract in the deanery of the same.

The vicarage there is worth in £ s. d. site of the mansion with garden vjs. viijd. rents and farms ij closes and meadows called Spittleflatt and Cokeshote close xs. one close called Sti-wardroode xs. and a certain close called Lytlyng iijs. iiijd.

Chap. VII. 180   HISTORY OF BARNSLEY.

Silkstone Vicarage.

and the rent of one close in Hoighland called Eventreacre vj*s.* viij*d.* one close called Fysherflatte vj*s.* viij*d.* the rent of five acres of arable land iij*s.* iiij*d.* one close called Vicar-cote v*s.* one barn with garden v*s.* tithes of grain xxx*s.* pension annually received from the prior of the aforesaid monastery £xiij. vj*s.* viij*d.* . . .   xvij   xiij   iiij

	£	s.	d.
Sum of the value above.	xvij	xiij	iiij

Which it is worth clearly.

	£	s.	d.
A tenth part thereout	—	xxxv	iiij

YORKSHIRE.

Chantry in Cawthorne Chapel.

Chantry of the Blessed Mary in the chapel of Cawthorne, in the parish aforesaid.

Master Richard Wygfall cantarist there.

The chantry there is worth in site of the mansion with garden, iiij*s.* ; rents and farms of certain lands and tenements in Cawthorn, c*s.* ; in all per annum . . . .

	£	s.	d.
annum	—	ciiij	—

Sum of the value above.

Which it is worth clearly.

	£	s.	d.
A tenth part thereout . . .	—	x	v

YORKSHIRE.

Chantry in Silkstone Church.

Chantry of the Blessed Mary in the church of Sixton.

Master Richard Rawlyn cantarist there.

The chantry there is worth in rents and farms in Sykeston, viz. mansion iiij*s.* certain closes

SILKSTONE CHURCH AND BARNSLEY CHAPEL. 181

xxxiijs.iiij*d*.rents and farms in Cawthorn & Darton xliijs.viij*d*.

Sum of the value above.

	£	s.	d.
	iiij	—	xij

Which it is worth clearly.

	£	s.	d.
A tenth part thereout . . .	—	viij	j¼

It appears from the Chartulary of Pontefract that Walter the prior granted to Herbert Preight the churches of Silkstone and Cawthorne, which latter is a member of the other church, with the tithes belonging to the same churches—to wit, to the church of Silkstone belongs all the tithes of Dodworth, and of Barnsley, and of Stainbrough, and of Thurgoland, and of Hoyland, and of Cumberworth, and of Bretton, and of Cheuveford. Witnesses : William Bygot and others.

BARNSLEY CHAPEL.

The parochial chapel of Saint Mary at Barnsley is in the Gothic style, and situate on rising ground to the north of the town. The previous edifice, which had accommodation for 500 persons, having fallen into decay, was taken down, except the tower, during the years 1820-21, and the present structure, which will seat 1,050 hearers, erected at the cost of £12,000, defrayed by a rate granted under the provisions of an Act of Parliament, by which power was given to purchase several houses, in order that the chapelyard might be enlarged. The bill was opposed in the House of Commons, which occasioned an extra expense of about £2,600 by the petitions for and against the rate. The interior is lofty and spacious, measuring one hundred and two feet by sixty-one. The east centre window is rich in tracery, in which are representations of the patron saint, our Saviour, and the four Evangelists.

Chap. VII.	182 HISTORY OF BARNSLEY.

The Tower.

The tower is cöeval with the body of the chapel taken down, and of good antiquity; the period of its erection, may be referred to the early part of the fifteenth century. On the west side thereof is a niche, in which has evidently been a representation of the patron saint; this the iron hand of Time has destroyed. Underneath are the arms of Keresforth —a fess embattled between three butterflies, and the inscription 𝕾𝖆𝖓𝖈𝖙𝖊 𝕸𝖆𝖗𝖎𝖊. The clock was placed in the tower about the year 1784.

Organ.

In the year 1787 the old organ was removed, and its place supplied with a better instrument (to which several additions have since been made). The organist's salary at that time was £10 per annum. Mr. John Asquith at present fills the situation of organist at St. Mary's Chapel.

Bells.

Previous to the eighteenth century there were three bells here, one of which was cast in the year 1647. Thomas Bridgehouse was then church-warden, and also for the year following. He went over to Pontefract at the time the castle was dismantled, and purchased lead for the reparation of Barnsley chapel, as appears by the following notices in his accounts :—

	£	s.	d.
For charges in going to Pontefract for buying lead	—	iiij	—
One fouther of lead	vj	—	—
Takeing downe of yᵉ timber and lead, and leading yᵉ timber, in ale and bread . . .	—	v	iiij
Payde in meate and drinke at yᵉ taking of yᵉ leads and binding upe yᵉ timber of yᵉ church	—	iiij	iiij
Payde to Thomas Bagshawe for mendinge clocke, making a barre to axeltree of yᵉ finger	—	iij	—
Payde to George Swindon for nayles to yᵉ church yeard gates	—	—	ij
Payde more to slatter	—	—	vj
Payd to John Dick for healping slatter to worke	—	ij	—

BARNSLEY CHAPEL. 183 Chap. VII.

	£	s.	d.
Payd in charges for yᵉ men and the drought that fettched yᵉ wood out of Mr. Armitage ground for yᵉ porch	—	j	—
Payde to Thomas Mellor, carpenter, in part of yᵉ worke for yᵉ church	—	—	iiij
Payde to Richard Haslam for three pecces of timber lyeinge at yeᵉ church side . .	—	xij	—

Bells.

The three bells before mentioned were removed in the year 1769 and five others substituted; another was added in 1772. The other two are undated.

The old chapel[1] being, as before stated, an ancient building, contained some objects of interest to the antiquarian. John Charles Brooke, " Somerset Herald," a native of Dodworth, has left us the following notes, which were taken in the year 1775 :—

The Old Chapel.

Brooke's Notes.

" In the south chancel, belonging to Keresforth Hill, there have been several inscriptions on gravestones, but so defaced by time, or covered by pews, as to be illegible. They probably belonged to the Keresforths. In the south wall is an old arched tomb, but the arms which might have shown to whom it belonged are defaced. Carved in ancient text characters in wood-work over the great east window :—

" 𝔒rate : pr : bo : statu : dni : ricardi : haegh : nuc : poris : monasterii : sci : Johis : ebagelisti : et : cobetus : ista : cenonc[2] : fieri : fecit."

Or in English :—

" Pray for the good estate of Master Richard

---

[1] Mr. Thomas Dale has a sketch of the old church in his possession.

[2] Probably *qui hanc* (*i. e. hanc fenestram*).

Chap. VII. 184 HISTORY OF BARNSLEY.

Brooke's Notes respecting the Old Chapel. Haegh, now prior of the monastery of Saint John the Evangelist and the convent of the same, who caused this to be made."

There were other inscriptions[1] in the chapel noticed by Brooke which have now disappeared.

On a Freestone in the North Aisle.

" Anne, d^r of Henry Wood, Gent., bapt^d Dec. 7th 1699, bur^d the 13th of the same month. William, son of the same Henry, bapt^d Jany 28th 1691, Buried March 1st 1699. John, son of the said Henry, was bapt^d Augt 9th & bur^d M^{ch} 24th 1702. Lyndley Wood, son of the said Henry, ob: 16th Dec: 1711, Ætat: 3 an. Mary-Dorothea, d^r of Francis Wood, Esqre was interred here, Sept: 2^d 1759, lamented by her friends aged 34 years & 2 months. Also John her younger brother who had the command of a detached Body of his Majesty's Forces in North-America under General Amherst, was slain there June 5th 1760, aged 25 years & 10 months."

On a Gravestone within the Altar Rails.

" Mary d^r of Henry Wood Gent: was buried Jany 19th 1673."

In the South Chancel belonging to Keresforth Hill, on a brass plate fixed in a Freestone Monument, now tumbled down and much broken. Arms and Crest of Armytage imp^g. Bosseville.

" Strenuus, Fortis, et Urbanus Invidiâ et Labore Invictus Qui Mores Hominum Multorum vidit et Urbes Gervasus Armytage Generosus jacet hic sepultus Post varios casus in regionibus remotis Incolumis in patriam Reversus Uxorem sibi adjunxit Priscillam Gulielmi Bosvile de Gunthwait Armigeri filiam Duas reliquit parvulas Elizabetham et Margaretam Castam Mœstissimamque Conjugem cum Vitam Morte Commutavit 9 die Julii 1691 Eliz.: pr: genit Obiit Sept: 23° 92° in Sinu patris Obdormiscit."

[1] These have been kindly furnished me by Albert William Woods, Esq., " Lancaster Herald."

THE OLD CHAPEL OF BARNSLEY. 185 Chap. VII.

On a Brass Plate fixed to a Gravestone. Arms and Brooke's Notes.
Crest of Armytage, a Mullet for difference.

" In Ingenuum Edwardum Armytage Gen : qui obiit 8º die
Mar : Anº Dom : 1673, ætat 37.

> Multa referre licet sed vix sat digna dolenta
> Desunt verba sed hæc capias certissima Lector
> Ingeniosus erat sociusq. fidelis ammicus
> Chara Noverca sibi et Soboles quod (crede Viator)
> Rarum est ille tamen literis aut arte Periti
> Charior ; ut spero, Superis charissimus exit."

On another Brass Plate in the same Chancel.

" Virgo Sponsa Christi Elizab: Armytage Latet hic sepulta
Cujus vitæ innocentia et spectata virtus eximia in parentes
religio, in pauperes Charitas Immota in Omnes Urbanitas Adi-
tum ad immortalitatem Aperuerunt 13º die Martii Anno Dom :
1685 Et ætatis suæ xliiº."

INSCRIPTIONS IN THE CHANCEL.

On a Gravestone.

" Here lyeth interred the Body of John Oxley of Barnsley,
Gent., who departed this life the 10th day of May, A.D. 1690,
aged 27 years. Here also lieth interred the Body of Francis,
the son of Francis Oxley, late of Barnsley, Gent. He departed
this life the 30th day of January, A.D. 1730, aged about 60 years.
Here also lieth interred the Body of John, the son of Francis
Oxley, late of Barnsley, Gent., he departed this life the 5th day
of Janʸ 1735, aged 29 years."

On a Gravestone.

" Here lyeth interred the Body of Wᵐ the son of Mʳ Richard
Pickering of Barnsley, Surgeon & Apothecary, & Sarah his wife,
he departed this life on the 30th day of Augᵗ A.D. 1749, aged 5
years & 6 months."

" Here also lies the Body of the said Mʳ Richᵈ Pickering,
who died the 20th day of June, 1754, in the 40th year of his
age."

On a Brass Plate.

" Here lies interred the Body of Richard the son of William
& Rebecca Ellison, late of Barnsley, Gent., who departed this
life Sept : 26th 1759, in the 49th year of his age."

Chap. VII. 186   HISTORY OF BARNSLEY.

Brooke's Notes
respecting the
Old Chapel.

Brass Plate, Chancel.

" Here lyeth interred the Body of Rebecca Wood, Relict of the late Francis Wood of Barnsley, Esq: and daughter of the late William Ellison, Gent: She departed this life 1st Nov: 1784, in the 72nd year of her age."

Brass Plate, Middle Aisle.

" To the Memory of John Deykin, Esqre, who departed this life the 25th March, 1788, aged 58 yrs."

On a Brass Plate in the Chancel.

" Here lyeth the Body of Robert Danyell, Gent., interred July 22^{d} 1676, aged 71 years. Elizab: his daughter interred Dec: 17th 1676, aged 4 years & 3 months. Edward his son was interred 14th June, 1692, aged 22 years & 4 months."

On another fixed to the same Stone.

"Margaret, the wife of Thomas Oxley, mother of Robert Danyell, bur: the 20th of April, 1647. Margaret, daughter of Robert Danyell, Gent., aged 4 years, bur^{d} 8th April, 1647. Jane, his daughter, aged 6 years, bur^{d} 14th Aug: 1651. An infant, bur^{d} the 3^{d} of Sept: . . . Marg^{t} the younger, his daugh^{r} aged 7 years, bur: the 14th April, 1656. Mary, the wife of Robert Danyell, bur: 20th Sept: 1662."

On another.

" Here lies the Body of Wm Marsden of Barnsley, Gent., who departed this life the 21st day of April, 1718, aged 53 years."

On another.

" Here lyeth the Body of Catherine, the wife of Henry Bowler of the county of Leicester, Gent., who departed this life the 27th of Oct: Anno 1711, aged 35."

On another.

" Here lyeth interred the Body of Henry Bowler of the County of Leicester, Gent., who departed this life the 3rd of June, Anno 1746, aged 68."

IN THE CHANCEL.

On a Brass Plate.

" Here was interred the Body of William, the Son of Daniel and Margaret Stopes of Barnsley, Mercer, who died the 30th of April, 1751, aged 8 months."

THE OLD CHAPEL OF BARNSLEY. 187 Chap. VII.

On a Freestone.[1]

Brooke'sNotes.

" Here was interred the Body of Richard Ellison of Pogmore, in the Parish of Barnsley, Gentleman, who departed this life on the 9th day of Sept : 169 , aged 43 years. Here also lyeth interred the Body of Richard, son of Richard Ellison, late of Pogmore, who departed this life the 14th day of July, A? Dom: 1699, aged 29 years."

On a Brass Plate on the same Stone.

" Here lyeth interred the Body of William Ellison, late of Barnsley, Gent., who departed this life on the 27th day of August, 1742, in the 58th year of his age."

On a Freestone near the last.

" Here lyeth interred the Body of Ann, the wife of Rich⁴ Ellison, late of Pogmore, who departed this life the 21st day of May, A.D. 1696, aged 46 years."

On a Brass Plate on the same Stone.

" Here lyeth interred the Body of Rebecca, Relict of Wm Ellison of Barnsley, Gent., who departed this life the 26th of Dec : 1747, in the 59th year of her age."

On another Brass Plate.

" Here lies interred the Body of John, the son of Wm & Rebecca Ellison, late of Barnsley, Gent. He departed this life March 1st 1759, in the 43rd year of his age."

About the year 1770 some thieves entered the vestry of the chapel, broke open the chest containing the old records of the town, and took them away. Portions were afterwards found by some reapers in the church field, but in a very decayed state.

The old Records.

Three chantries existed in St. Mary's, the fol-

Chantries.

[1] This is now in the churchyard, but the brass plate is wanting ; probably taken away at the time the church was rebuilt.

Chap. VII.   188   HISTORY OF BARNSLEY.

Chantries in Barnsley Old Chapel. lowing account of which is extracted from the *Valor Ecclesiasticus, temp.* Hen. VIII.:—

YORKSHIRE.

St. Mary's Chantry. Chantry of the Blessed Mary in the church or chapel of Barneslay, in the parish of Sylkeston.

Master Thomas Kirkby cantarist there.

The chantry there is worth in

	£	s.	d.
rents and farms there viz. in Barnsley per annum . . .	vi	—	xvij

Sum of the above value.

Reprisals, viz., in rent, annually to be paid to the prior of the monastery of Saint John the Evangelist at Pontefract . .

	£	s.	d.
Evangelist at Pontefract . .	—	xviij	—$\frac{1}{2}$

Sum of the reprisals above.

	£	s.	d.
And it is worth clearly . . .	—	ciij	iiij
A tenth part thereout . . .	—	x	iiij

YORKSHIRE.

St. John the Evangelist's Chantry. Chantry of Saint John the Evangelist in the aforesaid chapel.

. Master Alexander Lacy cantarist there.

The chantry there is worth in rents and farms of divers lands and tenements in Halifax . lxiijs. iiijd. Barnsley, xvjs. Rothwell xxvs. and in Cudworth, xvjs. iiijd. in all per annum . . . .

	£	s.	d.
annum	vj	—	viij

Sum of the value above.

Reprisals viz. in rent annually paid to the prior aforesaid

THE OLD CHAPEL OF BARNSLEY. 189 Chap. VII.

Chantries.

iiij*s*. alms annually distributed for ij obits[1] performed for the souls of William Symmes and William Issett chaplain founder of the said chantry, per annum . . .

	£	s.	d.
chantry, per annum . . .	—	xiv	viij
Sum of the reprisals above.	£	s.	d.
And it is worth clearly . . .	—	cvj	—
A tenth part thereout . . .	—	☸	vij$\frac{1}{4}$

YORKSHIRE.

Chantry of Saint John the Baptist in the aforesaid chapel.

St. John the Baptist's Chantry.

Master John Horne cantarist there.
The chantry there is worth in rents and farms in Barnsley cxij*s*. ij*d*. and farms in Ruston v*s*. in all per annum

	£	s.	d.
ton v*s*. in all per annum ..	—	cxvij	ij

Sum of the value above.
·Reprisals viz. in rent annually paid to the prior of Pontefract aforesaid xviij*s*. xj$\frac{1}{2}$*d*. and an accustomed rent paid to the chaplain for the service of the Blessed Mary aforesaid, xij*d*. in all . . . . . .

	£	s.	d.
xij*d*. in all	—	xix	xi$\frac{1}{2}$

Sum of the reprisals above.

And it is worth clearly . . .	iiij	xvij	ij$\frac{1}{2}$
A tenth part thereout . . .	—	ix	viij$\frac{3}{4}$

Dodsworth informs us that upwards of forty of these foundations existed in York Minster, the

Chantries in York Minster.

[1] Masses for the dead.

Chap. VII. 190 HISTORY OF BARNSLEY.

Chantries in York Minster. annual revenue of which exceeded twelve hundred pounds—an enormous sum in those days.

The following is a short account of the masses which were celebrated at these altars, as expressed in one of their endowments :—

" That amongst other suffrages of mankinds' salvation and restoration, the celebration of masses, in which God the Son offered himself a victim 'to God the Father for the health of the living and the repose of the dead; and before other things, on the day of atonement, they counted it meritorious chiefly to prosecute those things with respect to the multiplicity of masses, and the increase of Divine worship."

The chantries and all other foundations of a similar nature were swept away by a statute of Edward IV.

Pontefract Priory. In a list contained in the *Valor Ecclesiasticus, temp.* Henry VIII., of the possessions of the house of St. John of Pontefract, we find that the following amongst others, under the head of pensions, were payable by the monastery :—

	£	s.	d.
A pension annually paid to John Nicolls, perpetual vicar of Silkstone	xiij	vj	viij
A pension annually paid to John Hollingbrig, perpetual chaplain of Barnsley . . .	v	ij	—
A pension annually to Thurstan Gawkthorpp, perpetual chaplain of Cawthorne . .	iiij	xiij	iiij

We find the following in the *Computationes Ministrorum Domini Regis, temp.* Hen. VIII., concerning the possessions then late belonging to the monastery of Pontefract, county of York :—

	£	s.	d.
Barnsley rents and farms[1] *(firmæ)* . .	xlix	xvij	vj

[1] Spelman (in his Glossary) says "firma" means a rent or return, either pecuniary, or in corn, victuals, &c.

TESTAMENTARY BURIALS AT BARNSLEY. 191

	£	s.	d.
Dodworth rents and farms	xxij	xvj	iiij
Silkstone ditto	v	iij	ij
Silkstone rectory	xlij	ij	x
Barnsley and other places *cum perquis. curie*[1]	iij	xviij	—

Pontefract Priory.

TESTAMENTARY BURIALS AT BARNSLEY, FROM TORRE'S MSS.

Testamentary Burials.

Warde.—Ult. Junii, A.D. 1519 : William Warde of Barnsley made his will, proved 20 Sept., 1519, giving his soul to God Almighty, Saint Mary, and all Saints, and his body to be buried in the chapel of Barnsley.

Kaye.—A.D. 1525 : John Kaye of Barnsley made his will, proved 13 July, 1525, giving his soul *ut supra*, and his body to be buried in the High Where[2] of Barnsley church.

Keresforth.—26 Dec. A.D. 1550: Richard Kexforth of Kexforth Hill, in the parish of Barnsley, made his will, proved 16 April, 1551, giving his soul to God Almighty, and his body to be buried in the Lady Quere in the parish church of Barnsley.

Jessop.—14 Dec., A.D. 1591: William Jessop of Barnsley, yeoman, made his will, proved 13 April, 1592, giving his soul to God Almighty, hoping through Jesus Christ for salvation, and his body to be buried in the church or chapel of Barnsley nigh unto the font.

Wood.—23 July, A.D. 1662: James Wood of Barnsley, Gentleman, made his will, proved ———

---

[1] Du Cange (in his Glossary) says, with regard to this phrase, as follows :—"Perquisita curiarum sunt acquisita et addita curiis seu prædiis rusticis est enim curia prædium rusticum, possessio, &c.," and does not consider the words to relate to courts.

[2] (Qy.) Quire.

Chap. VII.

Testamentary Burials.

——, giving his soul *ut supra*, and his body to be buried in the quire of Barnsley church.

Armitage.—John Armitage of Keresforth Hill, in the township of Barnsley, made his will, proved —————————, giving his soul *ut supra*, and his body to be buried in the church of Barnsley.

Armitage.—22 Feb., 1673; Edward Armitage of Keresforth Hill, Gentleman, made his will, proved ————, giving his soul to God Almighty his Creator, hoping through Jesus X! for salvation, and his body to be buried in the S. Quire of the chapel of Barnsley.

The above are all the testamentary burials at Barnsley which are noticed in Torre's MSS.; and he gives no list of the incumbents, neither does he notice the chantries, which is a very unusual omission with him.

Dodsworth's Notes concerning Barnsley Old Chapel.

Dodsworth visited Barnsley chapel about the year 1620, when he noticed the arms mentioned below, to which I append short notices of the families to whom they pertain. He does not record any monumental inscriptions :—

Barnby.—*Or*, a lion rampant *Sable*, hung about with escallop shells, *Argent*. An eminent Yorkshire family, of Barnby and Midhope, the last heir-male of which was Thomas Barnby of Barnby, Esquire, living *temp.* Charles II., who left two daughters and co-heirs, the elder married to John Allot of Bentley, and Mary to Nicholas Bowden of Bowden, Esquire. The last male of the family of the Barnbys of Barnby and his wife lived to so great an age that they were both superannuated. They used to sit one on each side of the fire. The man died first, and a

THE OLD CHAPEL OF BARNSLEY. 193 Chap. VII.

few days after, the old woman asked where the old Dodsworth's Notes of Arms. man was who used to sit opposite to her.

Bosvile.—*Argent*, five fusils in fess *Gules*, in chief three bears' heads *Sable*. The family of Bosvile is of great antiquity; of which was Sir John Bosvile of New Hall, in Darfield, living A.D. 1252, who married Alice, daughter and heir of Hugh de Darfield, and their descendants resided there for many generations.[1] Branches of the family were seated at Braithwell, Conisbrough, Gunthwaite, Ravenfield, Barnsley, and other places. On the crest[2] and family name this epigram was written in the time of Queen Elizabeth :—

" *Dii tibi dent Bosvile, Boves villasque Radulphi,*
Nec villâ careat bosve, vel illa bove."

Which, rendered into English, would be :

" May the Gods give to thee, O Bosvile,
The oxen and towns of Radulphus,
Nor may the ox want a town,
Or the town an ox."

Burton.—*Argent*, a bend wavy *Sable*. Of this family was Sir John Burton, Knight, of Kingsley, who married Muriel, daughter of Thomas Bosvile of New Hall, Esquire.

Everingham.—Quarterly, *Argent* and *Sable*, a bend *Gules*. Seated at Stainbrough.

Midleton.—*Argent*, fretty *Sable ;* a canton of the second. This family was of Stockeld in this county, and descended from Sir Peter de Midleton, living *temp.* Edward II., son of William de Midleton and Agnes his wife, daughter of Nigel Boteler. The eventual heiress, Elizabeth, sister of William Midleton of

[1] Peter de Bosewill and Robert de Bosewill were witnesses to a charter of Robert de Holtham, vicar of Roreston ; dated at Bretton, A.D. 1296.—Harl. MSS. 4757.

[2] The crest of Bosvile is an Ox issuing from a holt of trees.

N

Chap. VII. 194   HISTORY OF BARNSLEY.

Dodsworth's Notes of Arms in Barnsley Old Chapel.

Stockeld, Esq., who died in the year 1763, married Sir Carnaby Haggerston, Baronet, and was grandmother of William Haggerstone Constable, who inherited the Stockeld estate, and took the arms of Midleton.

Keresforth of Keresforth.—Argent, a fess embattled *Sable*, between three butterflies *Gules*. This is quartered with the arms of another family (viz., *Azure*, two millrinds fessways in pale *Argent*). To whom these latter bearings[1] relate I have not been able to discover with certainty.

Vavasour.—Or, a fess dancette *Sable*, charged with a mullet *Argent*. Seated at Haselwood in this county; of whom was Sir Mauger le Vavasour, who accompanied the Conqueror, and is mentioned in Domesday Book. The last direct male-heir, Sir Thomas Vavasour of Haselwood, Baronet, died 1826, having devised his estates to his cousin, the Hon. Marmaduke Stourton, who changed his name to Vavasour, and was created a baronet in 1828.

Brooke's Notes.

Brooke says the north aisle of Barnsley church belongs to the Duke of Leeds as lord of the manor; the south to Lord Strafford, as owner of Keresforth Hill. Mr. Marsden bought the great tithes of Barnsley of the family of Wood of Burton, and sold them to the Duke of Leeds. And again he says that the Duke has the middle and north chancel, and takes a fee of ten shillings for every corpse buried therein. On the ceiling of the north chancel of the old church was the following inscription: "H.W. 1714."

Monuments.

MONUMENTS AND MONUMENTAL INSCRIPTIONS.

Few of the old memorials now exist, many of the ancient tombstones having been cut up and

---

[1] In some of the heralds' visitations they are stated to be the arms of Keresforth.

BARNSLEY CHAPEL. 195 Chap. VII.

used for paving the graveyard at the time the church was rebuilt. This does not reflect much credit on the officials concerned.

Monuments.

In the churchyard formerly was a stone bearing the following inscription :—

> " *Robert Chappel*,[1] *not tall,*
> *Though strong of Body once I was, now am I laid in grave,*
> *My trust is ever in Jesus Christ that he my sould would save.*"
> *Buried, 7th July,* 1645.

The memorials in the church are as follow :—

On a freestone monument fixed to the wall in the north chancel, surrounded with a black wooden frame :—

In the North Chancel.

> "PROPE REQUIESCIT.

> " Quicquid Mortale Gulielmi Denton in Artibus Magistri concionatoris olim in hac Ecclesia orthodoxi qui obiit vi Cal Julii MDCXXXXVI ætatis suæ XXX."

A monument fixed to the north wall in the same chancel of black marble, bordered with gray. Arms in chief *B.* three wild men passant in fess *proper* impaling party per bend sinister *Or* and *S.*, a lion counterchang'd. Crest: on a wreath a wild man *proper*, as in the arms.

> " Near this place lies the Body of Henry Wood of this Town, Gent., who married Elizabeth, daughter of William Simpson of Babworth, in the County of Nottingham, Esq., by whom he had issue 6 sons and 7 daughters, four of whom are here interred. He died May ye 4th 1720, aged 75.
> " Here also lies the Body of Henry Wood, Esq., his eldest son. He died April ye 28th 1741, aged 50.
> " The said Elizabeth died 31 Decr 1748, aged 81."

[1] Johnston says that this was the chief family at Barnsley in the year 1670.

Chap. VII. 196   HISTORY OF BARNSLEY.

Monuments in the North Chancel. Marble mural monument, north wall, north chancel, a tablet of white marble, on which is the inscription; under it two palm branches in saltire; above it a pyramid of gray marble, on which is a shield, with the arms (Baron) Palmer, *A.* on 2 bars *S.* 3 trefoils *A.* in chief a greyhound current *S.* collared *Or* quartering Bellasis *A.* a chevron *G.* between three fleur-de-lis *B.* (Femme) Armroyd, *B.* on fess *Or* ent: 3 doves *A.*, 2 eschallops *B..* Crest: on a mount *V.* a greyhound sej^t *S.* collar'd *Or.* In base of the pyramid an urn, in chief a lamp (S. R.).

" In Memory of Charles Palmer esq^r late of Thurnscoe Hall in this county who departed this life the 28th of August 1780 in the 56th year of his age.

> ' Of manners gentle, of affection mild ;
> In wit a man, simplicity a child.
> A safe companion and an easy friend,
> Beloved thro' life, lamented in the end.
> To name his virtues ill·befits my grief :
> What was my bliss can now give no relief.
> I·may mourn—the rest shall friendship tell;
> Fame spread his worth, for I knew it well.'

This Monument was erected by Mrs Anne wife of the above Charles Palmer esq^r as a mark of the esteem she had for him."

In the same chancel:

" In Memory of Ann Hargreave of Barnsley who departed this life the 16 day of January 1814 in the 88 year of her age."

" Sacred to the memory of John Ellison, M.D., Fellow of the Royal College of Physicians of Edinburgh. He was studious in his profession, of which he had a universal knowledge. A kind and affectionate husband, a faithful friend, and a truly honest man. Died 13 April, 1791, aged 57 years."

North Aisle.   *In the North Aisle.*

" Sacred to the memory of Joseph Hall, for upwards of fifty

BARNSLEY CHAPEL. 197 Chap. VII

years an ironmonger and seed merchant of this town, who died
the viii December, MDCCCXLIV, aged lxxv years.

Monuments in the North Aisle.

" By temperance and unremitting industry he raised himself
to comparative affluence; and by the exercise of strict integrity
in all his commercial transactions, he acquired the confidence
and esteem of a wide circle of friends."

" Sacred to the memory of John Clarke of Keresforth Hall,
who died November 13, 1850, in the 80th year of his age. Also
of Hannah, wife of the above, who died January 26, 1842, in
the 60th year of her age.

" This tablet was erected by their daughters, as a tribute of
love and affection to their memory.

" Near this place lie interred the mortal remains of Bart.
Hodgetts of this town, merchant, formerly of Dudley, who died
22nd December, 1830, æt. 40 years.

" This tablet is erected as a tribute to the memory of departed
worth."

" Near this place are deposited the mortal remains of Elizabeth, wife of Mr. Andrew Faulds of Marrow House, in the township of Worsbrough, to whom, in grateful and affectionate remembrance of her worth and virtues, this tablet is erected."

The only memorial of the Wombwell family is
a marble monument in the North Aisle :—

" In memory of Mr. John Wombwell, who was interred near
this place, yᵉ 21st of February, 1733, aged 63 years. And of
Elizabeth his wife, who was also here interred the 29th of May,
1745, aged 65 years.

" This monument was erected by their most affectionate son,
Mr. George Wombwell, merchant in London."

In the South Aisle.

South Aisle.

" In memory of George Miller of this town, stonemason, one
of the contractors for rebuilding this church. He died before
the edifice was completed, September 16, 1821, aged 57 years."

" Sacred to the memory of James Dow, M.D. ; during thirty
years a medical practitioner in this town, to the inhabitants of
which, rich and poor alike, he was endeared by his virtues,
worth, and usefulness. As a man, he was of an exalted and independent spirit, and of a nature social, beneficent, gentle,
and just. As a physician he possessed a profound knowledge of the science of his profession, and applied it with a
sensitive anxiety to justify the confidence and realise the hopes

Chap. VII. 198 HISTORY OF BARNSLEY.

Monuments in the South Aisle. of his patients; liberal and considerate—the success of his efforts was his happiest reward. As a friend, he was faithful, disinterested, and kind. As a citizen, he was the judicious and energetic advocate of freedom; the enemy of oppression, and the intrepid defender of the veritable rights of his countrymen. Above all, as a Christian, he was in truth and in deed the servant of his God; in humble imitation of the example of his Saviour, benign, compassionate, and charitable to all—esteemed, beloved, lamented. He departed this life on the 9th day of October, 1832, aged 57 years. As a reverent tribute to the eminence of his character, and in affectionate consciousness of their own loss, his townsmen have erected this tablet in memorable record of both."

"Sacred to the memory of George Clarke, late of this place, banker, who died April 1, 1814, aged 70 years.

"This tablet is erected by his sister, Mrs. Sarah Cawood, as a tribute of respect due to his memory."

"Sacred to the memory of Edward Taylor, and Sarah his wife, whom death long separated, but who now, through Him who is 'the resurrection and the life,' are reunited in that blessed and eternal state, where all separations shall for ever cease. The former died February 7, 1806, aged 62; the latter, August 12, 1836, aged 85 years. Their mortal remains are interred in the village of Cawthorn.

"This tablet is erected, not in praise of the virtues of the dead, but in order that those Christian graces which so eminently adorned their lives; and which are recorded on the page of local history, may be had in perpetual remembrance as a means under Divine Providence of stimulating others to the exercise of Christian charity."

South Chancel.

In the South Chancel.

" S. M.

" Of Richard Beckett, captain in the Coldstream Regiment of Guards, and brigade-major of the British Guards in Spain, who gloriously fell in the victorious battle of Talavera de la Reyna, the 28th July, 1809, Æ. 28."

On a neat marble monument, on which is pourtrayed the arms of Beckett :—

"To the memory of Joseph Beckett, Esq., merchant and banker, born in this town, August 31, A.D. 1751, who died February 11, A.D. 1840, aged 88 years. Also in memory of Mary his wife, daughter of the late John Staniforth, Esq., of

BARNSLEY CHAPEL.

199 Chap. VII.

Monuments in the South Chancel.

Hull, who, surviving her husband but two days, died February 13, A.D. 1840, aged 79 years. After being united 55 years, they were interred together on the same day in one grave."

"Sacred to the memory of Henry Clarke of this town, gentlemen, who died the 30th November, 1826, aged 85 years. Blessed are the dead which die in the Lord, even so saith the Spirit, for they rest from their labours."

"Near this place lieth interred the body of Mr. Francis Roper; he departed this life November 12, 1780, aged 84 years. Also Mary-Ann, daughter to George and Mary Roper of Leeds, merchant, who died ye 27th June, in the 8th year of her age.

"Also George Roper, ye son of Francis and Elizabeth, and father of the above Mary-Ann Roper, who died the 12th Feb., 1807, in the 58th year of his age.

"Also Elizabeth, the wife of Francis Roper, who died ye 27th November, 1809, in the 88th year of her age.

"Also John Cartwright Roper, the son of the above George Roper, and grandson to Francis and Elizabeth Roper, who died 27th February, 1810, in the 18th year of his age.

"Also of Richard, youngest son of the above Francis and Elizabeth Roper, died the 17th Sept., 1810, aged 58 years.

"Also John, the eldest son, died 9th March 1819, aged 73 years."

"M. S.

Gulielmi et Hannæ Marsden, qui cum in hoc vico quinquaginta annos, hospitaliter et utiliter vixerant; obierunt, ille 18 Mar., 1774, æt. 76; hæc 28th April, 1761, æt. 60, Johannes et Hanna, filius et filia superstites marmor hoc parentibus optimis posuerunt, A.D. 1793."

In the Chancel.

The Chancel.

A marble tablet, with the arms of Jackson, quartering Radcliffe, and the inscription :—

"Sacred to the memory of William Jackson, Esq., late of Beevor, descended from the ancient family of the same name, long settled at Edwardthorpe, in the parish of Darfield. He removed in early life to this town, where by diligent and successful application to business, he established the firm of Jacksons and Co., the extensive mercantile transactions of which were conducted with probity and honour.

"In the domestic circle he was an affectionate husband, and a tender yet prudent parent; in social life, a sincere and steady

Chap. VII. 200   HISTORY OF BARNSLEY.

Monuments in the Chancel.

friend, and an hospitable neighbour; as a citizen, a lover of peace and order, and a firm but temperate supporter of the institutions of his country.

"Ardently attached to the Established Church, he promoted, as well by his presence as by his contributions, the instruction of the rising generation in her principles, and to all local institutions, having for their object the amelioration of the condition of the poor, he was a cheerful and liberal benefactor.

"Courteous and unassuming in his manners, benevolent in his disposition, and uniform and consistent in all the relations of life, he lived universally beloved, and died greatly regretted on the 29th day of May, 1833, in the 74th year of his age, his townsmen testifying their sense of his public and private worth by voluntarily closing their shops and attending his mortal remains to the grave.

"To record her sorrow, and to convey to posterity the memorial of his virtues, his afflicted widow caused this monument to be erected.

"'The memory of the just is blessed,'—Prov. 10th, 7th verse."

"Here lies, in hope of a glorious resurrection, the Rev. John Mence, B.A. of Oriel College, Oxford, a most upright man, and of this flock for 35 years the faithful pastor, who departed this life October 19, A.D. 1761, in the 75th year of his age.

"Also the Rev. John Mence, B.A., son of the above named, who for 32 years was minister of the same church; he departed this life March 8, 1806, in the 72nd year of his age.

"Also the Rev. John Mence, M.A., Fellow of Worcester College, Oxford, son of the last named, for many years curate of this church; he departed this life December 1, 1816, aged 40 years.

"Also in the burial ground adjoining, William Cookes Mence, another son of the second-named John Mence, for more than 30 years an attorney in this town; respected by all, beloved and regretted by the poor, he departed this life, February 2, 1853, and in the 61st year of his age."

"Here lyeth the body of Mrs. Sarah Radcliffe, late of Barnsley, who died the 17th of July, 1792, unmarried, aged 66 years.

"Also the body of her beloved sister, Mrs. Hannah Radcliffe, late of the same place, who died the 20th of February, 1801, unmarried, aged 70 years. Leaving to posterity the most ami-

BARNSLEY CHAPEL.

201   Chap. VII.

Monuments.

able and unblemished characters. They were the only daughters of Thomas Radcliffe of this town."

In the adjoining yard are the following inscriptions :— *Inscriptions on Stones in the Graveyard.*

" Here lyeth interr'd the body of Richard Chappel, eldest son of Robert Chappel, who departed this life the 13th day of November, 1666.

" Here lyeth interred the body of Elizabeth Chappel, and daughter of Richard Chappel, who departed this life the 30th day of November, Anno Dom. 1668, and was aged 60 years."

There are other memorials of this family : ·

" John Chappel, buried 14th May, 1713, aged 62. Elizabeth, daughter of Richard Chappel of Barnsley, mercer, who died 1726. Mary, wife of Richard Chappel, 1738, aged 48. Ann, their daughter, 1746. Richard Chappel, 1748, aged 67. Richard, son of Richard and Mary Chappel, 1766, aged 42."

" Here resteth the body of Catherine, late wife and relict of Edward Oxley of Barnsley, yeoman, deceased, and sister to Thomas Garnet, gentleman, deceased, who departed this life the 4th day of July, and was buried the 6th day, Anno Dm. 1669, aged about 70 years."

· " Here lyeth interred the body of Sarah Bridgehouse, relict of Robert Bridgehouse, and daughter of Thomas Garnet, late of Barnsley, Gent. She died yᵉ 12th. day of February, An. Dm. 1699, aged 59 years and 8 months."

" Here lyeth the body of Francis Langley of Barnsley, mercer, who was buried November 7, 1675, in the 42nd year of his age. William, son of Francis Langley, was buried October 9, 1671. Francis, son of Francis Langley, was buried November 26, 167–. Ann, daughter of Francis Langley, was buried December 19, 1675. John, son of Francis Langley, was buried April 12, 1687, · aged 18 years. Robert, son of Francis Langley, was buried October 10th, 1692, aged 20 years."

" Helena uxor Joshuæ Anderws obiit j Junii, Ano. Dom.1675, ætat 26. Elizabeth, filia ejus obiit 6? ejusdem mensis et anni. Alcia Thrist amitadictæ Helenæ obiit 21 Februarii, Ano. Dom.

Chap. VII. 202   HISTORY OF BARNSLEY.

Inscriptions on Stones in the Graveyard. 1674, ætat 85.   Anna filia dicti Joshuæ obiit 17 Maii, Ano. Dom. 1675."

"Elizabeth, daughter of James Donford of Barnsley, Gent., was buried May the 4th, 1680. And also John her brother, died Sept. y⁰ 12th, 1689."

"Here lyeth interred the body of Thomas Ludlam, son of Mr. Stephen Ludlam, late of Barnsley, who departed this life the 24th day of January, in the 21st year of his age, Anno Domini 1689."

"Here lyeth interred the body of Thomas Littlewood of Barnsley, mercer, who departed this life 23rd day of March, 1691-2, aged 32 years. Here also was interred the body of Joseph Daykin of Barnsley, mercer and draper, who departed this life upon the 23rd day of September, Ano. Dni. 1720, aged 63 years."

"Here lyeth interred the body of John Littlewood, late of Ould Barnsley, who departed this life the 6th day of April, 1693."

"Here was interred the body of Catty, the daughter of John and Ellen Deykin; she departed this life the 6th of April, 1730, aged 14 months. Here was also interred the body of Ellen, the daughter of John and Ellen Deykin; she departed this life on the 17th day of May, Anno Domini 1733, aged 1 year and 3 months.

"Here was interred the body of Joseph, son of Joseph and Sarah Deykin; he departed this life May 12, 1694, aged 9 days.

"Here was interred Sarah, the wife of Joseph Daykin of Barnsley, mercer and draper; she departed this life 13th July, 1712, aged 50 years."

"Also lyeth interred the body of Elizabeth, the wife of Thomas Taylor of Barnsley, mercer and draper; she departed this life the 12th day of February, 1729, and in y⁰ 35th year of her age.

"Here also was interred the body of Elizabeth, daughter of Thomas and Elizabeth Taylor; she departed this life the 5th of February, 1729."

"Here lyeth interred y⁰ body of William, the son of John and Elizabeth Marsden of Old Barnsley; he departed this life the 30th day of January, A⁰ Dⁿⁱ 1728, aged 3 years.

"Here also lyeth interred the body of John Marsden, sen., of

BARNSLEY CHAPEL. 203 Chap. VII.

Old Barnsley, who departed this life on the 2nd day of July, Anno Domini 1744, aged about 63 years."

Inscriptions on Stones in the Graveyard.

" William, son of Foljambe and Anna Maria Wood, died 12th March, 1771, in the 2nd year of his age.

" Anna Maria, wife of Foljambe Wood, died 5th March, 1784, aged 33."

The following memorials relate to the family of Rooke :—

The Rooke Family.

" Resuscitationis spe Gloriosæ cineres Gervasii Rooke generosi conduntur hic sopiti qui senio gravis animi meretis gravior vera pietate gravissimus obiit, Anno Domini 1693, ætatis 79.

" Olive, yᵉ wife of John Rooke, Gent., son of the said Gervas, was buried the ninth day of November, Anno Domini 1721, ætatis suæ lxx.

" Here was interred the body of John Rooke, sen., Gent.; he was buried on the 26th day of June, Anno Domini 1724, and in the 84th year of his age.

" Here also was interred the body of John Rooke, jun., Gent.; he departed this life on the 12th day of September, Anno Domini 1734.

" Here was interred yᵉ body of Wilburton Rooke, who departed this life upon yᵉ 16th of August, A.D. 1706, aged 12 months.

" Also Michael Rooke upon yᵉ —— March, A.D. 1706-7, aged 6 years.

" Also William Rooke upon yᵉ 20th of February, A.D. 1709-10, aged 2 years, who were sons of William Rooke of Barnsley, apothecary.

" Also George Rooke upon yᵉ 10th day of February, 1714, aged 5 weeks.

" Also Anne, yᵉ wife of William Rooke, departed this life yᵉ 26th day of March, 1720.

" Here lieth the body of Gervas Rooke of Barnsley, Gent., who departed this life 4th June, 1763, aged 58 years."

THE REGISTERS.

Registers.

These records commence with the latter part of the year 1568 ; a few chasms occur here and there,

Chap. VII. 204   HISTORY OF BARNSLEY.

The Registers. but with these exceptions they are in an excellent state of preservation. Subjoined is an account of the marriages, baptisms, and burials, in the years enumerated below, from which some idea may be formed of the rate of increase of the population of Barnsley since the sixteenth century. A burial ground existed here as early as the reign of Henry III. :—

Abstract of Registers.

Year.	Mar	Bap.	Bur.	Year.	Mar	Bap.	Bur.	Year.	Mar.	Bap.	Bur.
1568	..	4	3	1660	3	8	6	1760	19	71	37
1569	3	37	16	1665	7	39	38	1765	21	77	36
1570	6	17	19	1670	10	33	50	1770	14	69	57
1575	11	25	24	1675	2	34	19	1775	6	64	53
1580	11	34	42	1680	9	55	33	1780	24	85	62
1585[1]	8	25	72	1685	4	31	40	1785	20	93	45
1590	16	44	23	1690	8	42	50	1790	13	104	52
1595	8	47	22	1695	5	41	51	1795	10	116	128
1600	6	37	16	1700	7	51	86	1800	12	138	71
1605	13	46	24	1705	5	37	38	1805	22	175	65
1610	8	40	28	1710	12	47	40	1810	28	107	202
1615	15	34	32	1715	10	55	26	1815	37	290	145
1620	8	42	33	1720	11	61	23	1820	25	290	111
1625	..	19	8	1725	13	56	35	1825	37	390	276
1630	8	29	30	1730	12	62	25	1830	38	324	147
1635	16	48	16	1735	7	60	28	1835	45	336	190
1640	17	70	44	1740	5	51	49	1840	44	282	325
1645	14	51	40	1745	7	53	26	1845	67	318	194
1650	..	17	39	1750	10	59	36	1850	71	246	242
1655	11	31	18	1755	6	61	36	1855	59	209	194

The Plague.   [1] The pestilence visited Barnsley in 1585, and carried off many victims. It will be seen that the number of deaths greatly exceeded that of the previous years, being more than double. During the prevalence of the Great Plague, in 1665, our ancestors, being fully aware of the ravages committed by this unseen and unwelcome visitor, were not backward in using proper precautions to prevent its entrance into this locality. Annexed is a copy of an order from the high constable of the wapentake of Staincross to the constables of Barnsley and other places, warning them of the prevalence of the malady in the West Riding, and directing what steps should be taken to arrest its progress. After requesting that the document be sent from

BARNSLEY CHAPEL. 205 Chap. VII.

The three greatest years of mortality were 1585; The Registers.
1832, when cholera added many victims to the
list, 295 burials being recorded in St. Mary's district; and 1840.

Subjoined are some curious extracts from the Curious
registers :— Entries.

"Ann, daughter of Elizabeth Trelis and John Copley, as it is
reported, was bap. the xxx July, 1569.

John Brone, son of Janet Brone, was licenced to goe from
Barnesley and seeke a service the x day of August, 1579.

William, son of Agnes Chadwick, bap. xvi February, 1581,
gotten by Robert Wilson.

Elizabeth Gene, ye daughter of Jane Gene, bap. 1st March
1581, gotten by George Bryge.

Twa Twyndles of Richard Turton, bur. xi Feb. 1583.

Sunday beynge the xvi June, one James Johnes, as he sayth,
did preache in Barnsley church without any lycence, that he
would shewe in the afternoon of the same day at after evenynge
prayer, 1588.

Edward Walker did preache in Barnsley church xviii Aug.,
1583.

one constable to another with speed, he says :—" By vertue
of an order from several of his Maties justies of ye peace for this
Ridd. by meanes of the continuance of the Plague, which by
the immediate hand of God is still continued at London and
sev'all places in this Rydeing, to the danger of the countery, it
is thought fitt, and accordingly ordered, that not only the ward,
but also the watch, be still continued within this division of the
sayde Rydeing, until upon good cause it be ordered to the contrary, and that the same be p'formed by every householder in
p'son, or by a sufficient man for that purpose ; and if any person
refuse or neglect the same, then the constable of each towne is hereby ordered to conduct such p'son before the next justice of the peace
to be bound over to the next sesshions. And it is further ordered,
y^t if any householder shall receive any p'son or p'sons y^t comes
from any infected or suspected place, for the same then the constable of each towne is not only to secure such p'son as comes
from any infected or suspected place, but also such p'son as shall
receive him, her, or them, and cause ye house where they are to
be shut up until such time as they shall receive order from the
next justice of ye peace for their reliefe."

Chap. VII. 206   HISTORY OF BARNSLEY.

The Registers.

Mr. Brooke did preache at Barnsley xxvii Sept., 1589.

Curious Entries.

Edmund Walker did preache at Barnsley, and would not showe his lycence to the curate, the x October, 1589."

Sir Gervase Cutler was baptised here. Amongst the entries, under the year 1593, appears the following:—

"𝕵𝖆𝖗𝖚𝖎𝖈𝖊 𝕮𝖚𝖙𝖑𝖊𝖗, 𝖋𝖎𝖑𝖎𝖚𝖘 𝕮𝖍𝖔𝖒𝖆𝖊 𝕮𝖚𝖙𝖑𝖊𝖗, 𝖇𝖆𝖕𝖙𝖎𝖟. 𝖗𝖗° 𝖉𝖎𝖊 𝕬𝖕𝖗𝖎𝖑𝖑𝖎𝖘."

"Richard Burges mad. himself away iv April, 1611.

Ould Halliday was buried xxiv May, 1614.

The man slayne with the tree was buried the i day of March, 1616.

Isaacke Waterhouse of Barnsley came to live at thay Ould Toun in the yeare of oure Lord God, 1651.

Richard Sprignall, that lived upon allmes, died v January, 1654.

Thomas Nettleship, a younge man that died at George Carr's, 2 March, 1654.

Tow sons of Margarett Sheppherds that was base begotten, was borne the 12 day of March.

Petter Clayton that hanged himself, died y[e] 28 day of March.

Richard Welles, lanteran macker, died 3 May.

Grace Hirst, an ignurrant boode, died 18 June.

Jane Foxley, an ould single woman, dwelt with Mr. Waterhouse, buried 5 June, 1669.

Ann, daughter of a poore woman that was brought to bed att John Fosterds, bap. 5 Dec. 1670.

John Blacker, bellman, buried, 16 Jan. 1671.

Samuel Truelove.

John Fish[1], died from wounds received from contents of a gun discharged by Samuel Truelove, 26 June, 1787, aged 24."

The Incumbency.

THE INCUMBENCY.

About the year 1300 the prior of Pontefract gave to the curate of Barnsley a pension of five pounds per annum, which was to be paid by the

---

[1] An account of this tragedy has been given in a work by Mr. Burland, entitled, "Sketches of Local Characters." Truelove died 24th April, 1789, aged 68.

BARNSLEY CHAPEL. 207 Chap. VII.

prior's lessees of the tithes of corn, hay, wool, and *The Incumbency.*
lamb; in Dodworth, tithes of wool, lamb; and
small tithes in Stainbrough, and tolls of two fairs
in Barnsley.

In 1592 the vicar of Silkstone commenced a suit *Chancery Suit.*
in Chancery, to which the curate of Barnsley was not
a party. The first decree is entitled, between Robert
Usher, clerk, vicar of Silkstone, plaintiff; and John
Wilkinson, John Hobson, Thomas Cutler, and Henry
Burdet, defendants. Trinity Term, 34th Elizabeth,
A.D. 1592. The substance of it is that the vicar of
Silkstone had always had a pension of twenty marks
from the farmer of the tithes of the rectory of Silkstone, namely, the tithe of hay, wool, and lamb, and
other small tithes of Silkstone, Barnsley, and Cawthorne; the tithes of corn, hay, and other small
tithes of Dodworth; with the tithe of wool and lamb
and other small tithes of Stainbrough; and the toll
of two fairs holden at Barnsley, one called " St. Paul
Fair," and the other " St. Elly Fair," whereof the
defendants were lessees (or farmers), and that the
defendants had withheld payment of the said pension
of twenty marks and certain other payments due
from them. Wherefore it was decreed by the Court
that the said defendants should pay the said pension, and the other pensions, synodals, &c., before
expressed in the shares therein mentioned.

It appears that after this decree there was still
some dispute about the matter, and the vicar still
remained unpaid; therefore a second decree was
made by the Court, empowering the Archbishop of
York to call the lessees before him, and compel
them, by such means as to him should seem good,
to pay all arrearages of the said pensions, &c., and
to appoint what portion should be paid by every
several lessee.

Chap. VII. 208 HISTORY OF BARNSLEY.

The Incumbency. Augmentation.

In consideration of the incumbent of Barnsley only receiving an income of £22 per annum for his services, the freeholders and inhabitants, on the 12th of October, 1714, agreed to enclose thirty-three acres of land from the common, provided the consent of the lord of the manor could be obtained, which, on application being made to him, being granted, that quantity of land was set apart for the incumbent, in conformity with the Act of Parliament made and passed in the 12th year of the reign of Queen Anne. The Rev. Thomas Peighen was then minister. It was my intention to have furnished a list of the incumbents of St. Mary's, could the same have been given satisfactorily, and in succession.

The Mence Family.

The Mence family, by whom the incumbency was held for several generations, came to Barnsley from Worcester in the year 1726.

The minister resided at the Old Town until 1737, in which year the parsonage was erected, which was further enlarged by the Rev. Benjamin Mence in 1796. A part of the building, projecting into the street, was taken down to widen the road by the trustees of the Shaw Lands in 1823, and by way of compensation, an addition of three rooms was built on a site adjoining the north side, on land given by Mr. Robert Richardson.

In 1733 the living produced £40 from land and £15 from fees. In 1805 the total annual income was about £100, while in 1816 the rents amounted to the sum of £180, and the fees to £30. The total amount now received by the minister is upwards of two hundred and twenty pounds per annum.

In one volume of the registers is an account of the property belonging to the church of St. Mary, in connection with which appears the following:—

BARNSLEY CHAPEL. 209 Chap. VII.

"And whereas, it is required of all rectors, vicars, and curates to show what hath been customarily paid in their respective parishes or chapelries for mortuaries and Easter offerings, marriages, christenings, and burials. The answer is: Mortuaries and Easter offerings are received by the impropriators;

Fees paid to Incumbent.

	s.	d.
For a marriage pursuant to the publication of the banns, two shillings have been usually paid to our minister	2	0
And to the clerk one shilling	1	0
And for notifying to the minister of another parish that the banns were published here	1	0
For a licensed marriage the accustomed dues to the minister are thirteen shillings and four pence	13	4
And to the clerk two shillings and six pence	2	6

Marriage Fees.

As to the burials, if the corpse be interred only in a winding sheet, in our chapelyard—

Burial Fees.

	s.	d.
The minister's dues are ten pence	0	10
The clerk's four pence	0	4
The sexton's four pence	0	4
But if the body is coffin'd—		
Then the minister's due is sixteen pence	1	4
The clerk's eight pence	0	8
The sexton's six pence	0	6

For every one buried in the body of the chapel—

	s.	d.
The minister's due is two shillings and six pence	2	6
Besides breaking up the ground three shillings and four pence	3	4
Which sum of three shillings and four pence the chapel wardens received formerly, till the time of our former incumbent, Mr. Thomas Peighen, to whom it was given by the courtesy of the town.		
The clerk's dues are two shillings and six pence	2	6
And the sexton's one shilling	1	0

o

Chap. VII. 210   HISTORY OF BARNSLEY.

Burial Fees.   For a burial in the chancel—

	s.	d.
The minister ordinarily receives five shillings .	5	0
The clerk two shillings	2	0
The sexton eighteen pence . . .	1	6

For a burial within the rails, near or about the Communion Table—

	s.	d.
The minister hath seven shillings and six pence .	7	6
The clerk two shillings and six pence . .	2	6
And the sexton two shillings . . .	2	0
For a burial in the North Quire—		
To the minister seven shillings and six pence .	7	6
To the clerk two shillings and six pence . .	2	6
And to the sexton one shilling . . .	1	0
For a burial in the South Quire—		
The minister's due is seven shillings and six pence	7	6
The clerk's two shillings and six pence . .	2	6
And the sexton's one shilling . . .	1	0

Patron and Incumbent. The living is in the gift of the Archbishop of York. Henry Robert Alder is the present incumbent, he having succeeded Robert Willan.

ST. GEORGE'S CHURCH.

St. George's Church.

This is a beautiful structure in the decorated Gothic style, the first stone of which was laid on St. George's day, A.D. 1821, in the presence of from fifteen to twenty thousand persons.

Freemasons. The Freemasons took part in the ceremony, and attended from the following places: Edinburgh, Wigan, Preston, Chesterfield, Hopton, Thornhill, Huddersfield, Sheffield, Rotherham, Wakefield, Leeds, and Doncaster. A lodge was opened in the Grammar School by Brother Andrew Faulds, W.M., and soon after twelve o'clock the procession moved

ST. GEORGE'S CHURCH. 211 Chap. VII.

off to the site of the church in the following order:— Procession of Freemasons.

Detachment of the Barnsley Troop of Yeomanry.
Children of the National School.
Mr. Rickman of Liverpool, Architect.
Rev. Robert Willan, Curate of Barnsley.
Gentlemen of the Town on Foot.
Two Tylers with drawn Swords.
Inscription Plate carried by the Master of a Lodge.
Two Stewards with Wands.
Music.
Junior Brethren.
Architect with Mallet.
Superintendent of Works with the Plan.
Deacons with Wands.
Secretary carrying the Book of Constitution on a purple
velvet cushion.
Registrar.
Treasurer carrying his Staff and the Bible with Deposits.

| Steward with a Wand. | { St. George's Lodge, (Doncaster) Banner. } | Steward with a Wand. |

Chaplain.
Warden.
P. Masters.
Masters.
Wine, Oil, and Corn carried by three Masters of Lodges.
Junior Warden with the Plumb.
Senior Warden with the Level.

| Steward with a Wand. | { Volume of the Sacred Law carried on a crimson velvet cushion. } | Steward with a Wand. |

Deputy-Master with the Square.

| Steward with a Wand. | } Friendly Lodge Banner. { | Steward with a Wand. |

Banner.
Sword Bearer.
The W. Master.
Two Stewards with Wands.
Two Tylers.
Operative Masons, not being Freemasons, with White Aprons.
Cavalry.

A bottle was deposited by the treasurer in a

Chap. VII. 212   HISTORY OF BARNSLEY.

Foundation Ceremony. cavity in the lower part of the stone, containing, amongst other coins, a sovereign, a half-sovereign, a crown, and a half-crown of George IV., over which was placed a brass plate, bearing the following inscription :—

"By the blessing of Almighty God, in the name of the Right Hon. and Right Rev. Edward, Lord Archbishop of York and Primate of England, on the 23rd day of April, A.D. MDCCCXXI, being the second year of the reign of his most gracious Majesty King George IV., Grand Patron of Ancient, Free, and Accepted Masons of England—Prince Augustus Frederick Duke of Sussex, Earl of Inverness, Baron of Arklow, &c., &c., Grand Master—the first stone of a new church, to be called St. George's, was laid by the Freemasons, in the presence of the Rev. Robert Willan, A.M., curate of Barnsley, and great numbers of the inhabitants of the town and neighbourhood. The entire expense of the building, amounting to £5,743 15s., was defrayed by the commissioners for building new churches, in his Majesty's name, out of the Parliamentary grant of £1,000,000. The site of the church and cemetery was purchased of Richard Pickering of Barnsley, M.D., out of a fund raised for the purpose by private subscription, and under the authority of two Acts of Parliament for building new churches, passed in the 58th and 59th years of the reign of his late Majesty King George III. Thomas Rickman of Liverpool, architect."

Consecration. The church was consecrated on the 22nd of October, 1822. In the interior thereof are the following memorials :—

Monuments. "Sacred to the memory of Susan, wife of Richard Pickering, M.D., who died the 4th day of July, 1831, aged 55 years. Also of Margaret, relict of the Reverend William Porter of Worsbrough, who died the 25th day of November, 1832, aged 81 years, universally respected."

"To the memory of the Reverend Matthew Mark, the first incumbent of this district church, in which for a period of nearly fourteen years he preached the gospel of Christ. He was a man of great integrity of heart, good sense, and piety

ST. GEORGE'S CHURCH. 213 Chap. VII.

Monuments.

unfeigned. A workman that needed not to be ashamed, rightly dividing the word of truth. To commemorate his worth, and to give an enduring testimony of the place he held in their esteem, a few of his friends caused this tablet to be inscribed. He died the 7th of April, A.D. 1836, in the 52nd year of his age."

" In memory of John Micklethwait of Shepcote House, in Ardsley, who died the xxix day of July, MDCCCXXXVIII, aged lxxix years."

" Sacred to the memory of James Lister of this town, merchant, who departed this life xxi August, MDCCCXLVI, aged lxxxii years. Also of Frances his wife, who departed this life xxiii June, MDCCCXLIV, aged lxxiii years. This monument, the last tribute of affection, was erected by their only daughter, Mary, the wife of Edward Newman, to record the worth of her revered parents."

" Sacred to the memory of William Dandison, who departed this life January 10, 1849, in the 61st year of his age. Blessed be the name of the Lord from this day forth and for ever. Amen."

The beautiful stained-glass window, representing the assumption of our Saviour, has only recently been added. The living is a curacy, valued at about £150 per annum, now enjoyed by the Rev. Richard Earnshaw Roberts, M.A., and in the gift of the Archbishop of York.

Curacy.

ST. JOHN'S CHURCH.

St. John's Church.

This edifice, now in course of erection, is in the early decorated style of architecture. Its total length is 106 feet, and extreme width 45 feet. All the seats, in nave and aisles, are to be free, and will consist of low, open benches, calculated to accommodate about 600 people. The estimated cost of

Chap. VII. 214   HISTORY OF BARNSLEY.

St. John's Church. the building is £2,000, towards which, including grants from the Ripon Diocesan Church Building Society, Incorporated Society, and Church Commissioners, £1,714 have been collected. Mr. Edward Newman gave the site; Mr. William Shaw of Stanley Hall, near Wakefield, the stone for the building.

Foundation. The first stone was laid on the 20th of November, 1856, and in it was deposited a copper plate, bearing the following inscription :—

> "This foundation stone, of St. John's Church, was laid by Edward Newman, Esq., the 20th day of November, 1856. Philip Boyce, architect; William John Binder, minister; George Ward, William Frudd, Joseph Fogg, Henry Wilkinson, members of the Building Committee."

Curacy. St. John's is a perpetual curacy, value £130, in the alternate patronage of the Crown and the Bishop of Ripon.

THE WESLEYAN CHAPEL.

Wesleyan Chapel, Pitt Street. This neat and spacious structure is situate in Pitt Street, and was erected from a design furnished by Mr. James Simpson of Leeds. Its style of architecture is Grecian, and it has accommodation for **Foundation.** 1,800 hearers. The foundation stone was laid, in the presence of about 3,000 persons, by Mr. Thos. Cope, a liberal contributor towards the undertaking, who was presented with a silver trowel, bearing the inscription :—

> "Presented to Thomas Cope, Esquire, as an expression of esteem, by the trustees of the Wesleyan Chapel, on his laying the foundation stone.—Barnsley, September 1, 1845."

THE WESLEYAN CHAPEL. 215 Chap. VII.

The munificent sum of £460 was collected at the different opening services; the first of which took place on the 8th of October, 1846.

Opening Services.

A brass plate was deposited in the foundation stone, bearing the following inscription :—

"In the name of God the Father, Son, and Holy Ghost, MDCCCXLV, the first stone of this Wesleyan Methodist Chapel was laid, in the presence of the Rev. Joseph Entwisle and Rev. Thomas Capp, ministers, and of Thomas Cope, John Cope, T. M. Carter, John Gelder, John Goody, Charles Harrison, Thomas Morley, George Moxon, R. R. Raywood, Henry Richardson, John Rollin, Joseph Smith, John Shepherd, John Twibell, James Taylor, trustees.

"This edifice is erected by subscription, at a cost of £5,000, under the authority of the Conference—Dr. Bunting being President."

The interior is well finished, and its greatest ornament is the grand organ, built by Hill & Son of London, which obtained a medal at the Great Exhibition of 1851. This was bought by subscription, is an instrument of great power, and much admired for its sweetness of tone. Mr. Wood is organist.

The Organ.

On the wall of the chapel is a neat marble tablet, bearing the following inscription :—

Monument to Mr. Keeling.

" In memory of the Reverend Ralph Ratcliffe Keeling, late superintendent of the Barnsley circuit, who died August 30, 1851, in the fifty-sixth year of his age, and the twenty-eighth of his ministry.

"This tablet is erected by the quarterly meeting, as a testimony of their deep respect for his manly and Christian virtues, and their cherished remembrance of his affectionate and judicious fidelity as a pastor of the flock of Christ, and an able minister of the New Testament. Thomas Cope, John Twibell, circuit stewards."

Chap. VII. 216   HISTORY OF BARNSLEY.

Wesleyan Methodists.

Wesley's preachers held services in this town upwards of eighty years ago, which were sometimes conducted in the Market Place; as at other places, they experienced much persecution, being frequently assailed by the mob with rotten eggs, dirt, &c.

Visit of John Wesley.

John Wesley himself once preached near to the same spot. In his journal is this entry:—

" Frid., June 30, 1786.—I turned aside to Barnsley, formerly famous for all manner of wickedness. They were then ready to tear any Methodist preacher in pieces. Now not a dog wagged his tongue. I preached near the Market Place to a very large congregation; and I believe the Word sank into many hearts. They seemed to drink in every word. Surely God will have a people in this place."

A few years after Wesley's visit a society was formed, and the services held for some time in a chamber in Eastgate. As the members and congregation increased, a larger place was requisite, and towards the close of the last century Westgate Chapel was erected, to which some additions have since been made. This is now the property of the Primitive Methodists, having been purchased by them for the sum of £525 after the erection of Pitt Street Chapel. The number of members in the Barnsley Wesleyan Methodist circuit, as given at the last Conference, amounted to 568, being an increase of 65 on the preceding year.

Westgate Chapel.

Primitive Methodists.

Independent Chapel.

THE INDEPENDENT CHAPEL,

situate in Regent Street, is an elegant structure in the decorated Gothic style, with tower and lofty spire; the foundation stone was laid on the 28th of November, 1854, by Mr. John Shaw of this town,

THE INDEPENDENT CHAPEL.　　217　Chap. VII.

ironfounder, to whom was presented a polished *Independent*
mahogany mallet, together with a silver trowel, *Chapel.*
bearing the inscription :— *The Founda-*
tion.

"Presented to Mr. John Shaw on his laying the foundation
stone of the new Congregational Chapel, Regent Street, Barnsley, Nov. 28, 1854."

Some silver and copper coins were placed under
the foundation stone, together with a copy of the
"Leeds Mercury" newspaper, and a parchment
document, on which was written :—

"The stone, under which this record is deposited, was laid
with due ceremony and sacred service, as the corner stone of a
place of Christian worship, to be called 'The Regent Street
Congregational Chapel,' for the use of a Christian church and
congregation in Barnsley, Yorkshire, the church being known as
the Congregational or Independent Church, which was first
formally constituted by the Rev. Mr. Docker, on Lord's day,
January the 9th, in the year of our Lord 1825, and has since
continued to meet in Salem Chapel, Blucher Street, Barnsley,
under the successive pastorates of the Revds. John Orange,
Joshua Armitage, and Benjamin Beddow. The structure, of
which this stone forms a part, including the school-rooms and
vestries, owes its existence mainly to the munificence of Mr.
William Shaw of Porto Bello, near Wakefield, who was a native
of Worsbro'-dale, near Barnsley, and who generously engaged to
contribute one-half of the cost, the English Congregational
Chapel Building Society giving a grant of £500, and the remaining portion being raised by voluntary offerings of the congregation and their friends. The estimated cost of the building,
exclusive of the land and of professional charges, was £3,978 1s.,
the freehold plot of ground having been purchased for £735.
The digging for the foundations was begun on the 28th Sept.,
1854, and the first stone was laid by the workmen on the 16th
October in the same year. In the name of the Father, and of the
Son, and of the Holy Ghost, to the glory of the only true God,
and Jesus Christ whom He hath sent, this corner stone was
laid by Mr. John Shaw (brother of the above named William

Chap. VII. 218   HISTORY OF BARNSLEY.

Independent Chapel. Shaw), one of the deacons of the aforesaid church, under the pastorate of the Rev. B. Beddow, during the eleventh year of his pastorate, on Tuesday the 28th day of November, in the year of our Lord, 1854, and in the 17th year of the reign of her Majesty Queen Victoria. The undermentioned persons were officially connected with the undertaking:—Rev. B. Beddow, pastor; John Shaw and Thomas Bellwood, deacons; William Shaw, Esq., and Sigsworth Simpson, T. Guest, John Huntley, B. Beddow, C. Harvey, John Shaw, John Naylor, Joseph Hawcroft, John Smorfit, John Wilcock, John Elliott, Samuel Bottomley Jackson, Wm. Park, Richard Ledger, Henry Rhodes, G. Rogerson, William Booth, A. Brown, and Jonathan Carnley, trustees. S. B. Jackson, T. Bellwood, W. Shaw (absent in Lisbon), Isaac Briggs (London), Sigsworth Simpson, Thomas Guest, John Shaw, Joseph Hawcroft, John Wilcock, Richard Sugden, George Rogerson, and Jonathan Carnley, building committee. Joseph James, architect, London. John Whitworth, superintendent of works. David Ainsworth, mason; Joshua Jackson & Sons,[1] Milns Bridge, joiners; William Brown, plumber and glazier; Charles Rogers, painter, contractors. 'Except the Lord build the house they labour in vain that build it.'—Psalm 127 v. 2. 'Let Thy work appear unto Thy servants, and Thy glory unto their children, and let the beauty of the Lord our God be upon us; and establish Thou the work of our hands unto us; yea the work of our hands establish thou it.'—Psalm 90, v. 16 and 17.''

This edifice was opened for public worship on the 25th of September, 1856, when the collections connected therewith amounted to the sum of £149.

Ancient Chapel.

ANCIENT CHAPEL.

A religious edifice formerly stood upon or near to the site of Messrs. Tee & Son's warehouse, but to what denomination it belonged does not appear to be known. While the workmen were excavating, previous to the erection of the premises above men-

[1] Jackson & Sons having thrown up their contract, the joiners' work was executed by Mr. Henry Harrison.

QUAKERS', CALVINIST, AND CATHOLIC CHAPELS. 219 Chap. VII.

tioned, a gravestone was found with a cross upon it. *Ancient Chapel.*
The name of Chapel Fold still adheres to the
place.

THE QUAKERS' CHAPEL.

Quakers' Chapel.

George Fox the (founder), and others of the
fraternity, visited this locality, and through their
preaching many converts were made, one of whom,
Gamaliel Milner, Esq., of Monk Bretton, about A.D.
1657, gave land at that place for a Quakers' burial-
ground, whereon a meeting-house was afterwards
erected, to which the Barnsley Friends resorted up
to 1816.   In the latter year the Quakers' Chapel at ,
Barnsley was built, and in it is preserved a brass
plate, bearing a curious inscription, which was formerly placed over the entrance to the burying-ground
at Monk Bretton.   Tradition says the first Quaker
that died in England was interred in this ground.

THE CALVINIST CHAPEL

Calvinist Chapel.

is situate near the Sheffield Road, and has a burial
ground attached to it.   Over the entrance door of
the building is the following inscription —

" *Domum tuam decet Jehova diuturna sanctitas.
Psal. xciii. 5. Ædificata erat publicis donis. Anno
Domini* 1778."

The place where the services are conducted is
only small.   A tablet records the death of the Rev.
Robert Ellis, who had been minister here for 45
years.

THE ROMAN CATHOLIC CHAPEL

*Roman Catho-
lic Chapel.*

(which has received the name of Holyrood Chapel)
is in the Grecian style, has a richly decorated interior, and a good organ.

Chap. VIII. 220   HISTORY OF BARNSLEY.

Roman Catholic Chapel.   During the Reign of Terror in France at the end of the last century, England offered a safe retreat from the scene of anarchy. Amongst the exiles were many of the French clergy, who spread themselves over England. The little Catholic congregation at Barnsley, who numbered about forty, were favoured with the services of the Rev. Vincent Louis Denis, one of the exiled priests. He entered on his missionary duty A.D. 1800 at Barnsley, Burghwallis, and Penistone, which he fulfilled until his death, in the year 1819. His remains were deposited in the churchyard at Penistone. Until 1821 the services were conducted in private houses, but the late Mr. Locke, with the assistance of the Rev. Benedict Raymont, vicar-general of York, and other friends, erected the first chapel, which was opened in 1824, and enlarged, so as to accommodate 600 persons, in 1832. The congregation at present numbers about 2,000. The Rev. Henry Cooke is priest.

Other Chapels.

OTHER CHAPELS.

There are other chapels: Salem Chapel, built by the Independents in 1825, and lately sold for the sum of £700 to the Wesleyan Reformers; a small chapel in Wilson's Piece, erected by the Primitive Methodists in 1824; the Wesleyan Association Chapel, containing 700 sittings, built A.D. 1829, with a spacious school-room underneath; the Methodist New Connexion Chapel, in New Street, containing 700 sittings, and a good organ; the Baptist Chapel, erected in the year 1849.

HISTORY OF BARNSLEY. 221 Chap. VII.

SUNDAY SCHOOLS.

Sunday
Schools.

Subjoined is a list of the Sunday Schools belonging to different denominations, with the number of scholars and teachers in attendance :—

Church of England—	Scholars.	Teachers.
St. Mary's	220	24
St. George's . . .	300	50
St. John's	269	32
Wesleyan—		
Pitt Street	228	46
Sunday School Union—		
New Connexion . . .	403	36
Independents . . .	263	32
Primitive Methodists . .	341	32
Baptist	147	21
Free Gospel . . .	132	16
United Methodist Free Church School	354	49
Christian Church (Salem) .	61	22

CHAPTER VIII.

THE CHARITIES.

Abstract of Returns of Charitable Donations (County of York, West Riding) for the Benefit of Poor Persons, 26th George III., 1786—page 1566—Staincross Wapentake. [*A more detailed account of some of these is afterwards given.*]

Name of the Parish, Township, &c	Names of the Persons who gave the Charity.	When given.	Whether by Will or Deed.	Description of the Charity, and for what purposes given.	Whether in Land or Money.	In whom now Vested.	Gross Amount of that given in Money. £ s. d.	Annual Produce of the Money. £ s. d.	Clear Annual Produce of that given in Land, after deducting the Rents issuing thereout. £ s. d.	Observations.
Barnsley.	Edmund Brookhouse.	A.D. 1493	Unknown.	To Build Almshouses for the Poor.	Money.	Overseers.	26 13 4	— — —	— — —	Expended accordingly.
				To the Poor, and occupied by them.	3 Cottages, &c.	Do.				
				To the Poor.	Rent charge.	Do.	— — —	— — —	0 16 8	
				Do.	Do.	Do.	— — —	— — —	0 16 8	
	Edmund Rogers.	1616	Will.	To the Poor.	Land Rent charge.	Do.	— — —	— — —	35 0 0	
	*Thos. Cutler.	1622	Do.	To the Poor of Silkstone Parish, which consists of this and five more Townships, to be laid out in Lands.	Money.	His Heirs.	†40 0 0	— — —	1 10 0	A sixth of the now Rent. † Now in Land. * Depending in Chancery. Vide Hoylandswaine.
	*Ellen Cutler, his widow.	1633	Do.	To the Poor of Barnsley Town and Silkstone Parish, a moiety to this	Land.	Do.			4 0 0	Or thereabouts.

	Donor	Date	How given	Object	Property	By whom paid	£ s. d.	£ s. d.	£ s. d.	Remarks
			Will.		Rent charge. Land.	Overseer. Dean of York Godfrey Wentworth, and others.			0 0 8	
	George Ellis.	1711	Will.	For books for teaching 20 boys & girls, to the curate for catechising them, and for apprenticing one of them.	Land.	Dean of York Godfrey Wentworth, and others.	— — —	— — —	18 16 8	This sum, £18 16s. 8d., issues annually from the said Trustees (called Head Trustees), being part of the Rent of a considerable Estate, unto certain local Trustees of different neighbouring towns, of which this town is one, and the local Trustees here are now—The minister, J. Deykin, Jos. Beckett, Geo. Clarke, and Thomas Hall.
	Samuel Allen.	—	...	To 40 Poor Widows.	Money.	Allen Watson.	— — —	2 0 0	— — —	Withheld for some years past—there is no reason for withholding it.
	Ann Grantham.	1748	...	To the Poor.	Do.	Wm. Broom.	50 0 0	— — —	— — —	Withheld. William Broom, Esq., of Manchester, acknowledges the donation, and gives hopes of payment, but neglects, and the inhabitants supine.
Hoyland-swaine.	Ellen Cutler, widow of Thos. Cutler.	1633	Will.	Two Closes in Barnsley, called the Upper or Farther, and nearer Amias Closes, to the Poor in Silkstone Parish.	Lands.	John Alderson.	— — —	— — —	18 0 0	An uncertain donation—nothing since 1779.
	...		Do.	The nearer Amias Close to the Poor of Barnsley and Silkstone Parish, viz.: to the Town of Barnsley one-half of the Rent thereof, and to Silkstone Parish the other half of the rent thereof. An allotment to said Closes on an inclosure.	Do.	John Malinson.	— — —	— — —	1 1 0	The rents have been withheld for a number of years, because of the difficulty of proving the right heirs of Sir Gervase Cutler. The business has been some time before the Chancellor, and it is expected Trustees will be soon appointed.

CHARITABLE BEQUESTS.

Edmund Brookhouse's[1] Bequest.—Extract from his Will.

Edmund Brookhouse of Doncaster, by his will, dated 24th May, 1493, gave as follows :—

" I also bequeath, for the building, curation, and reparation of three houses or tenements of alms by my executors undermentioned, to be sustained, built, and repaired, nigh to the burial-ground of the same town of Barnesley, 40 marks of lawful English money ; the first of which I will shall be in honour of St. Mary the Virgin, to be built on the southern side, and in the same, I will that my executors shall make, or cause to be made, three beds for poor impotent and lame men in the same hospital to be for ever entertained.

" The second tenement, in honour of St. John the Evangelist, shall be built on the northern side.

" The third I will in honour of St. John the Baptist, and it shall be built near Kirk Stile on the northern side."

The site of one of these was where now stands the old workhouse.

Mrs. Ellen Cutler's Bequest.—Extract from her Will, dated 27th November, 1633.

" Allsoe (in rgde for acknowledgm^t, and my owne humble thainks to God for his mercies to my sellfe, moste unworthie of them), I doe further give, will, and bequeath to my s^d sone, Sr Gervase Cutler, that one other close in Barnesley, called the Nearer or Narr Amyas Close, and beinge nearest to the s^d towne, and soe allsoe purchased as last affor^{sd}, viz., of one Robert Wood of Barnesley, and nowe, or late, beinge in the occupacion of one Thomas Andersone. To have and to houlde the s^d Nearer or Narr Amyas Close, wth all and singular the appurtenances and hereditaments to the same belonging, to my said sone, Sr Gervase

---

[1] These almshouses, about the time of the Reformation, came, it was not known how, into the hands of Matthew Wentworth, of Bretton, Esq., in whose possession they continued for forty years, until, in the year of King James, of England the 14th and of Scotland the 49th, an inquiry having been made by commissioners, under statute 43rd Eliz., Matthew Wentworth was ordered to restore said almshouses to the town, and to pay 33s. 4d. yearly to the churchwardens and overseers of the poor for the upholding and support thereof.

CHARITABLE BEQUESTS. 225

Mrs. Ellen Cutler's Bequest.

Cutler, and his heirs for ever. To the onely proper use and behoofe of the most needefull poore of Barnesley towne and Silkstone p'ishe for ever. And Barnesley poore to have the one-half yeare's rente every yeare whoolye to themselves, and Silkstone p'ishe poore thother halfe-yeare's rente wholie everye yeare to themselves, and to be distributed by my s[d] son, his heirs, and assignes for ever."

Mrs. Cutler died about 1635, and the first donation to the poor of Barnsley was made at Whitsuntide, in the year 1636, by order of Sir Gervase Cutler, in the presence of Richard Haslam, Edward Oxley, Percival Thryst, and Edward Robinson, churchwardens; Simon Carter, Richard Swinden, Francis Thompson, and Gervase Hinchliffe, overseers. When five of the recipients, who numbered altogether twenty-five, received the sum of two shillings each, and the remainder one shilling each. Amongst the names appears that of John Knitter Wyseman of Barnsley.

Edmund Rogers' Bequest.—Extract from his Will.

Edmund Rogers' Bequest.

Edmund Rogers[1], by his will, dated 11th January, 1646, after making certain devises and bequests in favour of Ellen Rooke and Alice Hinchliffe, wife of Edward Hinchliffe, and daughter of testator's brother, Thomas Meller—

" Gave and bequeathed all those his tythes of corne and graine, comeing, groweing, and reneweing of, in, and upon the fields in the territoryes of Thorpe Audline, and soe much of the fields in the territoryes of Wentbridge as were within the parish of Badsworth, and the laithe or barne he there built, and the three roods of land there which belonged to him, with theire, and every of theire, appurtenances, unto and for the use of the poore people of the town and parish of Barnsley, to be employed

---

[1] *Temp. Car.* I. Edmund Rogers was collector of the Queen's rents for Barnsley, which was part of the dower of Queen Henrietta Maria.—*Hunter.*

P

Chap. VIII. 226   HISTORY OF BARNSLEY.

Edmund Rogers' Bequest.

by the overseers of the poore there for ever towards the relief of the said poore there, being the rent yearely for ever reserved, and paid the rent of forty-six shillings and eight pence unto the poore people of Thorpe Audline, and part of Wentbridge aforesaid. And testator directed that Francis Watson and Hughe Allen should during their lives enjoy the said tithes and premises, paying thereout the rent of £10 and forty-six shillings and eight pence, and such other rents as issued thereout. Testator appointed John Armitage of Keresforth Hill, Gent., and Robert Wood of Monk Bretton, executors of his will, and directed them to pay the legacies following, viz. (amongst others):—To Mrs. Sandford of Silkstone, £30; to Mrs. Bateson of Barnsley, £10; to Mr. John Waterhouse, £50; to the three other children of Mr. John Waterhouse, testator's late landlord, £50; to testator's landlady, Mrs. Massie, £50; and £20 to be imployed towards the maintenance of a preacher at Middopp Chapel, and when the place is vacant, to the poore of Waldershelfe during the said vacancy; to the poor of Silkestone, £50; to the poore of the township of Kirkeby, £50, the profit of both legacies to be yearely employed respectively as aforesaid; to testator's tenant, John Swallowe, £10; to Mr. Hatefielde, vicar of Darton, £5; and testator desired his executors to

Moot Hall Clock.

bestowe £10 for the erecting of a clocke in the Towne Hall in Barnsley aforesaid; testator also gave £50 for and towards the erecting of a school-house in Barnsley; and £50 more for the erecting of a house for a preaching minister in Barnsley aforesaid; and testator desired Mr. Gregorye Armitage, Mr. Nicholas Broadley, and Thomas Wood to be supervisors of his will, and to help his executors; and testator's will was, that Thomas Smith should enjoy (amongst other things) the tythes in Barnsley after testator's executors had received one year's proffitt thereof, paying to the said executors for the remainder of the tyme, then to enforce by testator's lease £40 per annum. Witnesses to the will—Thomas Garnett, Robert Bower, Rowland Ottes," &c.

Jonathan Rhodes' Bequest.

Jonathan Rhodes' Bequest.—Extract from his Will.

Jonathan Rhodes of Glewhouse, in Worsbroughdale, county of York, by his will, dated 16th of June, 1653, gave to his cousin, Elias Oxley of Ardsley, and his heirs, the reversion of two closes of meadow, containing four acres, and called Collie

CHARITABLE BEQUESTS.   227   Chap. VIII.

Crofts, within Worsbrough-dale, after the death of Olive Rhodes, subject to the payment of 10s. a year to the poor of Worsbrough, and 10s. a year to the poor of Ardsley. The will then goes on as follows :— *Jonathan Rhodes' Bequest.*

"*Item.* I give unto the poore of Barnsley six shillings and *Barnsley Poor.* eight pence a year to be paid by the said Elias Oxley, his heirs and assigns for ever, forth of the rents. and profitts of the said two closes which I have given and bequeathed unto the said Elias Oxley, his heirs and assigns for ever, in trust, that he, the said Elias Oxley, his heirs and assigns, shall yearly pay, or cause to be paid, the said several sums of money to the said poore of Worsbrough and Worsbrough-dale, Ardsley and Barnsley, yearly, and every year for ever, forth of the said two closes and premises, after the decease of Olive Rhodes, my said mother.

"*My will and mind is,* that the overseers of the poore of the said severall towns for the time being shall receive the several sumes of money yearly for ever, for the use and behoofe of the said poore as before mentioned, at the feast of the Nativity of Christ. Only *my will and mind is,* that if the said Elias Oxley, his heirs and assigns, doe not pay yearly the said severall sumes of money as aforesaid, being lawfully demanded, that then it shall and may be lawfull to, and for the said severall overseers for the time being, and my executrix, their heirs and assigns, to enter and distrean, and the distress or distresses in the said promises, to lead, drive, and carry away, and the same to keep till the said rent be truly paid, with their arerages thereof, if any such, be satisfied unto the overseers for the poore."

George Ellis' Bequest.—Extract from his Will. *George Ellis' Bequest.*

The following is an extract from the will of Mr. George Ellis of Brampton, dated 24th January, 1711, relating to the National[1] School at Barnsley :—

" Also, I give and bequeath £6 13s. 4d. per annum for ever

[1] The National School was erected partly by the trustees of Ellis' charity, and partly by contributions from the inhabitants of Barnsley, A D. 1815, at a cost of £1,500 ; and a new system of education was adopted from Dr. Bell.

Chap. VIII. 228 HISTORY OF BARNSLEY.

George Ellis' Bequest.

for the teaching of twenty of the poorest boys and girls in and about the town of Barnsley, at Barnsley, to be chosen by my trustees for that school, to read the Bible and instruct them in the Church Catechism, and twenty shillings per annum for ever to buy them proper books, and ten shillings per annum for ever to buy them coals, and fifty shillings per annum for ever for putting out one of the said boys an apprentice to some trade every year, and twenty shillings for ever to the curate of Barnsley for the time being for his care and pains in catechising and instructing the poor children in the principles of the Christian religion. And of those my charities at Barnsley, I do appoint Thomas Edmunds of Worsborough, Esq., Mr. Henry Wood, Mr. John Senior of Dodworth, Mr. John Rooke, Mr. Joseph Dakyne, and the curate for the time being, to be trustees, or overseers and visitors, and I do hereby empower them and their successors to place and displace such schoolmasters or school dames as shall teach there, and such scholars as shall be taught there, as they, or the greater number of them, shall think fit. And my will further is, that when any of these trustees or overseers appointed as aforesaid for Brampton, and Wath, or for Barnsley, shall die, the surviving trustees or overseers appointed for such places respectively, or the major number of them, shall choose another honest man within six months into the room or stead of the person so deceased, and so successively for ever, that my charities may be preserved and employed according to the design and intent of this my will, and that the full number of trustees for each of those places, respectively, be kept up; and I do hereby give ten shillings per annum for ever to such of my trustees or overseers of my charities to Brampton or Wath as shall meet at Brampton once a year for placing or displacing master, dame, or scholars there, and putting out one of the poor boys an apprentice; and the like annual sum of ten shillings per annum for ever I give to such of my trustees or overseers of my charities to Barnsley as shall meet there once a year in like manner, and for the like purposes, which said several sum of ten shillings so given to my said trustees, overseers, or visitors of my charities respectively shall be expended in a treat at each of their respective annual meetings, the time and place whereof shall be appointed by the major number of the trustees or overseers for the several places respectively. But if the said trustees or overseers shall neglect to meet once a year for the purpose aforesaid, then my will is that the said ten shillings shall be withheld from the said neglecting trustees or overseers, and be

THE SHAW LANDS.

229 Chap. VIII.

applied to other purposes by my trustees first mentioned, and this so often as the aforesaid overseers shall neglect to meet once a year."

George Ellis' Bequest.

THE SHAW LANDS.

The Shaw Lands.

These composed a part of the possessions of the monastery of Pontefract, and consist of about 42 acres of land, which were on the 5th of May, 1558, conveyed by Ralph Bosvile[1] of London to Robert Thwaites[2] of Barnsley, for certain charitable uses, and were since that time continued by regular conveyances from one set of trustees to another till the year 1774, when all the trustees (who were mostly, if not always, twelve in number on every new appointment) were dead except two, viz., Francis Wood, Esq., and Thomas Taylor of Barnsley, Gent. On the 4th of April in that year, the two surviving trustees conveyed over their trust to thirty-two gentlemen and tradesmen of Barnsley and the neighbourhood. The uses to which the said lands are and have been always settled and conveyed are as follow, or to the like effect :—

" That the trustees shall pay forth and bestow all the yearly rents and profits by them, or any of them, to be in anywise lawfully made, had, received, and taken of, in, and upon the said mentioned premises, only in and about the commonwealth and

Uses.

---

[1] Bosvile had these lands from Robert Carr of Sleaford, Esq., who had them from Edward Fynes, K.G., Lord Clinton and Saye, who had them from the King, 16th of November, 5th Edw. VI., and they had before then been in the occupation of the churchwardens of Barnsley.—*Hunter*.

[2] Thwaites, by indenture, dated 10th Eliz., grants the same to Thomas Keresforth, sen., Thomas Keresforth, jun., Robert Keresforth, Robert Bayly, Richard Green, Rowland Oates, and others, to hold to the same uses.

Chap. VIII.   230   HISTORY OF BARNSLEY.

The Shaw Lands. Uses.

profit of the whole inhabitants, recent, now, and ever hereafter being within the said town and township of Barnsley, towards the making and amending of their common panniers and carts there for the true service of their prince or princes in their wars, paying their common tax or taxes, repairing of their church or highways, making or mending of their common butts, stocks, pindfolds, or wells therein and about, or belonging to things appertaining to the whole commonwealth of the said township of Barnsley, and if it fortune at any time that there be any remainder of the yearly rents and profits aforesaid over and above these articles aforesaid performed, fulfilled, and done, that then the same be put forth in a stock by the aforesaid feoffees and their heirs, partly by the advice of the greatest part of the most honest and discreet men, being inhabitants of the said town and township of Barnsley, to the intent to make some increase thereof for the profit of all the inhabitants aforesaid; and that the said feoffees, their heirs and assigns, or some of them, shall, from time to time, make new feoffees, for a continual performance of these articles."

Through the influence of a few of the trustees, and the sufferance, though disapprobation, of many of the rest, printed papers were put up in Barnsley announcing that the Shaw Lands would be let in lots in the vestry of St. Mary's Church, on the 8th of June, 1778. This was thought rather hard by the persons then holding, as some of them had been at much expense in the improving of their respective closes.

Tenants and Rents.

The trustees advanced the rents from thirty shillings to two pounds per acre, but no leases were granted on such advance, which was submitted to by the tenants, though not without great reluctance on the part of a few.

Subjoined is an account of the income derived from this property in the seventeenth century, together with names of the tenants at that period. It is headed—

THE SHAW LANDS.

231 Chap. VIII.

"*Moneys Rec. for Shawe Rentes by mee, Richard Chappel*, 1651. Rents in 1651.

	£	s.	d.
Imp. of Perceviall Thrist . . .	1	2	6
John Naylor	0	10	0
Mrs. Donford	1	10	0
James Thrist	1	0	8
George Ward	1	5	0
John Heaward	0	13	0
Richard Swindon . . .	1	8	0
Richard Bower	1	10	0
Dorothie Gillot	1	5	6
Richard Hinchliffe . . .	0	15	0
Mr. Garnett . . .	0	9	0
	£11	8	8

"*More Rec. by mee, Richard Chappel, Easter*, 1652.

Rents in 1652.

	£	s.	d.
Imp. of Mrs. Baiteson	1	13	4
Perceviall Thrist . . .	1	2	6
James Thrist . . .	1	0	8
George Ward	1	5	0
John Heaward . . .	0	13	0
Richard Bower	1	10	0
Dorothie Gillot	1	5	6
Richard Hinchliff . . .	0	15	0
Mr. Garnett	0	9	0
Widow Naylor . . .	0	10	0
	£10	4	0

" We, whose names are underwritten, doe alow of this ritourn for Richard Chappel, churchwarden for the years 1651 and 1652, and hath discharged it. Signed—John Armytage, James Thrist, Francis Thompson, Edward Oxley, Francis Usher, John Shepperd."

Below is a copy of a document, dated 22nd of October, 1696, which relates to the Shaw Lands, and to the misapplication of money left for charitable purposes:—

" We, whose names are subscribed, doe desire that such

Chap. VIII. 232   HISTORY OF BARNSLEY.

The Shaw Lands.

methods may be taken for the bringeing in of a deede of the Shawe Lands, which Mr. Bagnley hath clandestinely p'cured from John Oxley and Thomas Rhodes, two of the surviving feoffees, and likewise for bringing Mr. Joseph Dakins to accompt for all such moneys belonging to poore or minister of Barnsley, or either of them, which he hath recede, or hath in his hands, or hath misimployed, as councell shall advise.

" (Signed)—J. Rooke, Dan. Rooke, John Rooke, William Rooke, Jo. Witlick, Rich. Ellisson, Thomas Ellisson, Richard Woodcock, Francis Oxley, John Clarke."

The Grammar School.

THE GRAMMAR SCHOOL

was founded 18th of June, 1660, by Thomas Keresforth, Gent., for the support of a master who should teach and instruct free all such children as should come to the school to be taught that should be born within the township of Barnsley and Dodworth, whose parents should not be accounted to be worth the sum of £200 in lands or debtless goods, not demanding any penny of them or their parents until such children should be made fit for some university, or disposed of otherwise by their friends and parents. Those persons who should be worth more than £200 in lands or debtless goods should have their children instructed for half the amount paid at other schools in the neighbourhood, so long as they should think fit. The children of the donor's kindred and blood to be freely taught wheresoever they should reside, and the trustees to see that the poorer sort of children should be as well taught as the richer sort. How far the intentions of the founder are carried out others shall determine. The income is now £18 17s. 7d. per annum, and the fee-farm rents, and use of school premises, are estimated at about £50 a-year.

ADDENDA.

It seems that the Romans, during their sojourn in Britain, penetrated into the immediate neighbourhood of Barnsley.[1] Brooke in his MSS. gives a sketch of what appears to have been a Roman altar, which was found on Staincross Common in the year 1782, and, at the time he wrote, in the possession of Thomas Beaumont of Darton, Esquire. This fragment of antiquity bore the following inscription :—

Roman Altar.

DEO MAR
PRO SALVI
DD NN
IMP AVG

Brooke appears to have made a slight error in copying the second line ; the second word should no doubt be SALVT, and the inscription will then run as follows :—

"*Deo Marti pro salute Domini nostri Imperatoris Augusti.*"

Which may be translated thus—

"To the god Mars, for the welfare of our lord the Emperor Augustus."

I made application to Mr. Beaumont of Bretton Hall, thinking that he might be able to give some further information respecting the matter, but without success.

In the 10th Edward II., John Lord Mowbray had orders to array all the commonalty within the

Array of Commonalty, 10th Edw. II.

---

[1] Within a few miles portions of several Roman ridges may be still seen, and many Roman coins have been found.

HISTORY OF BARNSLEY.

Array of Commonalty, 10th Edw. II. wapentakes of Staincross, Barkeston, Agbrig and Morley, and the Soke of Snaith, in order to an expedition into Scotland.

Staincross given to Christopher Talbot for life. The King, in recompense of his services, granted to his beloved and faithful knight, Christopher[1] Talbot, the wapentake of Staincross, in Co. Ebor., for term of life of the said Christopher, with wafes and strayes, &c.

Granted to Thos. Clifford. Henry Vavasour was escheator of the wapentake of Staincross, and released it, when the King granted it to Thomas Clifford and his heirs.

Part of Queen Anne's Jointure. Queen Anne for jointure had (*inter alia*) the wapentake of Staincross.

Nevison the Highwayman. There was formerly a stone in Woolley Park bearing the inscription :—

" Here Nevison[2] killed Fletcher."

Barnsley Mills. A short account of the Barnsley mills will be found at page 121 ; since that sheet was printed, some additional information on the subject has come to light.

It appears that Isacke Waterhouse, a merchant of Woodhouse, near Halifax, was holding two mills at Barnsley (being then the King's mills) in 1608, in which year he instituted a suit in the Exchequer against Gabriel Keresforth and other inhabitants of Barnsley, in consequence of their sending corn to grind at the Abbey Mill of Monk Bretton, and others in the locality. The case was dismissed. And again, in 1637, during Easter Term, we find Sir Francis Wortley bringing an action in the Exchequer against Thomas Headen of Wood Hall Mill,

[1] He was third son of John the first Earl of Salop, and was slain fighting for the house of Lancaster at the battle of Northampton, A.D. 1460.

[2] No doubt the notorious highwayman of that name, harboured by Adam Hawksworth, the innkeeper of Ringstone Hill, who was ordered to have his sign taken down for so doing.

BANRSLEY MILLS. 225 Addenda.

in Darfield, for the same offence. The defendant proceeded to London on foot to appear in the cause, and was brought to ruin through the expenses.

One William Silvester held the mill at Monk Bretton of the King in 1638, at a rent of five nobles per annum, and like Headen seems to have ground a considerable quantity of the corn belonging to the Barnsley people, which excited the wrath of Sir Francis Wortley,[1] who instituted legal proceedings against Silvester, but from its being made appear that the Barnsley people were bound by no custom to grind their corn at the Barnsley Mills, and that those mills were not able to grind half the corn consumed by the townspeople, the case seems to have fallen through.

There appears also to have been a horse-mill at Barnsley belonging to Sir Francis Wortley, which was used chiefly for the grinding of malt; and another mill called the Queen's Mill, rented by Sir Francis Wortley of her then Majesty.

NEWSPAPERS.

The " Barnsley Telegraph " was the first newspaper issued here. In consequence of some dispute

[1] The oldest people in the neighbourhood were brought forward as witnesses in this case. William Shaw of Burton, who is described as being of the age of seventy-seven years, during his examination says, " that he knew Richard Boone, herdsman, who dwelt at Barnsley sixty years ago, carry corn and other grain to the Abbey Mill to grind for the space of nine or ten years together, for which he charged one penny per sack." This would be in the year 1578. Roger Burges said his father " used to carry oats thither to be made into shillinge and oatmeale;" and that there were above 300 householders in Barnsley. James Longbotham states that 240 of the householders are not able to keep or hire a horse to carry their corn; and we may gather from the remarks of Francis Ellis that the population of Barnsley in 1638 numbered from 700 to 750 souls, of whom 500 or 600 were " poore tradesmen," as wiredrawers, colliers, and labourers. And again he says, that the greater part are pitifully poor, and the rest are not able to relieve them without the help of the neighbouring towns. The Barnsley Mills appear to have been very much subject to backwater in time of floods in winter and to drought in summer.

HISTORY OF BARNSLEY.

Addenda 236

Newspapers. amongst the proprietors, its publication only extended over a period of six months—the last number having been issued on the 24th of December, 1852. It had attained a circulation of about 800 per week. The town was without a newspaper of its own, from that time till the 7th of April, 1855, when Mr. Pybus issued the first number of the "Barnsley Times," which is ably conducted, and has in a great measure supplied the requirements of the town and neighbourhood. Its circulation varies from 800 to 1,300 per week.

THE PRIORY OF MONK BRETTON.

Monk Bretton Priory.

The principal object of interest to the antiquarian in the neighbourhood of Barnsley is the remains of the priory of Monk Bretton. These are situate at a distance of about two miles eastward from the town, in the centre of rich pastures, through which the river Dearne takes its winding course. In one of the meadows is a well of excellent water, said to have formerly supplied the wants of the brotherhood. Proceeding in an eastwardly direction from the ruins of the priory along the valley of the Dearne, we come upon some beautiful scenery. On either side, the hills rise boldly to a considerable altitude, and are studded with the remains of those woods through whose glades in times gone by resounded the music of the priory bells, ofttimes striking welcomely the ear of some weary traveller,[1] and reminding him of his near approach to a spot where he might obtain rest and refreshment before proceeding on his journey.

[1] At most of the monasteries, travellers were furnished with lodging and diet for three days, without being questioned as to their business, but after that time they stayed not, unless they rendered an account thereof.

MONK BRETTON PRIORY.

237   Addenda.

Respecting the foundation of the priory, the following curious story appears in the Harl. MS., No. 798 :—

Story respecting the Foundation.

"There was at a place called Lound, neare adjoining, a young man called Lound, who rashly shooting of a peece at a haystack, set the whole towne on fire, whereupon, being troubled in conscience, was p'swaded, for the expiation of his offence, to build a cell at Lound aforesaid, which he did, and gave unto it the Great Lound and Lound Spring, which contayne each of them eighty acre, wch afterwards one Adam, son of Swane, removed to Bretton adjoining, commonly called Burton, and made it a priory, wch of the monks was called Monkbretton."

Some part of the above account is evidently incorrect, as fire-arms were unknown to our Saxon ancestors.

The house of Bretton was founded early in the reign of Henry II., and dedicated to St. Mary Magdalene. Adam[1] Fitz Swein (the founder) appears to have been a pretty considerable baron of the kingdom. Osbert, the archdeacon, who was one of the witnesses to the foundation charter, does not appear after A.D. 1160. Pope Urban confirmed it, and also Roger, Archbishop of York. This priory was for some time under subjection to that of St. John of Pontefract, and like that foundation for monks of the Cluniac[2] order.

The Foundation.

The acquisitions of the priory of Bretton must have been considerable, from the following account

Possessions.

[1] The note following was taken out of an old written book remaining in the hands of Robert Cooke, Esq., Clar. King-at-Arms, anno 1587 :—"Adam Swayn fut le primem fondeur du Prieure de Burton en le Com. de Yorke le g^t portoit en les armes ; Toupas a ung lyon passant Dyamont: whose daughter and heir was married to Mons, Roger de Montbegon."

[2] The reformation of some things which seemed too remiss in St. Benedict's rule, begun by Bernon, abbot of Gigni in Burgundy, but perfected by Odo, abbot of Cluni, about A.D. 912, gave occasion to the rising of the Cluniac order. They lived

Addenda. 238 HISTORY OF BARNSLEY.

Monk Bretton Priory. appearing in a Chartulary[1] of that house, now in the possession of Godfrey Wentworth, Esq., of Woolley :

Chartulary. " In this volume are contained all the charters, feoffments, confirmations, and quit claims of all the lands and tenements which belong, or by any title soever might belong, to the monastery of the Blessed Mary Magdalene of Monk Bretton, and the monks serving God there, according as in their places may more fully and at large be found.

" *Table of the Present Work.*—Firstly, of the original foundation of the above-named monastery, with the church of Roreston, Carleton, with other donations, Fasham, Cudworth, Monkbretton, Carleton, Erdyley, Darffelde, Mylnehouses, Hyll, Howland, Halton Minor, Halton Major, Byllyngley, Thryscho, Hykylton, Cadby, Adwyke super stratum, Doncaster, Wrangbrok, Newhal, Brampto., Wyntworth, Mekysburg, Wyrksburghdalle, Smythley, Barneby, Barghe, Swalyhill, Dartton, Cubley, Brokhows, Oxpryng, Wakeffelde, Ardyslaw, Roston, Aboldehagh, Notton, Darrton et Mapllwell, Morehouses, Wolley, Est Markham, Beghton."

The Library. In the Chartulary is an account of the library possessed by the monks of Bretton, of the fate of

under the rule of St. Benedict, but observed a different discipline. William, Earl of Warren, built their first house at Lewes, in the year 1077. They were all governed by foreigners, and had more French than English monks in them, and the greater part of their revenues was carried to the foreign houses of Cluni, La Charité sur Loire, and St. Martin des Champs at Paris, to which they were subject.—Dugdale's " Monasticon."

[1] Vol. 405 of the Lansdowne MSS. contains 65 parchment leaves of a chartulary of this priory. In 1633 this portion, with 35 more leaves, belonged to Sir Wm. Armyne. It now comprises charters relating to (*inter alia*) property at Scauceby, Tykhill, Melton, Wath, Coldelawe, Warkeworth, Doywellis, Tunstall, Holecumb, Akedene, Middelton-en-le-Peche, and Reddeburne, and Bulls of Popes Clement, Innocent, Urban, and Gregory.

MONK BRETTON PRIORY. 239 Addenda.

which valuable collection of books, with the excep- The Library
tion of two volumes, now in Mr. Wentworth's possession, viz., *Opus Regale de Persecutionibus Ecclesie*,
date 1509, and *Vetus et Novum Testamentum, transla-
tore Hieronymo*, date 1513, nothing definite is
known. Mr. Wentworth says, that when a little boy,
he remembers a quantity of rubbish being burnt,
amongst which appeared to be remains of old
books, which he supposes to have formed part of
this library.

Subjoined is a list of the priors of this house :— List of Priors.

Adam, Roger, 1267; William de Rihale, 1280, resigned
1291; William de Ebor., Richard de Halghton, 1305; William
de Went, 1323; William de Appleby, 1338; William de
Stainton, died 1349; Hugh Brerley, John de Birthwait, 1350;
William de Erdsley, 1385 and 1387; John de Crofton, 1404;
Thomas Dowdale, 1407; John Crofton, 1425; Richard de
Ledes, 1438 and 1484; William Battley, 1486; Robert Drax,
1494; Thomas Tickhill, 1504; William Brown, 1523.

Sir Nicholas Wortley, in his will, dated 1347,
directed that his body should be interred at the
priory of Monk Bretton.

Little now remains of the priory. Within the Present
last few years a great part of the ruins has been Remains.
removed, and the stone used for the erection of
farm buildings. Over the gate-house, which is still
entire, and now used as a barn, is a shield carved
in stone, on which apparently are pourtrayed three
covered cups. The arms borne by the house[1] appear, Arms.
however, according to Dugdale and other authorities,
to have been two covered cups and a cross patée.

Adam Fitz Swein, the original founder, bore for
arms—" *Or* a lion rampant, *Sable*;" but the arms

---

[1] It was customary among religious orders to bear the arms
of the founder wholly, or something varied. Sometimes they
assumed some new device where the founder's coat was not
known, or was uncertain.

Addenda. 240 HISTORY OF BARNSLEY.

Monk Bretton Priory. adopted by the monks were those of Lord Monteagle, a subsequent benefactor, according to the account of Norroy, King-at-Arms, *temp.* Hen. VIII.

Dissolution. In an account of various priories in Yorkshire and Nottinghamshire, at the time of their surrender, is a notice of Monk Bretton, which does not appear to have been hitherto published :—

A brefe certificate made upon the disolucione of div'se Monasteries and Priories ther, surrend^d in the Moneth of Novembre and of Decembre, in the xxxth yere of the reigne of oure Sovane Lord Kyng Henry the viij^t, as hereafter :—

The names of the howses with the kepers.	The clere valew of the possessions over the annual repsz.	The Nowmbre of th' abbotts and brethre, with ther pencions.
Monkebreton priorat. Thomas Ellis.	ccxlvj$^{Li.}$ xix^s iiij^d	Pori e. xl$^{Li.}$ xiij confr. e. lxxvj$^{Li.}$
The clere monay remanynge of the possessions.	The stok, stoore, and domesticall stuff sold, w^t detts receivyd.	Rewards, with the porcions payd unto the abbotts.
e. cxxx$^{Li.}$ xix^s iiij^d	e. ccccx$^{Li.}$ xj^s x^d	Priori e. lxx$^{Li.}$ Aliis e. iiij$\overset{xx}{x}$ij$^{Li.}$ viij^s ij^d
The remanes of the price of the goods and catall sold.	Leade and bells remaynynge.	Woodds and undrewoods.
e. ccxlvij$^{Li.}$ iij^s viij^d	Leade e. lix foth. Bells e. vij	e. clxviij acrez and cccc. oks of the comon.
Playte and Jewells.	Detts owing to the howses afforsayd	Detts owyng by the howses afforsayd.
Dcxlij uncz.	e. iiij$\overset{xx}{i}$ij$^{Li.}$ xij^s iiij^d	e. cxiij^s iiij^d

ADDENDA.

In the summer of 1762, which was remarkably dry, it was discovered, in a piece of ground east of the priory, and adjoining thereto, that the grass decayed away in one part in the shape of coffins, which induced Mr. Milner, the tenant under Mr. Wortley Montague, to open the ground, and two tombstones were found, nearly alike, as below:—

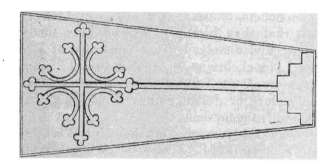

In Coles's MSS., vol. xxvii. page 205, respecting Monk Bretton Priory it is said, that the goods and cattle sold at the dissolution for £245 8s. 8d. The quantity of lead 59 fother, 7 bells, plate and jewels 642 ounces.

Speed states the *value* of Munke Burton Priory of Blacke Monkes, *temp.* Hen. VIII., to have been £323 8s. 2d.

In the Harleian MS., No. 798, written early in the 17th century, is the following:—"Dearne having received Cawthorne Beck, runneth by Barnsley smythies, iron works, formerly belonging to Burton Abbey, since to the King's assignes."

Dodsworth's MS. xxxii., in the Bodleian Lib., contains copies of three court rolls of Barnsley Manor (sometime the property of the Priory of Pontefract) of the years 1340 and 1341, and 23rd

242

HISTORY OF BARNSLEY.

Edw. III., lent him by Sir Gerv. Cutler of Stainber, Knt., 1632.

There was formerly a very fine warren on Barnsley Moor, held on lease for lives of the Crown by Sir Francis Wortley.

In the Cottonian M.S., Cleopatra E. IV., is a certificate to the King from George Lawson, Richard Bellasez, William Blithman, and James Rokeby, commissioners, dated at York, 15th of December, 1537, that they had " qwyetlye takine the surrenders, and dissolvyd the monasteries of Wyersoppe, Monckebreton, the Freers at Tykhill, Doncastere, Pontefracte, &c., where we perceyved no murmure or gunge in anye behalfe, but were thankefullye receyvede."

In a MS. survey of Yorkshire, by Warburton, made about 1720, he says:—" The market place (of Barnsley) stretches forth 7 poles broad on y° top, and 5 at y° bottom, and in y° middle stands y° Moat Hall." He says the town was remarkable for coals and wire, and mentions the Cross on Kirkgate.

CORRIGENDA.

PAGE 5, line 17, and following. This is contradicted in the Addenda, page 233; the information respecting the Roman altar having been obtained since the former sheet came out of press.—Page 14, line 4, *read* " Harold, &c., long to enjoy."—Page 18, line 5, *read* " Ilbert de Laci had," &c.—Page 20, side note should be opposite the first Latin extract from Dodsworth.—Page 51, line 14, *read* "Ottone de Tilli—English Otto."—Line 2 from bottom, *for* " confir-mavi quam habui," &c., *read* " calumpniam quam habui," &c.— Page 54, and Note—Speed, in his " History of England," mentions as sons of Henry II., William, Henry, Richard, Geoffrey, Philip, and John.—Page 58, line 14, *for* " persona," &c., *read* " pessona adven-erit dominici porci nostri in propriam curiam nostram missi sine contradictione aliqua quieti," &c.—Page 59, lines 2 and 3, *instead of* " some part of this charter is Monkish Latin," *read* " and granted that at the mast (*i. e.*, acorns, beech-nuts, &c.) season the swine of their (Richard and Matilda's) demesne sent into their own manor (or estate) should be free of pannage (the feeding of hogs on mast ; also money paid for such feeding—BAILEY)."—Page 67, line 16, *read* " Diacono ;" line 28, " Deacon."—Page 79, first line of transla-tion, *read* " Herbert de Silkiston."—Page 81, line 25, *for* "Domino," *read* " Dominus (Sir)."—Page 86, line 18, *for* " quarum una jacet," &c., *read* "quarum una dimidia acra jacet," &c.—Page 90, line 7, and Note : Bailey says " perquisites of court are those profits that come to a lord of a manor by virtue of his court baron, over and above the yearly revenues of his land ; as fines of copyholds, waifs, strays," &c.—Page 93, opposite line 25, *for* " 1248" *read* "1348."— Page 101, line 7, *for* " præscripto" *read* " præscriptos ;" line 8, *for* "ferent elect" *read* "fuerent electi."—Page 103, line 14, *for* " crofts" *read* " crofto ;" line 16, *for* " hæreditarie" *read* " hæredi-tario ;" line 28, *for* " protera" *read* "proterea ;" lines 34 and 37, *for* " prata" *read* " pratis."—Page 107, line 17, *for* " stakes" *read* " stocks."—Bottom of page 146, totals in the table of cotton and linen yarns, *for* " 168,707" *read* " 168,706 ;" *for* "203" *read* "2,603 ;"

244 CORRIGENDA.

for " 143" *read* " 2,783."—Page 196, date in the inscription on the monument to Gulielmo Denton, *for* " 1646 " *read* " 1696."—In the pedigree of the Laci family, *for* " Gilbert de Grant " *read* " Gilbert de Gant."—Wood's Pedigree: *for* " John Childers," *read* " John Walbanke Childers, Esq., of Cantley, High Sheriff for the County of York, 1858."—Beckett's Pedigree: Sir Thomas Beckett, 3rd baronet, had one brother (Christopher) and three sisters, not given in the pedigree, viz., Mary, Elizabeth, and Anne, who married Colonel Marriott. There are a few other minute errors in the printing, but not of any consequence.

SUBSCRIBERS' NAMES.

Those marked thus (*) have Two Copies.

The Right Hon. the Earl of Carlisle, Castle Howard.
The Right Hon. Lord Wharncliffe, Wortley Hall.
The Right Hon. Sir George Armytage, Bart., Kirklees Park.
The Right Hon. Sir Charles Wood, Bart., M.P., Hickleton.
The Right Hon. Sir Lionel Swinnerton Pilkington, Bart., Chevet.
Godfrey Wentworth, Esq., Woolley Park.
Godfrey Hawksworth Wentworth, Esq., Woolley Park.
George Edward Wentworth, Esq., Woolley Park.
William Digby Wentworth, Esq., 7th Dragoon Guards.
Frederick William Thomas Vernon Wentworth, Esq., Wentworth Castle.
John Wentworth, Esq.
Miss Wentworth, Woolley Park.
Charles Winn, Esq., Nostel Priory.
Richard Elmhirst, Esq., Lincoln.
Godfrey Higgins, Esq., Skellow Grange.
Edmund Beckett Denison, Esq., M.P., Doncaster.
Joseph Locke, Esq., M.P., Honiton.
Henry Spurr, Esq., Mayor of Scarborough.

Thomas Foljambe, Esq., Holme-Field, near Wakefield.
Charles Jackson, Esq., Doncaster.
*Major Daley, Sandhurst.
Thomas Taylor, Esq., Middlewood Hall.
Joseph Clarke, Esq., Eversley.
Mrs. Clarke, Noblethorpe.
Miss Beckett, Swinton Hall.
Messrs. Woodhouse and Jeffcock, Derby.
*John Freed Wright, Esq., Bilham House.
Rev. Henry Torre, Rector of Thornhill.
Rev. Henry Robert Alder, Incumbent of St. Mary's, Barnsley.
Rev. Richard Earnshaw Roberts, Incumbent of St. George's, Barnsley.
*Rev. William John Binder, Incumbent of St. John's, Barnsley.
*Rev. John Saville Hallifax, Edwardston House, Suffolk.
Rev. R. E. Batty, Ackworth Grove, Pontefract.
Rev. Henry Cooke, Catholic priest, Barnsley.
Rev. Benjamin Beddow, Independent minister, Barnsley.
Rev. William Thorpe, Rector of Misson.
Rev. Thomas P. Champneys, Vicar of Owston.
Rev. John Bell, Incumbent of Bolsterstone.

BARNSLEY.

Mr. John Ainsworth.
— William Allass.
— Thomas Allen.
— W. S. Armitage.
— John Asquith.
— G. W. Atkinson.
— Thomas Ayre.
— Thomas Blackburn.
— John Blackburn.
— John Beaumont.
Mrs. Bramhall.

Mr. Birch.
— W. R. Bamforth.
— George Birkenshaw.
— Joseph Bretherick.
— Edward Brady, sen.
* — Edward Brady, jun.
— Edwin Bygate.
— James H. Baron.
— Francis Butler.
— John Battman.
— William Brown.

SUBSCRIBERS' NAMES.

Mr. George Brown.
— Alexander Brown.
— John Cox.
— Jonathan Carnley.
— Henry Carter.
— John Clarke.
— James Cass.
— Robert Craik.
— John Carr.
— Miles Calvert.
— Benjamin Canter.
— Thomas Cope.
— Thomas Charlesworth.
— John Carrington.
— Joseph Dennis.
— W. J. Dandison.
— John Diggle.
— Thomas Dale.
— James Ellam.
— Anthony Edson.
— John K. Fox.
— Thomas K. Fox.
— James Fox.
— William Freeman.
— James Frudd.
— Samuel Fieldsend.
— H. T. Fletcher.
— Geo. Fletcher.
— Barnabas Gill.
— J. Gillott.
— William Gaunt.
— John Glover.
— Hugh Green.
— Gulliver.
— Moses Gelder.
— George Gelder.
— Thomas Guest.
— Joseph Goodyear.
— Moses Garner.
Mrs. Wm. Horsfall.
Mr. William Harvey.
— James Harper.
— Jepson Hartley.
— John Huntley.
— Robert Horner.
— G. J. Hamer.
— B. Harrison.
— Henry Harrison.
— Charles Harrison.
— William Harrison.
— Edwin Harrison.
— George Harrison.
— John Hanlon.
— James Hibbert.
— John Hibbert.
— Robert Hattersley.
— Isaac Hattersley.
— John M. Horsley.
— Isaac Hardcastle.
— William Hopwood.
— John Hargreave.
— W. J. Hindle, jun.

Mr. Edward Hedley.
— Joseph Hawcroft.
— Henry Haigh.
— James Ibeson.
— Robert Ibeson.
— John Iberson.
— Richard Inns.
*— Henry Jackson.
— William Jackson, Dodworth Road.
— Samuel B. Jackson.
— John Jessop.
— Samuel Johnson.
— J. G. Johnson.
Mrs. R. R. Keeling.
Mr. Charles Kilner.
— George Kay.
— Edwin Kay.
— Thomas Liddall.
— Samuel Linley.
— Thomas Lister.
— Richard Ledgar.
Miss Lockwood.
*Mr. John Lowrance.
*— William Lawton.
— Edward Lancaster.
— William Medlam.
— William Mallison.
— Joseph Mallison.
— Thomas Mirfin.
— Robert M'Lintock.
— James Milner.
— Henry Milner.
The Misses Mence.
Mr. Joseph Massie.
— Thomas Morley.
— Samuel Merryweather.
Mrs. Methley.
Mr. Charles Newman.
— Henry Nicholson.
— J. Outwin.
— William Oxley.
— W. A. Potter.
— J. S. Parkinson.
— Richard Parkin.
— Edward Parker.
— James Parker.
Miss Pickering.
Mr. William Peckett.
— George Pitt.
— Henry Pigott.
— Henry Payne, M.D.
*— George Rooke.
— James Rodgers.
— Charles Rogers.
*— G. J. Raley.
— R. R. Raywood.
— Richard Race.
— John Ray.
— John Robinson.
— Timothy Sykes.
— George Scales.
— Robert Steel.

SUBSCRIBERS' NAMES.

247

Mr. John Shaw.
— George Senior.
— Christopher Senior.
— M. T. Sadler.
— Thomas Smith, Church Street.
— Thomas Smith, Wesley Street.
— Joseph Smith.
— Richard Smith.
— Joseph A. Smith, Church Street.
— Elijah Sutcliffe.
— Richard Shortridge.
— John Schofield.
— George Scargill.
— John Shepherd.
— William Shepherd, Attorney.
— Joseph Sedgwick.
— Richard Thorpe.
— Henry Thorpe.
*— T. E. Taylor.
— F. H. Taylor.
— Amos Taylor.

Mr. William Tune.
— James Tiffany.
— George Travis.
Mrs. Thexton.
Mr. John Twibell.
— Joshua Wilkinson.
Mr. Joseph Wilkinson, St. George's Place.
— Robert Wilkinson, Dillington Castle.
— Joseph Wilkinson, Dillington Castle.
— Joseph Wilkinson, Wesley Street.
— Joseph Wilkinson, Plough Inn.
— John Widdop.
— George Willmot.
— William Wainwright.
*Mrs. Willan.
Mr. John Wilcock.
— Thomas White.
— Samuel Winter.
— William Ward.
— Matthias Wood.
— Joseph Woodruffe.

WAKEFIELD.

Mr. Henry Brown, Attorney.
— William Stott Banks, Attorney.
— John Henry Carter, Dentist.
— John Cryer, Bookseller.
— Benjamin Dixon, Deputy Clerk of the Peace.
— John Edward Dibb, Deputy Registrar, West Riding Register Office.
Messrs. Hicks and Allen, Booksellers.
Mr. E. B. Hick.
— Samuel Fozard Harrison, Attorney.
— Thomas Norris Ince, Clerk of the Peace Office.
— Henry Lumb, Solicitor, Deputy Steward, Manor of Wakefield.

Mr. Thomas Lamb, Bookseller.
— John M'Cabe, Bookseller.
— John Marsden, Solicitor.
— John Edwin Pickersley, Solicitor.
— Archibald Robertson, St. John's.
— Edward Shepherd, Governor of the House of Correction.
— John Scholey, Solicitor.
— John Stanfield, Bookseller.
— William Stewart, Solicitor.
— Henry Thompson, at Janson and Banks', Solicitors.
— William Wood, M.D.
— Joseph Williamson, Westmorland, Solici'or.

MISCELLANEOUS.

Mr. Henry Buckley, Ardsley.
*— Thomas Micklethwait, Ardsley.
— W. A. Potter, Monk Bretton.
*— William Day, Monk Bretton.
— Joseph Richardson, Monk Bretton.
— James Magee, Monk Bretton.
— John Stevens, Monk Bretton.
— John Harley, Monk Bretton.
— William Slater, Monk Bretton.
— James Battison, Monk Bretton.
— Thomas Armstead, Geelong, Australia.
— John Cooper, Derby.
— John Burland, Stainbrough.

Mr. George Surtees, Stainbrough.
— J. M. Barber, Liverpool.
*— M. H. Bobart.
*— Benjamin Bailey, Leeds.
— Henry Stooks Smith, Leeds.
— George Morley, Surgeon, Leeds.
— Edmund Bates, Leeds.
— John Greenwood, Leeds.
— Bertie Markland, Leeds.
— John Holmes, Leeds.
— James Wardell, Leeds.
— C. Hatfield, Doncaster.
— George Dunn, M.D., Doncaster.

248 SUBSCRIBERS' NAMES.

Mr. John Sykes, M.D., Doncaster.
— William Marratt, Doncaster.
— Walker, Doncaster.
— Cotnam Townsend, Doncaster.
— Henry Brooke, York.
— John J. Hawkins, Stockport.
— Thomas Reeder, Wath-upon-Dearne.
— James Thorpe, Wath-upon-Dearne.
— William Jackson, Wath-upon-Dearne.
— Charles Cocking, Wath-upon-Deane.
— Daniel Carnley, Wath-upon-Dearne.
— William Dixon, Newcastle, Stafford-shire.
— Thomas Davies, Huddersfield.
Mr. William Hick, Rotherham.
— William Walker, Rotherham.
— Richard Raywood, Darfield.
— John Wilkinson, Darfield.
Miss Elizabeth Haxworth, Darfield.
Mr. George Wilkinson, Darfield.
— George Mence Wood, Saiths, Darfield.
— William Littlewood, Edderthorpe.

Mr. John Haddlesey, Skellow Mills.
— Charles Reynolds, Skellow Grange.
— Charles Wemyss, Cannon Hall.
— Hatfield, The Aqueduct.
— Edward Lambert, London.
— James Womack, London.
— Thomas Caukwell, Cudworth.
— Edward Sanderson, Womersley Grange.
Mr. Thomas Walker, Sheffield.
— William Shaw, Sheffield.
— Henry Allen Spurr, Attorney, Wig-thorpe, Notts.
— William Taylor, Sen., Redbrook.
— William Taylor, Jun., Redbrook.
— Joseph Wigglesworth, Hemsworth.
— George Wigglesworth, Hemsworth.
— Charles Ward, Darton.
Miss Sarah Jackson, Callis Wolds.
— Lydia Jackson, Leavening.
Mr. William Peckett, Kexbro'.
— Frederick Ellis, Silkstone.
— Brown, Hickleton.

LONDON: HENRY VIZETELLY, PRINTER AND ENGRAVER, GOUGH SQUARE.

44

1st Quaker who } 219
1st   &   }
        Barnsley }

Catholic Church &c   220

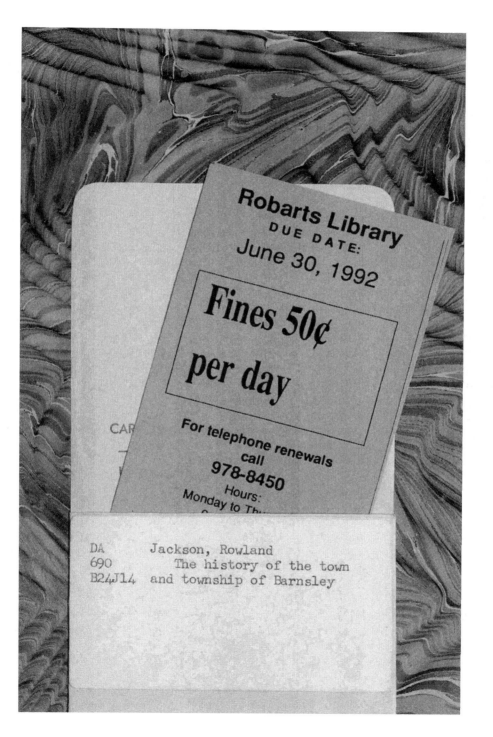

CPSIA information can be obtained
at www.ICGtesting.com
Printed in the USA
BVHW041553071221
623425BV00003B/158